The Bible Speaks Again

The Bible Speaks Again

A Guide from Holland, commissioned by
the Netherlands Reformed Church

With a Foreword by William Barclay

Augsburg Publishing House · Minneapolis

Translated by Annebeth Mackie from the Dutch
Klare Wijn: Rekenschap over geschiedenis,
geheim en gezag van de Bijbel
published 1967 by Boekencentrum N V
's-Gravenhage, Holland

© SCM Press Ltd. 1969
Augsburg Paperback, 1972
ISBN 0-8066-0931-1
Library of Congress Catalog Card No. 79-75400
Manufactured in the United States of America

Contents

Foreword by William Barclay

I have read this book with the very greatest interest and with the very greatest profit.

It states its own aims. It is 'one of its main objectives to help clarify matters'. It aims to stimulate the reader 'into giving the Bible another honest chance to show its living power'. It succeeds magnificently in its aims.

I know of no book which does so much and which does it so lucidly and so well. It deals with the history of the interpretation of the Bible and with the views which have been held of the Bible. Repeatedly it deals in the most masterly way with theological issues, such as, for example, solidarity and the idea of the Kingdom. Again and again it uses biblical passages in illustration of its statements and principles, and every passage is illustrated, as, for example, in the treatment of the Achan story and of the Parable of the Good Samaritan.

It is not an intellectual essay alone, although it is that. It is an appeal, an appeal to the church-goer, to the person who passes the Bible by, to the Roman Catholic Church, to the Jew. And all the time it is pleading for the Bible to be given a chance to speak for itself.

This book is astonishingly comprehensive. The early fathers and the modern radical continental theologians, fundamentalism and radicalism, history, theology, archaeology, linguistics – all are laid under tribute.

I am well aware of the danger of superlatives, but I believe that this is the best and most inclusive book on the Bible available. And one of its greatest qualities is that the most advanced technical scholar and the simplest Bible student will both be able to read it with profit. I wish it the widest possible circulation.

—

Introductory Note by the General Synod of the Netherlands Reformed Church

We consider ourselves fortunate in being able to offer this book to the public as an aid to the reading of the Bible. It was accepted unanimously by the meeting of the General Synod of the Netherlands Reformed Church of November 1966. In 1953 the Synod had already published *Teaching concerning Holy Scripture*. This book is intended as a test to prove that the Bible does indeed bring about an agreement among those who have felt its authority. Not a few people have expressed their scepticism about this agreement. It has therefore been an encouraging experience for the members of the committee which was in charge of the composition of the book – as well as for the Synod itself – that this scepticism proved to be unfounded.

The members of the committee mentioned, which was formed in 1960, were: Prof. Dr J. de Graaf, chairman; Dr T. Dokter, secretary; Prof. Dr H. Jonker, Dr B. Klein Wassink, the Rev. S. Meijers, Prof. Dr K. H. Miskotte, and Dr Th. C. Frederikse, who became responsible for reporting for the committee in 1961. He has written and re-written this book, in close consultation with the members of the commission and – in the last stage – also in consultation with the Synod and its Reporting Committee.

The whole commission is therefore collectively responsible for the basic concept, the contents and the plan of this book. It supports it fully, though, in the nature of the case, each of the members might perhaps have expressed himself differently here or there, or have underlined other points. But the members of the commission have left no doubt that the totality of their agreement has been interpreted by the author.

This book is about the Bible. Its intention is to put numerous problems, which keep recurring when the Bible enters the conversation in- or outside the church, into their historical background and context. Its principal aim, however, is to discuss the Bible from the inside, thus making it transparent. The basic thought of the book, therefore, is the Reformed insight *that the Bible carries its own authority*. This concept has been clarified with the help of biblical scholarship of the last hundred years.

When listening together to the Bible in this way, we do not stand behind defences in the conversation with our contemporaries, but on the contrary, there is a listening communication between us. This is true, both for the conversations between the different groups within the church, and between the churches, as well as for the conversation between the church and modern man who no longer lives in the community of any church. This book, which is in the first place intended as a helping hand for the reader of the Bible, therefore ultimately becomes a call to enter into this conversation, of which not only the aids, but also the promises and the possibilities, have been indicated. This should be a conversation between the members of the congregation, the so-called laymen, but it is also a conversation between theologians.

We hope that this book will help to bridge the gap that has developed continuously during the last hundred years between the biblical scholars and the man in the pew. It is also, in all modesty, a contribution to the theological conversation in so far as this is not entirely academic, but concerned with the well-being of the Church as the community which lives from and for the proclamation of the prophetic and apostolic word, by the grace of the Spirit.

> For the General Synod, Dr G. de Ru, *praeses*
> Dr E. Emmen, *scriba*

Introduction

In every Protestant church there is an open Bible in the pulpit. It does not lie there as an object of worship, but to be read and listened to.

This unobtrusive fact embodies a decision. The Bible is *the Book*. The Bible is *Holy Scripture*. It has its own, unique place. We declare the Bible to be the *Word of God*.

The unique significance of this remarkable book is not just accepted in the church; it is also the silent but nevertheless obvious presupposition of many who have become estranged from the church.

It is also obvious, however, that this plain fact must raise questions.

What caused the churches of the Reformation to put the Bible so emphatically in the pulpits?

What is the reason for this special place given to the Bible, not only in the church but also in society and civilization?

Is it right that the Bible should still have this astonishing authority?

Does the Bible not contain many mistakes and even offensive passages? Why, then, should it be Holy Scripture, the Word of God?

Is there not, beside all the use of the Bible, a good deal of misuse? How can we be sure of referring to the Bible in the right manner? Are not the separations and divisions among the churches significant writing on the wall?

This book sets out to answer these and similar questions honestly. 'Prepared to make a defence to anyone who calls you to account', as the apostle says in I Peter 3.15. It is always a bad business when people assume that one has to begin by 'accepting the Bible'. This is certainly not what we mean when we start from the definite assumption that the Bible has a special position. On the contrary: the more questions the better. It would be preferable, however, if these questions were not all fired off at once. That is why, in the first chapter, we invite the reader to investigate with us the role the Bible has played in the history of Christianity up till now.

Readers who do not have the patience for the first chapter can proceed at once to Chapter II. Here they will recognize their own questions more quickly. We hope that as they read on, they will want to go back to the first chapter again. In that case it could be used as a sort of appendix to the book.

I   The Bible in Christianity

A   The Bible on its Course through the Centuries

1. *The Scriptures of the Apostles and the First Congregations*

When we read the gospels and the letters of the apostles we often
overlook the many occasions where reference is made to 'the Scriptures'. Jesus says with great emphasis that he has not come to
abolish 'the law and the prophets' (Matt. 5.17). As a pious Jew
he had lived from childhood 'in his Father's house' (Luke 2.49). In
his death agony, words from the psalms rise to his lips. 'My God,
my God, why hast thou forsaken me?' (Ps. 22.1). 'Father, into thy
hand I commit my spirit' (Ps. 31.5). St Paul, too, breathed the
spiritual atmosphere of 'the Scriptures' (I Cor. 15.3). Some parts of
his letters really consist of nothing but quotations, as for instance
the well-known passage Romans 9-11. The letter to the Hebrews, by
an unknown author, is the same.

For Jesus and the apostles, the *Scriptures* (John 5.39) consisted of
the Law, the Prophets and *the Writings*. Together these three form
the books which became the *Scriptures* for the people of Israel. We
shall turn our attention for the moment to the division indicated
by these names.

The *Law of Moses*, indicating the first five books of the Bible, is
for the Jew the record of God's great deliverance which freed the
children of Jacob out of Egypt. That is the moment of the birth of
Israel as a people, through the waters of the Red Sea. At Sinai they
received the law of God and entered into history as a people. Again
and again we hear the prophets referring to this hour of birth.
'When Israel was a child, I loved him, and out of Egypt I called my
son' (Hos. 11.1). It happens again, very specifically, in Ezek. 16.4-11
(see also Amos 2.10). The stories of the patriarchs are the prepara-

tions for this miraculous birth. 'Look to Abraham your father and to Sarah who bore you' (Isa. 51.2).

Through this 'creation' of the people of Israel, the psalms and the prophets have their first vision of *the* Creation. It is striking how often these two are mentioned in one breath.

> *For the Lord is a great God,*
> *in whose hands are the depths of the earth,*
> *let us kneel before the Lord, our Maker!*
>
> Ps. 95.3-6
>
> *For the Lord has chosen Jacob for himself,*
> *Israel as his own possession. . . .*
> *Whatever the Lord pleases he does,*
> *in heaven and on earth,*
> *in the seas and all deeps . . .*
> *He it was who smote the first-born of Egypt . . .*
> *who in thy midst, O Egypt,*
> *sent signs and wonders . . .*
>
> Ps. 135.3-12

Psalm 136 refers in the same way to the miracles of creation and then to the miracles in Egypt, without any transition. Similarly Ps. 146.5 and 6; Ps. 147 and Ps. 148. See also Isa. 43.15: 'I am the Lord, your Holy One, the Creator of Israel, your King.'

Once this connection, so vivid and obvious for Israel, has been grasped, it no longer seems strange that the jubilant news of the creation of heaven and earth finds a place in *the Law*. So at this point we can already say that it is not necessary to read serious problems of science into the first chapters of the Scriptures. They are a reflection and an echo of God's salvation which has been granted to Israel, not a piece of physics or natural science. This does not detract from them; in fact, it adds something. They are a precious part of the 'Law'.

Indeed, the word *Torah* (law) in the Bible has a much richer sound than our 'law'. It would be better translated as 'signpost' or 'news of salvation'. To the Israelite it has the same sound as our word 'gospel'. Perhaps the best thing is to leave it untranslated. The Torah is like the hand of God which is stretched out mightily and irresistibly to Israel as his people. The Torah is the beginning and the foundation of the whole history of God's salvation. It has the character of a proclamation. For the Jew it is indisputably the most important part of the Scriptures.

Along with the Law comes *the Prophets*. Here we should not just think of Isaiah, Jeremiah and the other men of God whose writings have come down to us, but also of the books which describe history, such as Samuel and the Kings. The Prophets, in Hebrew *Nebiim*, contain an account of how the people of Israel lived with their Deliverer and Creator. It is well known that a critical note is sounded here. The people forget their Creator and Lord again and again, following other gods. Slowly but inexorably these writings draw nearer to the dark ending of the exile (586 BC).

The Writings, Hebrew *Ketubim*, are again of a quite different nature. They have their origin mostly in the period during and after the exile, and they are the answer of the faithful to God's deeds of salvation rather than a description of these deeds. They are a collection of songs, proverbs, wisdom literature and stories (Ruth), which may best be described, with some reservations, by the word 're-flection'.

> *Open my eyes, that I may behold*
> *wondrous things out of thy law.*
> Ps. 119.18

In Jesus' day, the Psalms and the book of Job, which consider in dramatic form why the faithful have to suffer, were the most important part of the writings.

Later Judaism liked to put these three groups together under the name of TaNaK. This is an artificial word, formed from the three first letters of *Torah*, *Nebiim* and *Ketubim*. The K is pronounced as the ch in 'loch'.

In the Church it became the custom to use the much paler and partly mistaken name *Old Testament*. It would be better to speak of *Law and Prophets*, as Jesus and the apostles used to do.

2. *The Bible in the Early Church*

The Christian Church accepted the Scriptures of Israel as a matter of course. Nevertheless we must stop to consider this for a moment, because Graeco-Roman culture, which is usually called Hellenism, breathed a very different spirit from that of Judaism. It is quite fascinating that in the very centre of this ancient, Gentile civilization round the Mediterranean there are time and again people who feel themselves attracted to this Jewish faith and to the confession of the unique God. Among the many Jews who emigrated during the centuries before and after the beginning of our era, there must evidently have been good ambassadors of Yahweh. Jesus refers to this missionary activity in Matt. 23.15. The Gentiles who hold themselves open for this and who even allow themselves to become part of Israel, are called proselytes, or God-fearing ones. We meet them repeatedly in the Gospels and in Acts. Cornelius, the Roman centurion of Acts 10, is one example. It is also said of Lydia that she worshipped God (Acts 16.14).

It was the so-called Septuagint, a Greek translation of the Old Testament originating from the second and third centuries before Christ, which must have contributed to the spreading of the knowledge of Israel's faith in the Hellenistic world. This must also have been one of the reasons why Paul often found a well-prepared soil among the Gentiles, while the Jewish synagogue rejected him. Such was the case in Antioch, in the heart of Asia Minor, where Paul, after reading from the Law and the Prophets, addresses himself to the 'men of Israel, and you that fear God' (Acts 13.16); but later he can only speak to the Gentiles, who accept the gospel with joy (v. 48). In this way there develops, alongside and together with the Jewish-Christian congregations, a church 'among the Gentiles'. That this causes many tensions is obvious from many pages of the Acts and the Epistles. 'Welcome one another, therefore, as Christ has welcomed you', Paul writes to the congregation in Rome, where this ecumenical question seems to have been a specially urgent one (Rom. 15.7).

What, is important to us in this context, however, is that the early Church of the first centuries, though it accepted the Jewish-Christian heritage of Law and Prophets, could not easily assimilate it entirely. This was because its difference from the Gentile-Hellenistic world of thought was too great. In the latter, beside the crude sensuality of decadent Roman civilization and the religious veneration of the passions in the old eastern religions, a strong desire for lasting happiness prevailed. Under the influence of philosophers like Plato and Aristotle and their spiritual following, people had come to see the world of the spirit and of the invisible as the only valuable one. This was what the best, the spiritual élite, strove after. Thus people came to long for deliverance from this transient life with its passing cares and joys. There was considered to be a great division, at times even an opposition, between the world of matter, of visible things, and the spiritual, eternal world. The latter was aspired after through asceticism and secret knowledge (*gnosis*).

When the gospel made its entry into this world, understandably the apostles soon found that they had to oppose not only vulgar and at times sensual paganism, but also the spiritual movements. Is this the reason why Paul had to issue a warning in I Cor. 8.1 against 'the knowledge' which puffs up? The same thing can be traced very clearly in the letter to the Colossians. 'Let no one disqualify you, insisting on self-abasement and worship of angels, taking his stand on visions' (Col. 2.18). We find the same thing, a little further on, in 'do not handle, do not taste, do not touch', and in 'appearance of wisdom in promoting rigour of devotion'. The whole section, 2.16-3.4, is worth reading in this context. It is not always certain whether the reference is to movements of Jewish origin, but the spiritual climate against which the apostle objects is clear enough.

Nevertheless, in the period after the apostles, the early Church – or perhaps it would be better to speak of the *young* Church – had to pay tribute to the ideas of the ancient and Hellenistic world, though the coarser growths of Greek-pagan concepts were not allowed to take root in the soil of the gospel.

The various forms of Christian gnosticism taught that matter as such was evil, and that Jesus had come to save man from his earthly existence through the true knowledge (gnosis). The idea that God himself created the material world was inconceivable to this system of thought. Jesus was only human in appearance; in reality he was a higher spiritual being. This mixture of pagan speculation and biblical themes might be compared to those movements in our day which combine Eastern and pan-religious ideas with certain elements of the Bible, such as Christian Science and Anthroposophy.

Marcion was influenced by gnosticism, though he remained closer to the gospel, because he considered as central the teaching on sin and grace which Paul had stressed so strongly. He did teach, however, that the God of the Old Testament was of a lower divinity, as he was responsible for the creations of the world of the senses. He therefore rejected the Israelite Scriptures. Over against the God of justice worshipped by the Jews he wanted to put the God of love, as revealed in the gospel. In the apostolic confession of faith, the rejection of Marcion can be clearly heard. 'I believe in God the Father, the Creator of heaven and earth.' Perhaps this also explains the emphatic confession of the 'resurrection of the body'.

Neo-Platonism began to exert a strong influence after the middle of the third century. This philosophical and religious movement teaches that the material world is only an emanation of the eternal divine being. There is therefore no direct opposition between matter and spirit, but a gradual transition from light to darkness, from spirit to matter and the reverse! It is known how this neo-platonism exerted a great and important influence on the Church Father, Augustine.

The Christian Church remained far from immune to all these philosophies. The spiritual climate was too much permeated by their thought. The opposition, or at least the distinction, between the divine being and the earthly life of the body became the great canvas on which the gospel is embroidered. This has had profound effects on the place given to the Bible and on the explanation of the Bible. The Law and the Prophets were accepted, but the colourful and very earthy and concrete stories of the Patriarchs, the Kings and the Prophets were spiritualized, most often through the use of the popular allegorical method.

To allegorize (literally: to say other things) is to give an explanation of Scripture by looking for a deeper significance behind the literal and grammatical meaning of the words. It was the Jewish scholar Philo of Alexandria, who was orientated towards Hellenism, rather than the Jewish rabbis, who did much to make this method popular. His aim was to make the crude and realistic stories of the Law and the Prophets acceptable to the intellectuals of his day. Thus he considered Adam to be the nous (spirit), while Eve was the image of sensual things. This seemed very clever, for when in Gen. 2.21 the spirit (Adam) sleeps, the senses wake.

The Church Father Origen, the great scholar and martyr from Alexandria who later lived in Caesarea (185-254), distinguished a threefold meaning in the Scriptures, corresponding to the threefold division of man into body, soul, and spirit. In this way he achieved a literal-historical, a moral and a spiritual-allegorical explanation of the texts. In his own world of thought this is less far-fetched than it seems to us. He was convinced that there is an invisible spiritual world, as it were parallel to the visible world.

Thus there is a corporeal, visible man, but also an inner, spiritual man. The names for things in the visible world can be used for the invisible one – a kind of poetic usage, as we use the words heart, light, high and so on. In this manner Origen solves the apparent difficulty in the biblical text that the blood is the soul (Lev. 17.11). Does this mean that the soul is also in the grave when the body lies there? No, because the blood of the human body corresponds to the soul of the invisible man.

Though Origen was later declared a heretic by the official church, his allegorical method was generally accepted. Thus Gregory of Nyssa (c. 335-394) explained the mystery of the cross by pointing out that the four arms point in all directions. The divine nature of Christ stretches itself out on the cross towards the whole created world, thus uniting it with the divine.

At that time there were, however, also those who wanted to keep closer to the literal and historical meaning of the stories. In general, the Church Fathers of the western part of the early Church, that is to say in Italy and North Africa, were somewhat more sober and restrained than the Greek Fathers in the East. But on the whole the allegorical method was accepted and used.

This digression was necessary in order to explain that since that time two questions have constantly recurred: first the question whether a text or a portion of the Bible must be taken literally, and second the problem of the relationship between the Old and the New Testament.

Until now we have only spoken of the Law and the Prophets which were accepted by the Christian Church as Holy Scripture. Alongside these, the *gospel* and the *apostolic letters* gained authority during the first centuries, though during the first century the Law and the Prophets were considered to be the real Scriptures. Gradually, however, these other writings acquired a place in the Church, as bearing authoritative witness from the apostles, who had seen the Lord with their own eyes. They kindled faith in Jesus as the Saviour. 'These are written that you may believe that Jesus is the Christ, the Son of God, and that believing you may have life in his name' (John 20.31). At first there was a long-drawn-out difference of opinion about some of the books of the Bible, such as Acts, the Revelation, and the Letter to the Hebrews, while II Peter and III John are definitely of a later date than the time of the apostles, so that they were only accepted later on. But by the end of the fourth century there is no longer any discussion, at least in the western part of the Church, and a Church Father in North Africa assumed the twenty-seven books which we find in the New Testament today to be authoritative or *canonical*.

The canon, a Greek word which means standard or list, is therefore the body of writings which the Church recognizes as Holy Scripture. As can be seen, the process of composing this canon was a lengthy one. From various notes made by the Church Fathers we can deduce how this process developed. Thus II Peter 3.15 mentions 'our be-loved brother Paul [who] wrote to you according to the wisdom given him, speaking of all this as he does in all his letters. There are some things in them, hard to understand, which the ignorant and the unstable twist to their own destruction, as they do the other scriptures'. Paul has already gained much authority, though he has to bear with some criticism. His letters are already mentioned with 'the other scriptures', which is surely a reference to the Law and the Prophets. At the end of the second century a canon is composed in Rome which does not quite tally with ours. This is called the Muratorian Canon. It contains one apocryphal book. But in 367 the famous Greek Father, Athanasius, lists our twenty-seven books for the first time and is supported by Augustine; the Synods of Hippo and Carthage in 393 and 397 subsequently recognize our canon. It is too early, however, to speak historically of the official estab-lishment of the canon. Only the Belgic Confession and the Council of Trent – at the time of the Reformation and the Counter-Reformation – give clear ecclesiastical pronouncements on the limits of the Holy Scripture. The apocryphal (hidden) books were also

*valued greatly. They have clearly been written to the model of,
and as a supplement to, the Gospels and Acts. There are, for instance, the Gospel according to St Peter, and the Acts of Thomas.
For the Church, however, they did not count as 'Holy Scripture'.*

These apostolic writings were referred to under the collective name
of *New Testament*. This name, too, is not a very good one, because
it seems to suggest that the gospel is new and independent from
'the old' one. It also lacks the feeling of a certain articulation and
nuance. For that reason it might be better to speak of Gospels and
Epistles, or just The Gospel.

In connection with the development which we have just traced,
we would like to make the following remarks.

1. The Church did not accept Holy Scripture because some
authority had declared that these books were the Scriptures, but
because the Bible established itself.

2. Conversely, it is also clear that there was a time when the
Church listened to and confessed the gospel, before our Bible had
acquired its form or shape, before it became our 'New Testament'.
The latter might be said to have come into existence in and through
the living Church.

3. The authority of the Bible, both of the Law and the Prophets,
and of the Gospels and Epistles, is practical and concrete. The
Church needs the Scriptures because they pass on the witness of
God's saving deeds in Israel and in the Messiah Jesus. That is why
the Scripture 'is inspired by God' and 'profitable for teaching' (II
Tim. 3.16). Its origin is interwoven with the history of God's salvation and is therefore established historically.

We shall end this section with a short note on the translation of
the Bible.

In Christian worship, the Septuagint was read and probably
translated into Latin by an interpreter, at least in the Roman part
of the world-church. The later Latin translations had their origin
here: there was the so-called Old Latin' (*Vetus Latina*), which is
sometimes called the *Itala*. This was a translation of the Law and
the Prophets via the Greek. At the end of the fourth century the
Church Father Jerome received a commission from Pope Damasus
to revise the translations of the gospels, and as a result of this he

also made a start with the translation of the Law and the Prophets from the Hebrew. Others probably continued this work, though tradition generally ascribes the whole translation into Latin from the original languages to this pious scholar of Bethlehem. Thus the *Vulgate* (literally: for the people) came into being, and it is to this day the official translation in the Roman Catholic Church. However, because church people were very attached to the 'Old Latin' version, it took a century and more before this undoubtedly much superior translation was accepted. In this respect, too, there is nothing new under the sun.

The Greek Church Fathers in particular explained the Bible in numerous treatises, sermons and meditations. Through the Christian church services in which it was read, it became very well known among the ordinary people, though of course extremely few were able to possess a Bible, as printing had not yet been invented.

3. *The Bible in the Middle Ages*

During the Middle Ages the Bible must have had a very important place in Christianized Europe, where civilization and Christianity were so closely connected. The Bible was without doubt accepted and honoured as *the* book of Christendom, not only in theory, but also in fact.

Art, too, bears an imposing witness to this attitude. During a church service Francis of Assisi heard the passage in Matthew 10 in which the Lord sends his disciples out without any possessions, and this made such an impression on him, that he dedicated his life in absolute poverty to the service of God and to works of charity.

At universities and monastery-schools, studies consisted for a large part in theology and explanations of the Bible. Those who aspired to a doctor's degree opened the promotion ceremony with a eulogy of the Scriptures.

Through catechism, morality plays, instruction and religious art, the knowledge of the Bible was spread among the people. In the later Middle Ages pulpits were brought into the churches, or sometimes built on the outside wall; the Dominican Preachers in particular made use of them to instruct the people in the Bible, though we must not think of the sermons of those days as exegetically responsible explanations of the Bible. But it remains true that a great deal of biblical knowledge became common property in this way.

A great contribution to this task must have been made by the Parisian chancellor Peter Comestor, who wrote the famous *Historia scholastica*, a history of the Bible which became very popular: a sort of children's Bible. This book was translated into many languages and even put into verse.

From all this it is clear that the picture which Protestant instruction evokes especially around the 31st of October – that during the dark Middle Ages the Bible was a forgotten book, which was rediscovered by Luther, deeply covered with monastic dust – is far too black and white a one.

All the same, there were several circumstances which prevented the Bible from exercising its influence properly. It would help our own attitude towards the Bible to see these conditions clearly.

1. The Bible was hardly available at all in the national languages, though there were some translations. The official *Vulgate* – in Latin – which had been accessible to the people in Latin Christendom, became in Western Europe a Bible for priests and scholars. In practice, people could get to know the Bible only indirectly. Here the great usefulness of Bible translations and editions, which we usually take for granted, stands out clearly.

2. The study of the Bible carried out by the scholars was curiously enough very limited in its originality. It was considered sufficient to collect the explanations of the fathers, in whose wisdom there was the greatest confidence, and to write these as adequate explanation beside, between and sometimes round the Bible texts. These are the so-called *glossaria*, which expanded with each generation till they became mighty volumes. More and more was collected, more and more was written, but an independent confrontation with the Bible was hardly possible.

In the eleventh and twelfth centuries the greatest scholars began to add their own theses to these enormous collections of old ecclesiastical explanations; in these theses they summed up the Bible dogmatically. They are called the *sententiae*. This is the origin of *scholasticism*. The aim of this system was to reconcile differences between the pronouncements of the Church Fathers into one beautiful unity through subtle reasonings and comparisons.

Though we owe much piety and many rich insights to this treatment of the contents of the Bible, it must be clear that the dogmaticians allowed theology to obscure the Scriptures.

Forewarned is forearmed: Christendom of later ages has never been very easily edified by the gratuitous repetition of truths.

3. The danger that the Bible itself would not be heard was made greater by the already mentioned, generally accepted teaching of the double meaning of the Scriptures. As Augustine had taught, it was not the letter which counted, but the contents. This left the way wide open for the allegorical method of interpretation, which might at times produce profound and beautiful things, which, when used in the sermon, might exhort, comfort or at times startle the congregation. But the truth of God's Word came through with difficulty. A few advocated a literal, historical and grammatically responsible explanation of the Bible, but they formed a small minority.

4. Because the general feeling was that it was necessary to find the hidden meaning of the Scriptures, a great need was felt for the authority and leadership of the Church, which alone could reveal this deeper sense. The Church was the only qualified interpreter of the Bible! Its key position in matters of teaching authority was not at all preposterous in a society where Church and Bible, Christianity and civilization, theology and science were entirely absorbed in one another, and considered as one entity. Thus the Bible was as it were covered by a dome of tradition and Church teaching.

For those who have grasped this situation, it is a striking turn of events when, at the end of the Middle Ages, the Bible sets itself in motion again, like the Sleeping Beauty after she had slept for a hundred years. There is an interesting demand for the Bible in the language of the people. The name of the English scholar Wycliffe may be mentioned here to represent many other known and unknown ones. Renaissance and Humanism announce themselves and, out of this unique awakening of a new era, the Reformation is born.

4. *The Bible at the Reformation*

It is remarkable that during the great years of Church reformation the Bible came through as a living power. 'And they are (in the

Bible) not just words which one simply reads, as is often thought; they have not been written to be discussed, but they are words to live and do', Luther writes in a letter which precedes the explanation of his beloved Psalm 118 (Weimar Edition, Vol. 31, I, p. 69). The historical conditions of Church and civilization created a favourable climate, but for us it remains a miracle from heaven how, through Luther's inward and outward struggle, the Scriptures begin to speak again.

It was no accident that the monk from Wittenberg made the liberating discovery that the sinner may be justified before God, because God pronounces him just. His passionate study of the Bible, and especially his intimacy with the Psalms, led him to this revelation. He experienced the Bible as the book of the God who speaks. He came to understand the Scriptures as a liberating gospel that spoke to him.

During the stormy developments after he had put up his ninety-five theses, he began to understand more and more clearly that, against the Pope and the Council, he could only appeal to the Scriptures. His declaration to the Diet of Worms on April 18th, 1521, that he was overwhelmed by the Scriptures, that his conscience was a prisoner of the words of God, is historically of world importance. From that day on, an appeal to the Bible would always arouse respect and attention in Christendom.

The basis for Luther's spiritual victory in Worms had curiously enough been laid when he suffered defeat in the summer of 1519 in Leipzig at the hands of the cunning debater Dr Eck. The latter forced him to acknowledge that the Council of Constance of 1415 had wrongly rejected the theses of Jan Hus. In those days, it was unheard of that a Council could be fallible, and Luther himself would never have put this suggestion forward. But his defeat in the discussion at Leipzig taught Luther that he would have to proceed with only the Scriptures for support.

The Reformation in Switzerland, in Zurich and Geneva, with which the names of Zwingli and Calvin are specially connected, is the historical illustration of Luther's discovery. The Bible begins to show its powers. The exciting and colourful events of the Reformation of the Church bring all sorts of other factors into play. The national consciousness awakens. A new, independent and free spirit stirs in the universities. Calvin had received a thorough train-

ing in the Humanities in Paris, where he had studied Law. It was
to be the work of his lifetime, however, simply to let the Bible
speak. His *Institutes* are not so much a dogmatic system as the
organization of biblical material according to certain insights which
are indicated by the *Creed*, or Apostolic Confession. His Bible commentaries, which grew out of his daily work of explaining the
Scriptures to his congregation, to ministers and students (who came
from many European countries), are a special monument to the Bible,
which conquered hearts and minds through the impression it made.
'We repose in the Word.'

It is obvious that Calvin's clear and astute French mind felt com-
pelled to give reasons why the Bible occupies this unique place for
the faith. Luther had discovered and experienced this emotionally
in the course of his turbulent struggle, but Calvin reflects on the
reason why. In chapters 6-8 of the first book of the Institutes we
find therefore, for the first time in the theology of the Reformers,
a 'Teaching concerning Holy Scripture'. It is wonderful how Calvin
here, with certain touch, and each time in different words, knows
how to hit on the real secret of the Reformation. The Scriptures, we
hear again and again, do not derive their authority from any
ecclesiastical institution, nor from all sorts of reasonings and proofs:
they exercise their dominion in the hearts of the faithful because the
living God speaks in them.

This does not have to be accepted on the authority of another
person; it is simply true when one wants to become a disciple, a pupil
of the Scriptures. At that moment its superior forces will be discovered, not subjectively, but as a divine truth which establishes
itself. To prevent a misunderstanding, it must be added at once that
Calvin accepted, with the whole Church, the divine origin of the
Bible as self-evident. But for Calvin, the certainty of this is not
based on a pronouncement of the Church, nor on a mysterious inner
feeling; it comes from the Bible itself. In his commentaries he
often calls this simply 'the Spirit'. This is how he should be understood when he speaks for the first time so emphatically of the hidden
witness of the Holy Spirit, through which God's truth is sealed in
our hearts. This is how the Reformers discovered and experienced
the superior force of the Bible.

It is interesting and important to understand the similarity and the difference between the Reformers properly so-called and the humanistic movement which is represented, among others, by the scholar Erasmus of Rotterdam. Church and civilization owe an immense debt to them, too. Their motto 'back to the sources' – *ad fontes* – prepared minds for an absorbed reading of the Scriptures and for open-minded and scientific study of them. Erasmus prepared a Greek edition of the New Testament with great scholarship and ability. The humanist Reuchlin, who wrote a Hebrew grammar, taught Luther his Hebrew.

The humanists, who in Germany, France and the Netherlands at least, remained entirely Christian and within the Church – Erasmus remained a faithful son of the Roman Catholic Church – also emphasized really basic aspects of the Christian faith. They stressed love, tolerance and service, which characterize the Christian life. Erasmus held that Christ and the apostles had rejected war. There is absolutely no reason to speak arrogantly of this moralism. In this they followed some of the pre-Reformation movements, such as that of Wycliffe, the Bohemian Brethren, and in the Netherlands the Brethren of the Common Life in Deventer, to which Thomas à Kempis and Geert Grote belonged. Compared with these men, the Reformers themselves were much more warlike. Calvin and his actions in particular cannot be freed from the charge of harshness. But the characteristic difference is found in the way in which the Bible was appealed to. Here we have a clear departure. For the humanists the Bible was a source from which one drew insights and rules. It was read as a new law, which could be made use of beside the tradition and the authority of the Church. Wessel Gansfort, one of the forerunners, lays down calmly that in the case of a difference between the two authorities of Bible and Pope, the Bible should always command the greater respect. For him these are still two comparable entities. For Luther and Calvin, however, passion suddenly flares up. For them, the Bible is not just a source in which they can find truths and precepts; it is the Scripture in which they meet the living God and his message.

5. *The Continuing Importance of the Bible in Church and Society*

People do not often stop to consider the enormous influence which the remarkable discovery of the great Reformers had on the civilization of the countries of Western Europe. The word 'influence', however, must be used with some care. Influences can be described and measured. They are a matter of more or less, they are quantitative. But the Bible itself, as the Reformers discovered, is qualitative and absolute. It is a message which demands conversion and faith. These are difficult to measure or register. They take place, if all is well, very definitely, and not only inwardly in the human heart; in some sense, they are intangible. We might call them existential, if we may employ this much abused word. We must say this emphatically before we enumerate briefly the 'influences' which the Bible has had on the life of the Church, the nation and society.

The Bible became the focal point in services in the Protestant churches from then on. This meant that the sermon came to be the most important part of the life of the church for nearly all church-goers, and this is still true today. Whether this is right we shall not discuss for the moment.

Authority on Family But the Bible came to be used at home, as part of family life; it occupied a place of honour, especially in earlier days, when family prayers at meals were the rule. In this way, many generations acquired an intimate knowledge of the Bible.

As churchmen gained access to the Bible, it became possible for them to form a competent judgement on matters concerning the gospel and the faith. This was the source of a stream which, after many obstacles, ended in our day in the much discussed coming-of-age of the layman. The Reformed character of our churches, with synods and presbyteries, is clearly connected with this. The minister is not the only one who should have a say, though in practice this may often be the case.

Because people wanted to read the Bible for themselves, education became of vital importance with the Reformation. Though this development had begun before the Reformation, it gained momentum with it – it was concerned with the education of the ordinary man. Unlike humanism and the Renaissance, which were an affair for scholars and artists, the Reformation has contributed greatly to the development of the schools. It could be said that the school was the offspring of the catechism. The child has rather outgrown the mother.

The *Statenvertaling* (the first official translation of the Bible into Dutch, comparable to the Authorized Version) has had an immense influence on the Dutch language, and therefore on its culture. It is not surprising that the cultural history of Christendom has been

introduced as a subject in secondary schools. Now that many people
no longer come to know the Bible in and through the church, because of secularization, it is felt that our civilization cannot be
understood without a knowledge of the Bible.

Finally, it is impossible to divorce the whole development of de-
mocracy in the Netherlands, in England and in America, from the
Bible which came to occupy such a central place through the Reformation. We have already mentioned the feeling of church
members that they share in the responsibility. The progress of
Calvin's Reformation, through Dutch Protestantism and English
Puritanism, to the North American States born from the love of
liberty of the colonists, is too involved for us to discuss here, but
that there are connecting links is clear. Without being political
followers of Groen van Prinster, that conservative Dutch statesman
of the nineteenth century, we can rationally agree with his famous
saying that Calvinism contains both the origin and the guarantee
of our constitutional liberties.

We will now leave this connection between the Bible and culture
aside, in order to focus more clearly on the questions which concern
us most closely in this book. The same questions came to the fore
when the Bible came into the limelight during the Reformation.
For that reason we will see in the second part of this chapter how
our ancestors framed and answered these questions.

B Questions and Answers

1. *The Orthodox Period: The Inspiration of the Scriptures*

The term *orthodox* is used to indicate the theology which was developed after the Reformation in Lutheran and Calvinist countries,
and which left its mark on the life of the Church. We are speaking
of the period stretching from the middle of the sixteenth to the
end of the seventeenth century.

After the struggle for religious freedom had been won – in Germany in 1555 with the religious treaty of Augsburg, in Switzerland
before that, and in the Netherlands much later – the Reformed
churches had time to reflect on the implications of the Reformation
for the Church. The harvest of the Reformation witness was stored

in the barns of theology. To counteract the Roman Catholic Church, which was again advancing rapidly, it was essential to work out the characteristic dogmas of the 'new teaching': justification by faith alone, the relation between faith and works, the new doctrines relating to the sacraments and the organization of the church. Theology was studied with passion at the universities, which in those years were the centre of spiritual and ecclesiastical life. A great deal of theological knowledge became common property among Protestants in this way. Yet it is also true that much of the thought of these theologians remained hidden in the libraries for many centuries. It is worth noticing that in the twentieth century Karl Barth has given renewed attention to orthodox theology, using many of its finer theological distinctions critically but positively for his own dogmatic work.

There were some good reasons why orthodoxy came to be forgotten. It had acquired a bad name. The pious zeal and sagacity of these theologians was spoilt by a fighting spirit which in retrospect must be called an unholy fire. The German Lutherans in particular were always ready to judge their opponents fiercely. Calvin and his spiritual descendants, the Calvinists, or Reformed, were more inclined to look for agreement and unity, though they were also capable of judging sharply when they felt the truth was at stake.

It is, however, better to enquire into the background of this type of theology before joining in the chorus of the many who consider theology, and particularly dogmatics, nothing but useless squabbles which cause hot heads and cold hearts.

A clear trait of the theologians of this period is their emphasis on clarity and *certainty*. In this they were in line with the Reformers. The writings of Luther and Calvin, as well as their confessions, which are the echo of these writings in many countries, sound a triumphant and confident note. 'A true faith is not only a certain knowledge or understanding . . . but also a certain confidence . . .' according to answer 21 of the Heidelberg Catechism. The Reformers had rediscovered the certainty of salvation. But this need for certainty was also a sign of the times. People were no longer content to accept without further argument the authority of the church or the old philosophers, as, for instance, Aristotle had been considered the final answer to all objections in the

Middle Ages. Renaissance man wanted to discover the truth for himself.

Typical of the spirit of those days is the philosophical method of *Descartes* (1596-1650), who exerted a great influence on his contemporaries. He was a clear and profound thinker, seeking for the basis of all certainty in the midst of all kinds of unproved ideas. As a mathematician he was much impressed by the infallibility of calculation and mathematical thought. The exactness with which our mind can proceed from one conclusion to the next made a great impression on him. He strove to find the same certainty for the deepest questions which always occupy man. The final ground for everything he found in the thought of man itself. *Cogito ergo sum* (I think, therefore I am). It is a curious detail, indicating how much Descartes remained a child of his time, that he found the guarantee for the reliability of our philosophical laws ultimately in the concept of a deity, who, as the perfect being, has no desire to deceive feeling and thinking man. He wanted to be a faithful Christian, but he gave to human reason the task of finding the unity between faith and knowledge.

We shall not examine this philosophy in detail, but must content ourselves with the remark that it is characterized by a rational lucidity. One feels that this is the beginning of rationalism. The essence of things is captured by a continuous train of thought.

Later orthodox theologians (e.g. Voetius) were radically opposed to Descartes because of his basic premise, but it cannot be denied that they are indebted to his method of thinking. For them, the certainty of the faith of the Reformation period became basically an intellectual certainty. They strove to find a theological system which proceeds step by step, through logical conclusions, to the final revelation of God's truth.

The sharp polemical tone characteristic of these theologians must be judged against the background of this rational certainty. A rational truth is sharp and clear, without shades of meaning or depths. Anything not in agreement with this has to be rejected. Rationalism may lead to fanaticism.

Another characteristic of orthodox theology was its strong attachment to written confessions which had been accepted once and for all. These were specially important to orthodox Lutherans, partly as a result of the situation in Germany. The cause of the Reformaion there was linked with the side chosen by the ruling princes. In the religious peace treaty of Augsburg of 1555, the well-known principle cuius regio, illius religio *was laid down: the subjects of each state must adopt the faith of their ruler or, at least, that faith would be counted as the official one. This tied those in favour of the Reformation to the Augsburg Confession (dating from 1530, but revised in 1540); this confession, together with other confessional documents, was incorporated into the* Book of Concord *in 1580. Thus these writings acquired a legal significance.*

In Reformed orthodox theology, which may be said to begin with Beza (1519-1605), Calvin's successor in Geneva, this attachment to written confessions was initially unknown. It was hindered by the spreading of Calvinism to several countries – Switzerland, France, the Netherlands, Scotland, Poland and so on. Each written confession had its own character. Nevertheless, the Reformed churches did not remain exempt from this legalistic confessionalism. Later, Bavinck wrote tersely: 'At the time of the Reformation people confessed their belief, later they believed their confession.'

Lutheran orthodoxy was unfortunately also modified by the difference, dating from before 1555, between the real Lutherans and the Philippists, the followers of Philip Melanchthon. This led to various disagreements, and was one of the causes which led to the destruction of the hope of unity between Calvinists and Lutherans which Calvin had longed for so ardently.

Yet there was also a feeling, above all because of the common struggle against Roman Catholic theology, that it was impossible to consider the other party as the false church. This led to the elaboration of the contrast between fundamental and non-fundamental articles of faith, and in particular to the distinction between the visible and the invisible church. Even then, however, these distinctions proved themselves unsuitable for the foundation of real, ecumenical unity.

The preceding sketch of the theology of the period will help to throw light on the most important doctrine which has been perfected by orthodox theology, namely *the inspiration of the Scriptures.* That was the reason for this rather long preamble.

The demand for certainty in doing theology brought with it the need for a fixed and undoubted starting point. The Church of Rome ultimately found this certainty in the teaching authority of the church. Orthodox theologians naturally looked for it in the Bible, which was right in the Reformed setting. One is reminded of Luther at Worms. But when it came to the reason for this authority, different routes were taken. Luther and Calvin simply based everything on the Bible; they stressed the decisive power of the Bible itself. The written confessions did the same. The Bible convinces because of the message it brings. The word is sufficient. This is what Calvin meant by his teaching on the *inner witness of the Holy Spirit.* The word of the Bible is alive, it is one with the Holy Spirit (see above, p. 26).

The orthodox theologians, however, went one step further. Regardless of its contents, they wanted a guarantee that the Bible is the Word of God. They found this in the doctrine that the Bible was at the time inspired and written through and under the direction of the Spirit of God. By teaching this, they guaranteed absolutely the theological authority of the Scriptures. Lutheran theologians especially took this very far. Some of them taught that the Hebrew vowel-signs had been inspired. But the Reformed side was also acquainted with this *mechanical inspiration.* Heidegger, Reformed Professor in Heidelberg and Zurich (1633-1698) formulated it thus: 'the Holy Scriptures are the Word of God, of which the Holy Spirit is the author, in the Old Testament through Moses and the prophets, but in the New Testament written by the evangelists and the apostles and set forth in the canonical books, so that they teach the church completely and clearly about God and divine matters, being the only standard of belief and life, tending to salvation'. Note the words *so that*: the teaching is necessary to form a guarantee. Everything has to be complete and transparent!

This teaching can be linked to an old tradition. In the Bible there are two texts which are often quoted as proofs. 'All scripture is inspired by God (theopneustos in Greek) and profitable for teaching' (II Tim. 3.16). 'First of all you must understand this, that no prophecy of scripture is a matter of one's own interpretation, because no prophecy ever came by the impulse of man, but men moved by the Holy Spirit spoke from God' (II Peter 1.20,21). Among the Jews there is no real teaching of biblical inspiration; we

find it for the first time in the writings of the Hellenistic Jew Philo
(first century), who connects inspiration specially with ecstasy.
The human consciousness is eliminated. Some of the Church Fathers
at that time speak of the writers of the Bible as a flute or a lyre of
which the Spirit of God makes use. Later, people (e.g. St Augustine)
speak less ecstatically of the Holy Spirit dictating the Bible. Though
the idea of the inspiration of Scripture in some form is held fairly
generally in the Church until and throughout the Middle Ages, it
plays no very important role. It only serves to express that this
is where God's Word is found. Because the basic guarantee of God's
saving truth lay in the authority of the Church, no need was felt
for a clear teaching on inspiration. It only became a sensitive point
towards the end of the Middle Ages when the Waldensians,
Wycliffe and other free movements appealed to the Scriptures
against the Church. As we have seen, the Reformers did not need
to elaborate the doctrine of inspiration as a guarantee. Calvin always
said that prophecy or doctrina (teaching) is contained in the Holy
Scriptures. But when orthodox theology enlarged on this teaching,
it identified the canonical books of the Bible with the Word of God
in such a way that no justice was done to the working of the Holy
Spirit which gives life to the written Word and illumines the heart.
The Bible thus becomes one massive revelation of truth, which is
at our disposal. Because of its direct origin from the Holy Spirit
who is the author, the Bible has to be called divine, and it bears
the characteristics of God, namely authority and certainty, suffici-
ency and transparency. Taking this as the starting point, it must be
said that the orthodox theologians have said some very fine things
about these qualities. For them, too, the authority of the Scriptures
was contained in them, and not in the Church or the Council, or
in human understanding. At this point they made a distinction
between historical authority and normative authority. That is to
say, not everything is relevant to faith and salvation, but Scripture
does contain everything that is necessary for salvation. The difficult passages have to be explained with the help of the sections
which are clear. This is the famous comparison of Scripture with
Scripture. Even though the Bible is essentially transparent, explanation is necessary; and, besides, the point is not to know it
theoretically or outwardly. Only when the Scriptures are approached
with the desire to find salvation can their real truth be perceived. It

is better always to take the literal meaning, though this may be composite and itself point to a figurative use of language. This is a sound rejection of unbridled allegorical exegesis.

This orthodox doctrine of inspiration has exercised an enormous influence on Protestantism; it can be said that it has until this day dominated the discussion on the authority and the meaning of the Bible. It is a proof of great respect and love for the Scriptures, and it gives expression to that insight of faith which accords a unique place to the Bible in church, which has never been lost since the Reformation. The doctrine of inspiration also led theologians to study the Bible with great exactness, including the text of the original languages. Some of the orthodox fathers acquired fame in this field.

We must also not neglect to point out that this period of orthodoxy was not only characterized by theological disputes. The beautiful hymns dating from that time are proof of a living and deep piety. Paul Gerhardt, the famous Lutheran poet of spiritual songs, lived in the orthodox period. Johann Sebastian Bach served the church of his day with his music.

Nevertheless, it must be said that the starting-point and the character of this theology have created many difficulties for later generations, causing much damage both in the church and in the pastoral field, because they imposed a yoke on hearts and minds which could and should have been avoided. A reaction was bound to follow. We shall hear about this in the next section.

2. Pietism: The Bible as a Book of Devotion

Pietism is that broad spiritual movement in which all the emphasis is laid on personal experience and application of the Christian faith. In the long run the heart could not find satisfaction in the cold virtuosity of the sermons of orthodox preachers, attempting to polish the numerous facets of the pure truth.

> *Though Christ were born a thousand times in Bethlehem,*
> *But not in me, so would I still be lost.*

In opposition to the objectiveness of orthodox theology, subjective hearts and minds began to claim their rights.

Pietism manifested itself in various forms in the countries of

Central Europe. It had a deep and sometimes lasting influence on the life of the Church and on spiritual developments. The force of its appeal is still evident in many spiritual songs. Church hymns which breathe this spiritual atmosphere are often more popular with congregations than the psalms, with their sturdy and classical melodies from the days of the Reformation.

In the Netherlands, pietism could be linked to the mystic traditions of the late Middle Ages. Ever since the Brotherhood of the Common Life, out of whose midst came Thomas à Kempis, author of the fervent and devout booklet *The Imitation of Christ*, the people of the Low Countries had felt an attraction to the introspective life. A Christianity which was experienced more personally thus found easy access. In the church, but especially on the edge of church life, in the sects, it has taken an important place since the beginning of the eighteenth century. There is great variety in the forms it took, varying from mystic, unbiblical fanaticism to a pattern linked closely to the Bible and the Confessions. But they all had this in common: theological truth became a matter of the heart and could only be truly experienced subjectively. This led to a great interest in the way of salvation and in questions of guilt, penitence, personal conversion and enlightenment.

In Germany, where Spener and Francke (at Halle) were very well known, this spiritual movement mostly had results in the practical application of the gospel, though the life of faith in Francke's environment was sombre. He was bitterly serious in matters of faith and conversion. But this same seriousness drove him to action. His orphanage in Halle quickly became famous. Christian social work, the diaconal side of the life of faith, began to take shape here for the first time. The concept of mission was also born. We should also mention here the name of Count Zinzendorf, the founder of the community of the Herrnhuters, which practised Christianity with childlike joy.

In England, 'the cradle of evangelistic preaching' (W. Perkins), pietism found a completely new expression in Methodism; here we are above all reminded of the names of John Wesley (1703-1791) and George Whitefield. They also laid great stress on conversion and on a personal experience of salvation, but the people thus 'awakened' were encouraged to go and preach the gospel and win more souls for Jesus. Whitefield was the first to hold an open air service, near

Bristol, and this practice had tremendous results later. Wesley gave their revival movement a much tighter organization, which eventually led to the formation of the Methodist Church. Since then, revival movements have recurred many times, especially in the Anglo-Saxon world. They show a type of militant, witnessing Christianity, of which the Salvation Army is to this day a good example.

Pietism, which had at first been reviled fiercely by some, while the Church and the theologians often refused to take it seriously, worked as an active salt in both the Church and the world. What would have become of the Church, indeed what would have become of Europe, if the dew of pietism had not watered the spiritual life in the period of drought?

All sorts of objections can, of course, be brought against this widespread movement. It paid more attention to sinful or converted man than to the saving work of Christ. There was the danger of salvation by works. It lacked awareness of the Church. It had a legalistic spirit. It is easy to point out these things in some of its more extreme manifestations. But what preaching of the Christian message, be it in or outside the Church, ever escapes entirely from objections of one-sidedness? Who can claim to have the whole gospel? Which existing church can claim to be 'catholic' here and now?

We are therefore bound to say that, in the situation created by orthodox theology and churchmanship of the seventeenth century, the pietistic reaction was not only understandable but also beneficial. But at the same time we must not lose sight of the fact that pietism could never conquer the orthodox attitude, because these two had a common basis. The liberating discovery of the Reformers had been that God addresses himself personally to man in the gospel, declaring him to be his child; later theologians had made this into an objective system, in which the Christian had to believe in order to acquire a personal share in it. In the well known distinction between *fides quae creditur* (the belief one holds, the content of faith) and *fides qua creditur* (the belief with which one believes, the act of 'believing') these two sides, the objective and the subjective one, can be clearly seen. What had been a living unity for the Reformers was divided into two parts. After orthodoxy had pushed the objective side forwards, the pietists added the subjective one. 'Object' and 'subject' have to be put side by side, and then the latter is the essential. This became the theme of 'the further Reformation'. Orthodox theology had divided the starting point. It fell just short of the original level, the liberating beginning of the Reformation. In the following centuries, Church and theology suffered continually from the division. *Herman Friedrich Kohlbrugge* (1803-1875), the fascinating preacher and theologian from Elberfeld, had a sudden vision of how to overcome it. This enabled him to preach with the same passion as the first Reformers, that the sinner is not only justified in Christ, but also sanctified. It is said of him that when asked where he had been converted, he answered: 'at Golgotha'. There can be no clearer expression of the unity in the tension between objective and subjective salvation. Kohlbrugge appears as a lonely and interesting figure in the nineteenth century.

The close relationship between orthodoxy and pietism may also be made evident by the fact that for some orthodox theologians they almost met. A worthy example of this is the Utrecht Professor Gisbert Voetius (1588-1676), who introduced into the Netherlands the 'further Reformation' referred to above. He urged 'the practice of godliness', *praxis pietatis*, which he himself took very seriously, as was evident from his sober and pious conduct in a period in which great pureness of doctrine was not always matched by a sanctification of the conduct of life.

Another indication of the close connection between orthodoxy and pietism is the fact that the teaching on the inspiration of the Bible was simply transferred from the former to the latter. This teaching had long been common property, so that it was accepted without further reflection. The Bible was God's revealed truth, which is at man's disposal. Where orthodox theology had used it to unfold the Christian message of salvation, pietism employed it for devotional exercises. In both cases the Bible was a store of texts which served to confirm their own truth. It is fortunately not necessary to suggest that this excluded the possibility of deep insights and real biblical thoughts being put forward with great intimacy and power. The Puritan J. Owen (1616-1683), who was highly regarded in certain pietist circles, and the Erskines, whose sermons are loved to this day, bear a telling witness to their love of the Scriptures. We must also mention with praise the exegetical work of the father of the so-called Wurttemburg pietism, J. A. Bengel (1687-1752), from whom come the well-known words: 'Apply yourself wholly to the text, apply the text wholly to yourself.'

3. *The Enlightenment and the Birth of a New Era:*
The Bible as a Book of Religious Experience

Since the late Middle Ages, spiritual and political movements had come to life which ran like clear mountain streams beside, or sometimes in, the same course as the main stream of Church life. We are referring to humanism, the Renaissance and the beginnings of free science and arts. Such names as Wycliffe (d. 1384) in England, Petrarch (d. 1374) and Lorenzo Valla (d. 1457) in Italy, Reuchlin (d. 1522) and Copernicus (d. 1543) in Germany, Erasmus (d. 1536) and Hugo Grotius (1583-1645) in the Netherlands and Descartes (d. 1650) in France, indicate but a few of the most striking rapids in these waters. They represent the questioning of the human spirit which, in youthful wonder at its own potentialities, begins to free itself more and more consciously from the authority of tradition, church and political powers, which it has come to consider as superfluous or restricting.

During the period of orthodox theology this current remained dammed up, or partly underground, because in the Protestant countries Church and theology put a heavy mark on public life through the authority of the inspired Bible which guaranteed the truth of its revelation. But simultaneously with the pietistic reaction, the humanist current began to gather force, ending up in the middle of the eighteenth century in the *Enlightenment* (Aufklärung), which forms a mountain lake in the history of the West European spirit. This lake, clear but rather shallow, dominates the landscape and becomes the origin, through the spiritual currents which it feeds in its turn, of the nineteenth century and its many varied spiritual movements.

A few of the most brilliant names must suffice to find our bearings. In England there are empiricist philosophers such as Locke (d. 1704) and Hume (d. 1776), who allowed only experience as a source of knowledge; in France we find Voltaire (d. 1778) with his sharp pen, and the sensitive Rousseau (d. 1778); in Germany the subtle Lessing (d. 1781) and the powerful philosopher Kant (d. 1804), who towered head and shoulders above all the others. Kant saw in the thought-patterns of the human consciousness the irrevocable, basic assumptions of all real knowledge, while in our moral awareness he found the source and norm of all truly moral action.

For our purposes it is not necessary to give an extensive description of the Enlightenment; a short character sketch will do. There is optimism and faith in the progress of man and mankind. There is great faith in the possibilities of science and rational thought. Tired of vehement and often melancholy theological disputes people set great store by tolerance. There was a growing conviction that the biblical revelation coincides exactly with what man learns from common sense and from the nature of things. Therefore we find no criticism or rejection of the Bible as the revealed truth, but instead an ever-growing tendency to consider it merely of practical value, or perhaps just superfluous. In France there was sharp criticism of the Church, which proved itself, on the Roman Catholic side, extremely corrupt. This was one of the reasons why the Enlightenment in France ended in the great revolution of 1789. Elsewhere this criticism took the form of condescending indifference – what is today known as 'not being against it'. Rationalism is the word with which to typify the Enlightenment as a whole.

If one had to make a judgement of this movement, then it would be well to note that many in the church today are less negative in their attitude towards it than used to be the case.

In the first place it is clear that in the spiritual atmosphere of those days the breakthrough of the Enlightenment brought a real liberation. In his book *The Bewitched World* (1691-1693), the Dutch preacher Balthasar Bekker exposed the contemporary belief in witches and devils as a superstition for the first time. In the Calvinistic Netherlands this cost him his office as minister, but he saved many 'witches' from the stake. The freedom to form and confess one's own convictions without social or political coercion is a real benefit for which we must thank the Enlightenment, even though the word 'toleration' – which is often used to avoid a discussion on matters of principle – today sounds rather threadbare and hardly positive to us. The scientific passion which cleared a wide path for free research, even if some sacred cows were killed in the process, would never have blossomed in our European civilization without the Enlightenment. It is right that a later generation should be honest about this, even though, seen from a distance, the limitations and the superficiality of this naïve faith in progress may seem more obvious to us.

But in the second place we must also put the question whether, from within the Christian faith, which the Enlightenment secretly undermined and sometimes openly attacked, this independent and free questioning and probing of the human mind should not be judged positively: man come of age! We discerned him already in a pre-natal state during the period of the Reformation (see above, pp. 27ff). Is it not true that the Enlightenment continued in its own way along the valid line which begins in the Gospel itself, where Paul writes: 'I speak as to sensible men; judge for yourselves what I say' (I Cor. 10.15)? This argument was persuasively advanced by Dietrich Bonhoeffer, the martyr of World War II, in his *Letters and Papers from Prison*.

In any case, however, we must ask ourselves with what weapons we want to fight the rationalism of the Enlightenment (which we meet, of course, even today), if we are to defend 'the truth' of the Bible. Before we know where we are, we find ourselves in the same situation as that in the well-known story of I Sam. 4 and 5, where the Israelites carry the Ark of the God of Israel before them against the uncircumcised Philistines as a guarantee of his powerful presence. They discover later that no victory over the enemy can be forced in this way, and suffer a humiliating defeat. Did not orthodox theology similarly carry Holy Scripture as the inspired word of God, in order to have a safe starting point for the attack against the un-Christian philosophy of Descartes, who elevated man and his reason to the throne? But when this 'humanistic' thinking gets stronger, as the Philistines did in the story, and when devout pietism – which, like the godly Eli, had remained outside the battle with trembling heart – can offer no real help, then defeat becomes inevitable. A curious controversy between a certain Pastor Goeze and Lessing is a clear example of this.

This discussion raised as much dust in the theological and ecclesiastical world of those days as the Bishop of Woolwich's 'Honest to God' did in our time. The scholar Samuel Reimarus from Hamburg had written a number of papers on biblical and ecclesiastical topics in which he pointed out many contradictions in the Bible, especially in the narratives concerning the crossing of the Red Sea and in the

resurrection narratives. This is the real beginning of 'biblical criticism'. He reached the conclusion that the Bible must be completely
unreliable, and that nothing could be preserved of the Christian
faith apart from a general religious belief in a god: deism. Reimarus
did not publish these papers out of fear of the reaction of the church
and science. Lessing found them in the Hamburg library, and, impressed by their scholarly force, he published them in 1774 under the
name of 'Wolfenbütteler Fragmente' (Fragments from Wolfenbüttel).
Lessing supported the critical position of the 'unnamed author',
though he did not share in his conclusions. He considered the core
of the reports in the Bible correct, and therefore he wanted to uphold God's revelation in the Scriptures. This he considered essential
in bringing mankind to an understanding of a general natural
religion, such as he believed Jesus to have taught. The 'historical
truths' of the Bible, which Lessing therefore generally accepted in
spite of the undeniable contradictions in the information given, are
nevertheless incapable of forming the basis of intellectual truths,
general religious ideas such as the existence of God, the creation of
the world, sin and moral progress and the immortal soul. He accepted
the resurrection of Jesus, but did not base his faith on that. Since
that time, the distinction between 'the letter and the spirit' which
Lessing had made has been used again and again to explain difficult
points in the Bible. Pastor Goeze of Hamburg, who made himself
the mouthpiece of the opposition, felt quite rightly that this approach
gave a mortal blow to the heart of the Christian faith, while the
Bible as the source of the gospel was left out of things. In his fierce
and not always very dignified retorts, however, he could do little more
than give a rather unscientific denial of the scientific theses of the
'Fragments'. He attempted to 'harmonize' the contradictions in the
biblical narratives. His starting point, which was the orthodox
position of inspiration, left him no other choice. Everything in the
Bible simply had to be correct historically. This made him easy game
for Lessing. Those who frame a doctrine of inspiration by the Holy
Spirit, however true this may be, are, according to Lessing, lost. 'He
betrays what is to him the real point. It is not the credibility of
the resurrection, which could suffer from irreconcilable contradictions
among the evangelists, but his concept of theopneustia, once and for
all absorbed. His concern is not the Gospel, but his dogma.' It is
exhilarating to read the arguments which flowed from Lessing's

agile pen, and which are as valid against Goeze as they are worthy of serious reflection today.

But in the meantime, with the victory of Lessing and his much more radical associates, the Ark of Scripture had fallen into the hands of Philistines of the Enlightenment, who honoured man and reason above all things. In this case, too, however, the story of the Ark is not finished; in the eighteenth and nineteenth centuries we find a curious sequel.

In the Bible story the Philistines placed the Ark with great respect in the temple of their god Dagon – behind this lies the very plausible pagan idea that gods exist to help and serve man in various circumstances, and that the God of Israel is also suited to such purposes. Similarly, the Enlightenment does not want to reject the Bible, but it wants to fit the Bible into its own philosophical framework and use it there. Thus the Bible becomes the book of human religiosity – instead of the book of God's living Word which comes to man. People hear and read in the Bible only those things that already seem familiar from the ups and downs of their own spiritual life. This combination of Bible and human religiosity proved to be less simple than the men of the Enlightenment had thought in the first flush of their victory – just as the priests of Dagon found to their disappointment that the two religious entities, the Ark and Dagon, did not tolerate each other very well. But this makes the history of the church and of theology in the nineteenth century, after the Enlightenment, such a fascinating period. It is the history of a new Protestantism, in which man tried to bring about new syntheses, or even a higher unity between the Bible and religion, faith and science, church and culture, God and man, Christ and the modern times.

It is obvious that we cannot give the history of this whole, varied development here. We must be content to indicate in a few words the different ways in which people attempted to achieve these various ends.

In the first place, there is the way of undiluted rationalism, which was at its most vigorous at the height of the Enlightenment, but which has many followers to this day. Impressed by the results of the sciences, man only takes note of what can be measured, counted or observed, neglecting the deeper layers of human existence, or the wider contexts of world and spirit. The causal-mechanical image of the world is the only one; there is no room here for 'miracles'. In a discussion of the Bible everything that has not 'really' happened is relegated to the realm of fables, unless a rational explanation can be found. Thus the resurrection of Christ can be explained by saying that Christ was only apparently dead. The classic example of this rationalism is that of the teacher who told the visiting minister that he no longer believed, because he had his teacher's certificate. This kind of rationalism often leads to materialism as a philosophy. Only what is tangible or concrete is accepted.

Much more profound and fascinating, but for that reason perhaps more dangerous to the Christian faith, is the *idealism* which has been symbolized for ever in the name of the philosopher Hegel (d. 1831). It is not intellect, but the Spirit, that explains and contains everything that exists. Here we are not concerned with a cold 'truth' which is unalterable (twice two makes four), but again and again contradictions are absorbed into a higher synthesis and thus the history of mankind and of the world proceeds towards an ever-increasing realization of the Spirit, in which God's Spirit and the spirit of man are one. All civilizations, but especially Christianity, and more particularly the proclamation of Jesus, can be considered and placed in one large, wide context. Contradictions in the Bible itself do not need to create offence. They have their significance and their meaning, because together they make a higher synthesis possible, which in its turn will be the beginning of a further development.

These rarefied speculations are strange to our generation, but if we take the trouble to understand them, we may feel their tremendous charm. The controlled and mild optimism, the great relief that all things, even the most incomprehensible and disturbing ones, have been allocated their place in the great whole – all this moves the philosopher who has understood it to quiet gratitude. It is not surprising that several of the great theologians, disturbed by the vulgar noise with which the Enlightenment kicked over so many of the old and accepted truths, took refuge in this idealism which was at once modern and conservative. It offered the possibility of appreciating and restoring to doctrine many of the ecclesiastical dogmas.

Outside academic circles, the effects of this idealism remained small, but traces of it can be found wherever people speak of the high and spiritual 'truths' which can also be found in the Scriptures. Ordinary, concrete stories in the Bible do not create any difficulties, nor do miracles or the crudely realistic stories, because they are considered as wrappings for profound ideas, and thus are stripped of their real meaning. It is not the form or the presentation of the biblical material which is important, but the spiritual contents. This is a return to the allegorical explanations of the Middle Ages and the preceding centuries. It is clear that in this manner the Bible is also prevented from saying more than what is already contained in the human spirit.

Yet another, completely different, entry into the Bible is made by those who consider human feelings the key to all religious attitudes. Here it is the way of *individualism* and *romanticism* which seems to offer new perspectives. Everything that I, in my personal experience, recognize as true and real, is valuable. Proofs are superfluous, because in inner contemplation I perceive at once how and what I may and must believe of the transcendental or inner-spiritual world of the divine. The German philosopher Jacobi (1743-1819) built his philosophy on this; he did not want to surrender to the reasoning intellect, but instead proceeded from the intuitive certainty which lies irrevocably behind every proof. Goethe (1749-1832) gave these ideas vivid and glittering expression in his extensive literary *oeuvres*. '*Gefühl ist alles, Name ist Schall und Rauch*', according to his Doctor Faustus, who could not find satisfaction for his deepest needs in the sciences.

Friedrich Schleiermacher (1768-1834) exploited these ideas for faith and the church. To those who looked down on religion from their scientific heights, he pointed out that both the highly prized knowledge and moral action had to have a common source, which he called feeling. This must not be confused with sentimentality or superficial sensitiveness. This deep point he indicated as the seat of religion. Religiously, the Christian feels himself absolutely dependent on the impression which emanates from Jesus. The Church is the community of all those who experience this and pass it on to others.

Since that time there has been an uncountable host of people who insist that religion and Christianity should not be discussed, and that everyone must feel and experience for himself what and how he must believe. In this climate of thought people may have the greatest respect for the Bible, but they will choose from it only those things they find beautiful. In this atmosphere in particular, the Bible is limited to being a book of human religious attitudes.

Finally, there is the way of the ethos, the deed. Following in the footsteps of Kant, the core of the human personality is seen in the moral judgements and actions of man. In this context the Bible is only heard when it lays down ethical demands or exhortations, or where it calls to action. Anyone can recognize this philosophy in a popularized form, in the cry that what matters is to do the right thing; the Christian faith is absorbed in morality. This is the popularized form! The men who saw in the ethical understanding of the Bible the solution of the synthesis of Bible and human consciousness – such as A. Ritschl (1822-1889) and many other theologians in the second half of the nineteenth century – in principle intended much more than a cheap moralism. Their concern was not for the fulfilment of fixed commandments or generally accepted norms of behaviour, but for the inner moral decision to hear the call of God's kingdom, which they discerned in the words of the Prophets, and more particularly in the words of Christ.

In this climate of thought it seems obvious to distinguish between what is lower and what is higher in the Bible. It is felt that there is a development in moral awareness in the Bible. The morality of the deceiving Jacob in the stories of the patriarchs is not as elevated as Amos' stern demands for justice and righteousness, and the crude war tales of the times of the Kings belong to a lower level than the wide and noble flights of thought of a prophet like Isaiah. The climax of moral development is then found in the radical gospel of love and forgiveness of Jesus himself. Law and gospel are one, God's love and God's demands coincide.

These last remarks lead us to the first of the three points with which we want to terminate this section.

1. In our very rough sketch of the roads followed by the Church and by theology in the nineteenth century we have indicated that these roads were *culs-de-sac*, but it is not our intention to deny that along these roads real and true things have been discovered. On the contrary, the sober honesty of rationalism, the broad and mild

vision of idealism, the profound and intimate approach of the individualists or the moral earnestness of the last group, all this must never be lost. They all contain truth, biblical truth. We owe the theologians of the new Protestantism respect and gratitude. Nevertheless, the right solution cannot lie in putting the Bible in the temple of 'the human personality', that idol of the nineteenth century. At the most this can only be a detour through the confusion created by man, though God is still the guide. But the Scriptures have to return to their own place, just as the Ark had to come back to Israel.

The story in I Sam. 5 tells us, not without irony, how the image of Dagon fell off its pedestal after every well-intentioned effort to put the Ark alongside it. Have we of the twentieth century not seen how the harmonious and optimistic image of man of the previous century fell into fragments, even though the priests of modern philosophy attempted to stick it together again and return it to its pedestal – and what else could they have done? Is it that the development of the concept of man and of philosophy, this crisis of our certainties of which existentialist thought knows, takes place entirely outside the quiet strength of that strange power, the Bible?

2. Here we should mention one curious figure of the nineteenth century who opposed these efforts to achieve a synthesis, though Church and world did not understand him, the Dane Kierkegaard (1813-1855). His protests and objections were garbed in the philosophical concepts and patterns of his time. But he saw the 'infinite, qualitative difference between time and eternity' more acutely and clearly than anyone else. The scandal of the cross cannot be fitted into the religious thoughts of man, not even into those of Kierkegaard. That is why his message to the world is put into such strange camouflaged and indirect terms. The echo of it was only captured in the twentieth century.

3. The development described was in the first place the concern of the philosophers and the theologians. The life of the Church, especially in Germany, continued fairly quietly along the lines indicated by orthodoxy and pietism. Naturally, the ideas of the Enlightenment and of the later movements penetrated, but the ordinary church-folk heard only from a distance the noise of the

battle being fought on the front-lines. It was, however, precisely this vague information and this unconscious influence which did so much harm pastorally and spiritually. It is no wonder that the situation in the churches became so confused. 'Parties' began to form, particularly in the Netherlands, where there was most interest in this spiritual battle – the Dutch are a nation of theologians. The main opposition was between the orthodox and the liberals, who in the second half of the nineteenth century were often called 'modernists'. On the one hand, people wanted to maintain (more or less moderately, though sometimes very strictly!) the old teaching which had been passed on, which in practice meant the same type of theology and preaching as in the period of orthodoxy and pietism. Others, however, wanted to make room for the new insights into faith and the Bible.

We hope that it is clear from what we have said that it is impossible to indicate plainly which side is right and which is wrong. Hoedemaker's remark, 'Together we became ill, together we must get better', is very true.

But people always like to judge by a few simple standards. One of these now became how one viewed the Bible. Those who were 'orthodox' were considered to be under obligation, on the basis of the inspiration of the Scriptures, to accept unconditionally everything that is found in the Bible. Those who called themselves 'liberal' were prepared to allow the scientific examination of the Bible, or *criticism* of the Scriptures. But this brings us to a matter with which the whole further development was closely connected. The Bible became the subject of detailed research in an entirely new way.

4. Historical Criticism of the Bible:

The Bible as a Literary Document

The Reformers and the Humanists in the sixteenth century already had an eye for what would later be called biblical criticism. Luther had some doubts about the Letter to the Hebrews and about James, because they differed in content from the writings of Paul. He barely counted them among the canonical books of the Bible. Calvin often speaks quite openly about the differences between the evangelists, which he either tries to reconcile, or else considers unimportant. Erasmus rendered a service by editing the Greek *text* of the New Testament. This clearly showed the differences from the Vulgate.

Luther made grateful use of Erasmus' text for his translation of the Bible. Erasmus also discovered that not all the epistles were written by the apostles themselves. The Church Fathers had already discovered this, too.

But a really scientific examination of the Bible only finds a break-through during and especially after the Enlightenment. During the nineteenth and twentieth centuries the movement produced an imposing monument of scholarship, witnessing to deep respect for the Bible. In the first period, the historical and grammatical research seemed to contemporaries to be of a mostly negative character. The origin of the various books of the Bible was verified and the discovery for example, of the fact that Moses could not have been the author of the first five books, as had been accepted traditionally, caused a great shock. There was also a sensation when it was discovered, through careful reading and comparison of the language and contents of these books, that the stories and the material came from different sources which had later been combined into the form which the books now have. This meant that they had had a long history of development.

A clear criterion for the distinction between sources was the use of the name of God. In some parts only the name God (Elohim) is used, but in other parts we find the name YHWH, which cannot be pronounced, and which expresses the great glory of God. In translations of the Bible this name is best rendered by Lord. The Jews do not pronounce this name, but in the Scripture readings they use the word adonai, which means 'Lord' or even 'master'. By differentiating between the uses of the name of God it is indeed possible to distinguish different stories in Genesis and Exodus. Any reader can make a test by comparing Gen. 1.1-2.3 with Gen. 2. 4-25. Here we discover two creation narratives side by side. The first story describes in detail the creation of heaven and earth, in which the creation of man is only one feature, mentioned in verses 26-28. The second story, on the other hand, is mainly concerned with the creation of man (or men), for which the creation of the earth, or at least of the grass and the trees because of a fertile mist coming out of the earth, forms merely a background. This so-called source theory explains inconsistencies in the sequence of the stories; as when, for example, Jacob first deceives his father in chapter 27, and then in chapter 28 again receives his father's blessing as if nothing had happened. Such discoveries were made by Professor Kuenen (1828-1891) of Leiden, among others.

The books of the prophets were also subjected to a careful analysis, which soon made it clear that many of these books were not by one author, but were composed of many parts which were, in terms of time, sometimes far removed from each other. The most famous of these was so-called Deutero-Isaiah, a title used to indicate Isaiah 40-55. Isaiah himself lived in the time of Ahaz and Hezekiah (Isa. 1.1), about 740-690 BC, that is to say nearly a century and a half before the Babylonian exile (568 BC). But in Isa. 40 and the following chapters the return from the Babylonian exile is foretold, and we find ourselves in the time of the Persian King Cyrus, who allows the exiles to return to Israel. This was about 530 BC. It would be necessary to have recourse to complicated devices to maintain that these chapters also dated from the time of Isaiah, or that they could even be from his hand.

In the same way a careful comparison of our four gospels taught that these give a very different picture, in detail, of Jesus' life and activity. In John, the cleansing of the temple takes place in chapter 2, and Jesus is several times in Jerusalem, while the other three evangelists put the cleansing of the temple after Jesus' entry into Jerusalem and just before the Passion (Mark 11.15-18). People had long ago been struck by the fact that the Gospel of John has an entirely different character and tone, but it became a well-known problem among scholars, how the similarities and differences between the three other evangelists should be explained; this was known as the 'synoptic problem'. The fact emerged through all this that we cannot be sure that many of the sayings attributed to Jesus were in fact spoken by him, at any rate in those particular words. In Matt. 10.10 we read that the disciples may not take sandals with them, but in Mark 6.9 it is stated emphatically that they must wear sandals. People began to suspect that the composition of the gospels had been a long process, influenced by the ideas of the early Church. Then the awkward question came up as to which words of Jesus had been 'real' ones, and which had not. The fact that various scholars contradicted each other was one reason for criticizing the 'criticism'. The fact that it was precisely the conservative scholars who tried to preserve as many texts as possible as 'real', while the more radical ones tended in the opposite direction, made the whole affair even more suspect to congregations.

The date and the origin of the apostolic letters were also subjected to a thorough examination. Were all the letters really written by the authors mentioned in the Bible and upheld by tradition? The uncertainty about the letters to the Ephesians and to the Colossians, as well as about those to Timothy and Titus, continues. It is generally accepted that II Peter was not written by Peter, but by another author. In the period of orthodox theology, the fact that the early Church did not take these questions quite so seriously had been kept quiet. Therefore all these matters came as a shock to the faithful.

It was during this period that biblical criticism began to acquire such a bad name. Many ministers and especially many theological students suffered from a crisis of conscience. To say 'the prophet' when referring to the unknown (to us, at least) voice of Isaiah 40 and the following chapters, left the matter neatly in the open as far as the congregation was concerned, but of course that was no solution. Sometimes congregations were upset because of scriptural criticism from the pulpit. Some of the epigrams of de Genestet still put this very pointedly for us:

> My understanding and my faith
> live together but can't agree,
> Truly it is good to see
> Such a blest confusion.

After the first somewhat stormy period, however, it gradually became clear that the Bible has a remarkable tolerance. After it had been crucified by negative analysis, it rose again from the grave, though somewhat scarred, with such life and splendour that it was more impressive than ever. New dimensions appeared, and did so precisely because people had worked with the Bible in a matter-of-fact and human way, as if it had a genealogical register of authors and influences, just as Jesus has a genealogical register of ordinary sinful ancestors. Now the contours became visible, nuances began to speak. The contradictions proved to be fruitful. The stories in Genesis seem nearer home to us when we pay attention to the differ-

ing styles of the various sources. The Elohist speaks of God as
powerful, majestic, high and exalted. The Yahwist pictures God as
'walking in the garden' (Gen. 3.8), having ordinary and almost
humble contact with the children of men, intimate and familiar.
Is the God of the Bible not both?

The same is true of the preaching of the prophets, which is much
better understood against the background of their time. The discovery that a certain section of a prophecy must have been written
many years later may give it a certain bias which renders the whole
proclamation much more eloquent. The same thing holds for the
distinction between the gospels. It proves to be an enrichment of
them. Precisely the things which have been omitted or added by
the evangelists may draw attention to something which they wanted
to pass on as witness at that moment. Matthew gives a much less
colourful account of the healing of the leper (Matt. 8.1-4) than does
Mark 1.40-44. He ends with the words: 'Show yourself to the priest,
and offer the gift that Moses commanded for a proof to the people.'
In this way he stresses Jesus' attitude towards the Jewish law.
Though Jesus came with the full consciousness of the salvation he
was bringing, he nevertheless does not want to break the law. This
must be made clear to his opponents. Mark, on the other hand,
concludes with the surprising spreading of the news. This is what
is important to him. Here the struggle against, and the victory over,
the demons and evil forces play an important part. This element is
found much less in Luke. There the gospel has a much more 'human'
framework against the background of the poor, the despised and
the lost. In John, on the other hand, it is often as if we were
participating in a high church liturgy. The words of Jesus are
exalted and majestic, as in John, chs 6, 10, 14-17 and in many other
beautiful sections. This style is unknown to the other gospel-
writers.

Similarly it is enriching to see the difference between the early
letters of Paul to the Galatians and to the Romans on the one hand
and the later, post-Pauline, epistles on the other. In the former we
have the fierce preaching of grace alone, justification by faith. In
the latter, especially in Ephesians and Colossians, we meet with a
tone of fulness and of 'spiritual blessing' (Eph. 1.3), with an echo
of cosmic distances, heights and depths, heavenly regions and particular words such as unity (Eph. 4.1-6) and fulfilment (Eph. 3.19),

which introduce a spaciousness and splendour which we do not meet with elsewhere.

Research into the original text of the Bible, backed up by the findings of many very old manuscripts and by excavations which have extended our knowledge of the history and the culture of the peoples of biblical times, came gradually to be understood as a valuable help in the real understanding of the Bible. It opened up like a whole world, rich and infinitely varied; and yet, in spite of all this diversity it formed one whole, even though differences came to light which we have not – or not yet – been able to reconcile.

This is obviously the case with the well-known problem of the biblical view of 'life after death'. The patriarchs died and 'were gathered to their people' (Gen. 25.8; 35.29), a somewhat vague expression which stresses strongly the awareness of community which is so characteristic of the people of Israel. In the Law and the Prophets the impression which is mainly conveyed is undoubtedly that man in his totality is mortal. Man is mortal and fleeting, a mere breath (Ps. 39.5), as the grass (Isa. 40.6). After that, it is not said that the soul endures, but that 'the word of our God will stand for ever' (Isa. 40.8). The same tone is heard in Eccles. 12, where the 'eternal' home is not an image of 'heaven', but of the grave. The return of the spirit to God (v. 7) alludes to Gen. 2.7, where God breathed the breath of life into man. As soon as God takes away this breath, however, man dies (Ps. 104.29; 146.4). Only occasionally do we find in the Law and Prophets any feeling of being safe with God, as in Ps. 73.26: 'My flesh and my heart may fail, but God is the strength of my heart and my portion forever.' Of Enoch we read that 'God took him' (Gen. 5.24), and the story of Elijah's end is obviously also an exception to the general idea that death is an end without anything afterwards. Alongside this, or later than this, we find the idea that the dead go to Sheol, the realm of the dead, where they lead a shadowy existence: Job 14.13; Deut. 32.22; Amos 9.2 and many other texts. Jacob also speaks of 'going down into Sheol' (Gen. 37.35). In the Bible we find every now and then a reference to a book in which all the names have been written (Ex. 32.32; Ps. 69.28; Isa. 4.3; Dan. 12.1; Phil. 4.3; Rev. 3.5; 13.8; 17.8; 20.12; 21.27). This is probably connected with the important part played by the word 'remember' in the Bible.

The murderer on the cross asks Jesus, 'remember me when you come in your kingly power' (Luke 23.42). It is terrible when the memory of someone is blotted out or destroyed (Ex. 17.14; Deut. 32.26; Isa. 26.14; Ps. 9.6; 34.15). In later Judaism there arises the idea of 'resurrection', which must not be confused with immortality. This 'resurrection' coincides with the day of judgement, which in Amos is a judgement over all the nations, through which Israel will be freed and justified. It is the 'day of the Lord' for which people long in vain, according to Amos, because that is the day on which their own people will be judged (Amos 5.18). In Jesus' day the idea of such a general resurrection is accepted everywhere by the Pharisees, and also by the people, but the (conservative) Sadducees object to it. This explains the well-known trick question put to Jesus about the woman with the seven husbands (Mark 12.18-27). 'In the resurrection, whose wife will she be?' (v. 23). Alongside this there is also somehow a current idea that directly after death one is carried to 'Abraham's bosom', as Jesus' story about the rich man and the poor Lazarus (Luke 16.19-31) testifies. Obviously, this is a concrete elaboration of 'gathered to his people' in Genesis, while the idea of Sheol is also much more elaborate. Jesus accepts these images, and in this way they have become the norm for the Christian Church. Then there is the word of Jesus to the murderer on the cross: 'today you will be with me in Paradise' (Luke 23.43). This word is repeated in II Cor. 12.3 and in Rev. 2.7, but when Jesus speaks of the house of my Father with its many rooms (John 14.2), as well as in Revelation and in other places, we meet with the same thought of 'being in blessedness' even before the final phase of the plan of salvation begins, and the Kingdom of God becomes visible to all eyes in judgement and glory. Paul speaks intimately and simply of 'being with Christ' (Phil. 1.23), but much more emphatic is the expectation in both Gospels and Epistles of the breaking through of the Kingdom of God through the Coming of the Lord (I Cor. 15.50-58; I Thess. 4.13-18, and other places). It is also striking that, in the Gospels and Epistles, there is hardly any interest in the question of the 'hereafter' (an ugly, unbiblical expression), because it pales in the tremendous light that shines out from Easter. Because of this light the congregation of Christ is aware of being part of a new and glorious era, 'the age to come' (Mark 10.30). 'Through him you have confidence in God, who *raised him from the dead and gave him glory, so that your faith and hope are in God' (I Peter 1.21). 'But you are a chosen race, a royal priesthood, a holy nation, God's own people, that you may declare the wonderful deeds of him who called you out of darkness into his marvellous light' (I Peter 2.9).*

At the end of Chapter IV we shall go into this further. At the moment our conclusion is that it is not so simple to say in a few words exactly what the Bible teaches about 'the life after death'.

For professional theologians and ministers alike, we must mention the standard work by G. Kittel. This is a theological wordbook in which all the words and concepts of any importance in the New Testament are explained, together with their development and significance, inside as well as outside the Bible. Consultation of this work may prevent people from associating a word with a certain idea because of its sound, giving it a meaning which it does not possess. No wonder that this work is considered indispensable to every minister for the preparation of his sermons, at least if these are intended as *biblical* preaching.

All this has been intended to show that the study of the Bible as a historical, human document has yielded a new revelation of God's salvation.

After this slightly exalted praise of the positive results of historical criticism, we must not conceal the fact that there continue to be difficulties.

What should our attitude be when it appears that during the long verbal transmission which preceded the composition of the Bible into book-form, historical events have been added to, elaborated upon or coloured? In profane literature, this would usually be called a saga. Can and should this word also be used in connection with some parts of the Scriptures, especially in the Old Testament? The stories of the patriarchs, the miracles that took place during the conquest of Canaan, the figure of Samson, the miracle stories of Elisha and the curious adventures of Daniel: does the significance of these stories for our faith diminish if we apply the word saga to them? Is it necessary to prove at all costs that such episodes 'really happened', and should we in any case believe this? If not,

what is the right and honest way out of these difficulties? In
Chapter III.B we shall go into this more deeply.

The word legend *refers to miraculous stories of saints of the early
church and of the Middle Ages. In the apocryphal books we find
what are clearly legends about Christ and the apostles, as well as
others. But is there not some legendary material in the Acts, on
the periphery, as it were? When we read in Acts 5.15 and 16 that
even Peter's shadow could heal the sick, this makes a different impression from the resuscitation of Dorcas in Acts 9.36-43. In the
latter story Peter speaks and prays; the former smacks slightly of
magic.*

A second, much discussed point is the occurrence of mythological
representations, not only in the Law and the Prophets, but also in
the Gospels and Epistles. The word *myth* is generally understood
to indicate a general and eternal truth – particularly the course of
nature as worshipped by pagans – embodied in story form. The
myths of Isis and Osiris in Egypt recount the eternal return of the
seasons and the ever new wonder of fertilization. By mythological
images are meant those images of heaven and earth, angels and
devils, good and evil, gods and Satan, which form the framework in
which the pagan myths take place. It is generally admitted by
scholars that the biblical story of salvation can definitely not be
called a myth. But is it not obvious that the Bible makes use of
a mythological framework? Should such images as a three-storied
universe, angels, Satan, dragons, be considered as the contents of
the biblical message, or as the form out of which we have to free
that message? The New Testament scholar Rudolf Bultmann has
insisted on 'demythologizing'. But do we not run the risk of losing
the contents together with the form? Is it possible to separate the
two? We do not want to conceal these thorny questions, nor do we
pretend that we can suggest a simple solution. We do ask, however, that other people do not offer glib 'solutions', which probably do little justice, either to faith or to scholarship.

The same is true of the third problem, that of the *historical* reliability of the gospels. Is it unbearable for the Christian faith that
some words, or texts, some sections or stories, prove not to be
historical? On the other hand, it is true that the gospels have an

atmosphere of living reality which simply cannot be denied. Historical touches, the filling in of small details, the correction of one evangelist by another, the very careful portrayal of the suffering of the Lord, even though each of the evangelists gives separate details which sometimes contradict each other (for example, the day of Jesus' death – before or on the day of the Passover) – all this cannot be denied to have reality, even by the scholars. We intend to discuss these questions further in what follows. Here we can only raise them, as our concern for the moment is the historical picture.

It seems right to close this short survey of scholarly criticism with an indication of a few of the points of view which emerged in the course of these studies.

1. In the Bible we find a *development*. The enthusiastic and ecstatic *prophesying* of the time of King Saul (I Sam. 10.10) has a different nature from the manner in which such prophets as Isaiah and Jeremiah bring their divine message. The former is close to 'speaking in tongues', as is favoured by the present-day Pentecostal Movement; the latter could be compared to the statements of the Netherlands Reformed Church 'for government and nation'. *Legislation* in Israel also developed considerably in the course of time. Most of the laws we find in Deuteronomy date from the centuries just before the exile, and were unknown at least in the time of the judges. In the same way, it seemed possible to note a clear difference in the *image of the deity* held by Israel and in the Gospel. The words of Jesus to the Samaritan woman seemed to indicate this : 'The hour is coming and now is, when true worshippers will worship the Father in spirit and in truth' (John 4.23). Once started on this track, men soon faced the question, which point in the development represents the real truth, God's own revelation? People began to ask about what was highest, what was lowest in the biblical message. It was supposed that what at first lay hidden in the Scriptures, contaminated by all sorts of primitive ideas, was gradually purified by the Prophets and the Psalms, to emerge finally with Jesus in ultimate purity. Not revenge, but absolute love. No earthly imagery, but everything spiritual. In this way people sometimes spoke of 'progessive revelation'.

This view has proved to be untenable in the light of further research. It cannot be said to be entirely satisfactory for the Christian faith, which would like to accept the Bible as a whole. Yet it contains a core of truth. The vision of a 'progression', of a history, will also prove to be of value to the understanding of the Bible. It is not so much a storehouse of divine truths as a book of the *history of salvation*.

2. It was discovered that the Bible is not isolated from the surrounding nations and cultures, but that *influences from outside* can be clearly detected in the Bible. The Bible is, after all, a Semitic, eastern book. When people first began to realize this, they could not resist the temptation to explain the Bible as much as possible through other influences, thus depriving it of its own original character. But here, too, the new fashion contained its own antidote. The very comparison with this extra-biblical world of thought underlined the special and separate character of the Scriptures. A nice example of these influences, by the way, is the second marriage of Abraham to Hagar, which provokes such sophisticated questions from the catechism classes. 'Why can't *we* have more than one wife nowadays?' But this story of Genesis should be seen against the background of old Babylonian laws. If the first wife proved to be infertile, one was allowed to take a second wife.

Gradually the following influences were distinguished.

(*a*) Babylonian and Egyptian civilization and religion. Particularly in the creation narrative of Gen. 1, the story of the serpent in Gen. 3 and that of the flood, there is a clear connection with the Babylonian myths of the creation and with the Gilgamesh epic. The background of Gen. 1 is the then current Babylonian representation of the heavens as a fixed dome (the firmament), which contains the waters which were above it. But where the Babylonian myths recount the eternal struggle between the god of light and the ancient dragon (Tiamat) from which the earth has its origin, the Bible speaks of the sovereign words of God, which summon the light and the stars that are to serve the good creation of God, the stage on which the history of God's relations with man will be enacted. The hero Gilgamesh is looking for the herb of life. This reminds one involuntarily of the 'tree of life' in paradise, of which Gen. 2 speaks. Gilgamesh loses this herb to the serpent through no fault of his. This is the eternal tragedy of the fate of man. But the biblical story speaks of guilt through which man comes to know trouble, suffering and death.

(b) The influence of later Jewish thought on the Gospels. For the explanation of the Sermon on the Mount (Matt. 5-7) in particular, a knowledge of rabbinism is indispensable.

(c) The oriental mystery religions and syncretism (the mixture of local Hellenistic religions) were also considered for a long time to be the source of all kinds of ideas, especially for the New Testament. The words in I John 1.7, 'the blood of Jesus his Son cleanses us from all sin', were supposed to refer to one of the sensual mystery religions, in which the blood of a slaughtered bull dripped on to the worshipper. It was thought that behind the sacraments of baptism and communion lay also the sacramental experience of unity with the deity of these religions. But it is rather the case that Paul warns his congregations repeatedly not to join in with these pagan ways. 'Therefore, my beloved, shun the worship of idols' (I Cor. 10.14). 'You know that when you were heathen, you were led astray to dumb idols, however you may have been moved' (I Cor. 12.2).

(d) The *gnostic* currents in Jewish and Hellenistic thought must also be discounted. Where the mystery religions were highly realistic and sensual, gnosticism (see above, pp. 17f.) has a pagan religion which sets out to convey spiritual knowledge and high and heavenly wisdom to its initiates. It despised matter and the body. It used to be thought that there were gnostic speculations behind the majestic opening of the Gospel of John about the Word which was in the beginning with God. In general, the exalted language of John, the repeated use of such words as Light, Life, Truth, and also especially the opposition between the Spirit and the flesh (John 6.63) were believed to be influenced by gnosticism. A more careful reading, however, showed that the reverse was true: John stresses that the Word has become *flesh*. That is where we find grace! (John 1.14). The letters of John also stress that Jesus has come in the flesh (I John 4.2). In I John 4.15, a much-quoted verse, the emphasis does not lie where it is usually supposed to be in theological discussion. We should read: 'Whoever confesses that Jesus is the Son of God . . .' The point here is not the 'son of God', but Jesus, the man! We have to confess that Jesus was a man; that is what the apostle wants to underline. Thus gnosticism is a position which is attacked by the Gospel.

(e) In our opinion, the great significance of the Law and the

Prophets for the Gospels is still underestimated by professional theologians. This is because so often in the Church Christian thought and the Christ himself are read into the Old Testament in a rather cheap manner. This is not the intention! But it does become more and more evident that the absolute and obvious cohesion and unity of both the Testaments has to be remembered in order to understand and sense the real meaning of what the evangelists and the apostles want to say to us.

3. In recent times, attention has been drawn to the particular character, the special literary structure of the various parts of the Bible, specifically of the Gospels, but also of the Law and the Prophets. We do not find a continuous report of how things happened in the Gospels. They consist of short, rounded-off pieces, pericopes, which have evidently been composed in this way by the author with the intention of making a point, of putting a special message across. It is the same in the other books of the Bible. There are stories and songs, liturgical pieces and letters, wisdom and contemplative literature, and all these parts have their own special function. They are meant to say something. The point is not just, and sometimes not at all, to give a historical report, or information about a general truth; what matters is the *message*. The evangelists confess, witness, the psalmists sing, the writers of the books of Judges and Kings show their prophetic criticism of the people by and through their story.

For this fertile approach we have to thank a small number of German scholars, e.g. K. L. Schmidt, Martin Dibelius, and Rudolf Bultmann, who have made this method of historical and literary research, called 'form criticism', prominent. Old Testament scholars, such as Gerhard von Rad and Martin Noth, have successfully applied the same method to research into the origin of the books of the Bible.

From what has been said it is evident that in recent times it has been particularly worthwhile to make a scholarly study of the Bible as a human, literary document. The Church should make full use of this in her preaching, and with an easy conscience. Is our preaching not often somewhat shallow and lacking in conviction because we dare not risk a real confrontation with the Bible?

5. The Bible and Moral Questions

One curious thing about the Scriptures is surely this, that they rule and work even when divorced from the learned problems which surround the Bible. While in the previous century the scholars were busy in their studies and pulpits subjecting the Bible as a literary document to a penetrating scrutiny, it became apparent that the Bible itself was becoming effective in a new manner. Even in the pietistic period, strong impulses towards mission had emanated from the Bible as well as towards social awareness and evangelism, especially in Germany and England. Spener and Francke in Halle are the men who cared for the orphans, and with the names of Zinzendorf and Carey, the panorama of worldwide mission begins to unfold.

William Carey, the highly gifted shoemaker, in whom were combined a passionate love for the Gospel and a vigorous sense of business, represents for us the miraculous growth and development of missions in the nineteenth and twentieth centuries. He collaborated in the foundation of the famous London Missionary Society (1795) and he realized then that mission should not be carried on from Europe, but by the converts from the pagan nations themselves. For that reason he exerted his great gifts as a linguist in the cause of the translation of the Bible into many languages and dialects of India. This is, of course, the root of the work of the Bible Societies, in which England also led the way.

The whole development of missions in the nineteenth century is such a miracle of the power of God's love that it leaves us speechless. While church life in the nineteenth century on the whole hardly made an encouraging impression, the heirs of pietism and Methodism, in their simple but stubborn faith and tremendous missionary zeal, guided and even directed world politics of their day. While the West European countries founded their colonial empires, the parallel current of the missionary movement is already groping ahead to things which in our time are only beginning to be discovered by the secular world. The younger nations could not forever remain under tutelage, but would have to become fully adult members of the community of nations. The nations of Asia and Africa should in their own way receive and develop, not just western technology, but also such things as advancement, science, medical care and neighbourly services. Can all this be divorced from the root which has been given in the Gospel of Jesus Christ? To this question the missionary movement gave its own unmistakable answer with impartiality, if also with the limitations and weaknesses which were characteristic of the missionary methods of the previous century. This answer is still of world-wide historical significance.

For the Protestant missions, the Bible was the central force. Can this also be said of the Roman Catholic mission? We must not detract from the blessing and influence which spread from it. In general, the missionary fathers and sisters were a refreshing example of Christian charitable love and devotion to the work of the Kingdom of God. But from the Protestant side we cannot escape the impression that the factor of the establishment of the power and influence of the 'Catholic Church' was always present. If this were true, could it be that this is one of the causes of the fact that in younger nations and countries which are predominantly Roman Catholic, the political, cultural and social development has often remained behind in comparison with countries where the Protestant missions were mainly at work?

Though it is not our intention to give a complete survey, we must also refer to Christian *social work*. It is untrue that the Christianity of the last century was unaware of the social distress of the working classes. On the other hand, it is certainly true that the official church circles had little or no feeling for the social justice which should have been brought about in the age of growing industrialism. Partly because of this the swelling stream of *socialism* became anti-church (though there were other reasons). It is generally accepted that the socialist labour movement took over the task of the Churches here. But we must not make the mistake of seeing in this proof that the power of the Bible is limited. It may even be that the opposite is true. To the shame of the many churchgoers, crowding round the pulpit with their Bibles open, it must be said that in this case the fruit did fall far from the tree.

It would be difficult to deny that the *abolition of slavery* is also a fruit of the Bible, even though there was much opposition to it in the Netherlands, especially in church circles. Da Costa lost a great part of the respect men might have felt for him, by being sharply opposed to abolition. But in the United States of America, the great champion for the slaves was John Brown, a descendant of a strict Calvinist family.

For us today it is beyond dispute that the leaders of the movements to which we have briefly referred were driven by the biblical message of the love of Christ for those who are lost. The harvest of this work is gathered by the Church today, when much of it is given a place inside the Church as *diaconia*, whereas previously it originated in private societies and persons.

There is, however, no reason for us to speak condescendingly of the 'diaconia' of earlier days. When the government was doing absolutely nothing against poverty, physical and social distress, the diaconia of the Church was in fact the only help available. Care for the poor, orphanages and old folks' homes were in the last century the hands of Christ stretched out to the destitute and the helpless.

In our own time other questions trouble the Christian conscience. Should we not declare war on war in the name of the gospel of peace? Since the First World War a strong pacifist movement has grown up, which is in part very consciously governed by biblical motives.

In the atomic age this problem acquires a special relevance and a more intense actuality. The discussion round the report of the Synod of the Netherlands Reformed Church on *atomic weapons* is partly strictly technical, but it is also of a direct biblical nature. Must, or even may, the Christian who lives with the Bible accept contemporary atomic weapons? What responsible risks can the Christian take in this field? This is the question of the practical application of biblical insights. In this field opinions are still strongly divided.

There is a similar division of opinion concerning *colonialism* and *racial discrimination*. And then there is still the matter of the *position of women*. The Netherlands Reformed Church has admitted women to its ministry, but the uncertainty about the rightness or wrongness of this from the biblical point of view still continues. It should also be remembered that it is not too easy to distinguish between a biblical and a purely human motivation of certain insights. For each generation anew the question is how to bridge the gap between the Bible and the question of the day. How and when does the Bible show its convincing and indisputable authority? This is another of the questions which caused this book to be written.

6. A Provisional Balance Sheet:

Can the Bible Assert Itself?

If the signs are not deceiving us, it can seriously be said that in this twentieth century the Bible is again on the march. It looks as if the Bible is asserting itself in this modern age. It is not superfluous to make the point in passing, because there are all sorts of indications that the opposite is true.

The *secularization* of our national life is a continuing process which must not be ignored. The connection between the Church and modern man is becoming less and less obvious. The protecting influence of Christian tradition and morality is decreasing steadily. Thus the churches and the church workers often have to wage a disheartening battle against increasing irreligiousness. The crowd of those who 'no longer believe in all that' seems to be ever on the increase.

Knowledge of the Bible, which as we well know was so sound in earlier days, is now much less so.

The much discussed *welfare philosophy* and the increasing *materialism* of our attitude to life which goes with it do not create a favourable climate for listening to the Bible and really paying attention to it. This last point, however, is at times stated too glibly. Welfare is not in itself something to which the attitude of the Bible is negative. Abundance and blessing are biblical words which must really not be understood in a purely 'spiritual' sense. Material joys and privileges may be received as good gifts from God, even on a national scale. It may even be that they – in contrast to poverty – create the conditions in which to find time and opportunity to study the Bible. Nevertheless, our present prosperity remains a somewhat ambiguous affair. It does not appear that the Bible's 'chances' are improved by superficiality, hurry, urbanization and all the other things connected with them.

All the same, we wonder whether these much-discussed features are really characteristic of our time. Are these not rather the offshoots of the nineteenth century, in which the middle-class mentality of faith in successful man waxed fat? Is it really the case that those who turn away from the Bible and the Church with such self-confidence are the ones who look to the future, the ones who are progressive and representative of our time? The typically nineteenth-century arguments which they can so often be heard to advance against the Church make one rather suspect the opposite.

In any case, there are indications that there is a transition in progress. The following points strike one as significant:

Widespread and close attention can always be counted on where animated and creative ways of confronting modern man with the Bible have been discovered. Radio and television programmes on subjects connected with the Bible always attract widespread attention. Evidently there are many people who, exactly because they no longer are in contact with the church, have arrived at a point where they long for honest information and thorough reflection on what the Bible has to say. The experience of church workers often provides remarkable examples of this. Not only the striking experiments, but also the ordinary Bible-study groups where the Bible is freely discussed, are always fascinating.

Contemporary poets express in their writings an encounter between the Scriptures and modern man, which is at once convincing and authentic. The recent metrical versions of the Psalms and the many experiments with sung portions of the Bible are significant. This is not the versifying of Christian poets on the subjects of Christian truths, but the inability to be detached from the Bible, in spite of oneself.

> *We speak and understand each other well*
> *A Jew called Jesus comes and passes by.*
> *Is it naïveté or existentialism?*
> *He has already gone to Golgotha.*
>
> A. Marja

In the state schools the demand for religious instruction has increased. Evidently large groups of the population have a desire to give the young more knowledge of the Bible than earlier generations have received.

Finally, it is very striking that in the Roman Catholic Church of today so much more attention is paid to the Bible than there used to be. There is a growing theological trend, the practical result of which is to create a deeper interest in the Scriptures. The encyclical *Divino afflante spiritu* of 1943 was not so much the cause as the result of this. Here more room is given to historical research into the Bible. It seems beyond dispute that in this respect Rome owes much to the age-long study of the Bible by the Reformed churches and by non-Roman Catholic scholars.

These developments, of course, have a background. They are not completely detached from the times. Since the First and Second World Wars a spiritual revolution has been in progress. The relative quiet and self-assurance of the nineteenth century have come to an end. Among numerous trends, often somewhat inaccurately summed up under the name of *existentialism*, the best ones are feeling towards a new evaluation of man. The effect of two world wars, the awakening of the East, and the staggering discoveries of modern technology and science have thrown man off balance. But is it not true that in all these things the Church was a few steps ahead of the world, just as theology was ahead of philosophy?

It is certainly a fact that during the 'twenties and 'thirties a striking revolution took place in theology, connected with the name of Karl Barth (b. 1886), which restored the Bible to its central position in a violent and much disputed manner. A new 'Theology of the Word' conquered the pulpits. A strange awakening spread through the world of the churches, bringing with it the removal of much dead wood, which should not be regretted. The *ecumenical movement* can no longer be omitted from the picture of our times. Through it, contacts between churches all over the world have increased tremendously. The problem of the explanation of the Scriptures plays an important part in these contacts. Does all this not contain indications of the living power of the Bible, which is letting its voice be heard again today? In the coming chapters, we must make an honest effort to listen keenly to this voice of the Bible.

II   The Bible Must Speak for Itself

1. *The Free Bible: Word and Spirit*

The Church does not just put the Bible as 'the Word' in the pulpit; it also likes to see the Bible in the hands of the people. It is not surprising, however, that this causes some confusion in hearts as well as in minds. When questions concerning the Bible are being discussed, two extremes stand out clearly.

On the one hand, there are those who accept the Bible as 'the Word of God' with certainty. This is done in such a way that the Bible does not inspire only great confidence, but also a deep respect. For many people the Bible at once becomes completely beyond discussion: 'I accept it the way it is written', they say.

On the other hand, there are those for whom the Bible has irrevocably lost any authority. They have heard of biblical criticism, of errors and mistakes. The modern view of the world and theories of evolution have created a conflict between Bible and science. In short, 'they no longer believe in the Bible'.

Between these two extremes there are some who are looking for a new approach to the Bible, but most people have given up altogether. For practical purposes the Bible still has a great authority for many, but in the background uncertainty is gnawing at their beliefs, thus preventing a decision of faith.

We are flattering ourselves with the hope that the reader who has had the patience to follow the strange course of the Bible through the history of the centuries has begun to see some light. With us he has discovered that the difficulties surrounding the Bible are the natural result of this development. He will therefore also understand that it is impossible to dismiss without further discussion either of the two attitudes described. Here, too, the saying holds that to understand much is to forgive much. But a compromise, an uncertain standpoint between two extremes, will not do either. What can we say instead?

To clarify the starting point that we have in mind we recall the story of Thomas (John 20.24-29). When Jesus appears for the second time, he meets Thomas' unbelief with the invitation to touch his marked body. This shows our Lord's great certainty. 'Thomas, you could not accept the message out of the mouth of the others, but here I am. See and touch.' And then Thomas surrenders.

We do not intend to use this well-known gospel story as a proof. Nor do we give a complete explanation of it. We want to use it as an illustration. In our opinion the Bible comes to meet man with this same attitude of conscious certainty. The Bible is prepared for the fact that it is not accepted as the Word of God on the authority of others. It is not put out by doubts, questions or objections. The Bible does ask, however, that we do not evade a meeting, and that we really touch it. At that point the Bible can speak for itself. We think that then the Bible will yield its secrets, and that a strange authority will begin to influence us. To this authority we may surrender, though we do not always want to. If we do so, the Bible comes to life for us in wonderful ways. The Word is also Spirit. God speaks to us through his Word and Spirit, as the fathers of the Reformation liked to put it. This has also been the experience of a great many others, as we saw in the previous chapter. This was what happened in that wonderfully transparent Easter story of the Walk to Emmaus (Luke 24.13-35). When the stranger speaks to the two men, the Bible begins to live. 'Did not our hearts burn within us while he talked to us on the road, while he opened to us the scriptures?' (v. 32). The same thing happened to the eunuch in Acts 8 when Philip explained the Bible to him (v. 35). This was also the world-shaking experience of Luther, who could not at first understand, in his study-cell, the obstinate verses, Romans 1.16-17, until suddenly the liberating light dawned, and these very words became for him 'the door to Paradise'. We could also mention the names of Augustine, of J. G. Hamann, and of H. F. Kohlbrugge who went almost mad with joy at the discovery of the comma in Romans 7.14. But there are also many unknown, ordinary men and women who have discovered something of the surprise which the Bible has in store for us, so that there is suddenly light, not once, but many times. This is why in the church service, before the reading from the Scriptures and the sermon, a prayer is said asking for 'the illumination of the Holy Spirit'.

The new and surprising urge to study theology in the twentieth century is in great measure due to a new discovery of the Bible. We have already mentioned the name of Karl Barth in this context. In the words of the Dutch theologian K. H. Miskotte: 'Among Roman Catholics, as well as among orthodox and liberal reformed, we find a more intense concentration on the explanation of the Bible than has been the case for centuries' . . . 'the secret of the church is that something happens there; the Word happens. Surrounding this inner secret is a zone of contemplation, of approach, of closer contact. Leaving aside the Word that penetrates, there is an occupation with Scripture as the witness of the Word, as a sphere of wisdom, as a companion and guide . . .' 'This is the case, not where the Bible is dismissed with a formal recognition of authority, not where it is used as a store of arguments, nor where it serves as green pastures where the disturbed soul may graze here or there; that is to say: not where a few proofs or a few pious words are fished up out of the confusion, but where the Scriptures open out as a world where one may tarry, out of which one may live . . .'

Here three remarks may help to refute some prevailing misconceptions:

1. To believe, in the sense of the Bible, should not be confused with simply 'to accept' on authority. If they were the same thing, we could not let the Bible loose in this manner. The story of Thomas is so illuminating because it illustrates clearly that believing in the biblical sense is not opposed to seeing and touching. Like many others in the Bible, Thomas comes to believe through seeing and touching. As another example we quote I Kings 18.39, where the people, on seeing the fire from heaven, confess Yahweh in the words: 'The Lord, he is God', words which Thomas almost makes his own. On the other hand, 'to believe' in the Bible is not the same as to see, nor is it the necessary consequence of seeing. The word is moreover used in varying shades of meaning in the Bible, which we cannot discuss more fully at the moment. But one of the main themes of the Bible is that people come to belief and confession through seeing and hearing. A good comparison is the boy who sees a girl *and* falls in love with her. The falling in love has its own secret, but at the same time it is obviously connected with the seeing. The be-

lief tends to become a blind faith, an acceptance of things with which one has no inner relationship.

This is certainly also not the intention of the famous beginning of Hebrews 11, where faith is 'the conviction of things not seen'. It is, however, a 'conviction', it contains an 'assurance', and it summons our 'understanding' (v. 3). This wonderful opening of the Letter to the Hebrews collapses when one bluntly equates faith with blind acceptance.

That the opposition between seeing and believing is nevertheless often drawn is also due to a misunderstanding of the end of the story of Thomas, where the Lord says: 'Blessed are those who have not seen and yet believe' (John 20.29). This saying should not just be taken as a reproof to the 'doubting' Thomas, who really loved his Master intensely. He was so overcome by the wounds of the cross that he was unable to open his heart to the Easter message. In his so-called unbelief he was therefore much more believing than those who 'accept' the miracle of Easter without further ado. It is rather that these closing words are to be of help in removing the stumbling block for all who come after Thomas, and who can no longer witness the appearances of the Lord. Instead, they will have the testimony of the apostles. But it would seem most unlikely that they have to overcome their doubts alone, and accept their faith solely on authority. No, the same attitude which Thomas was allowed to have towards his risen Lord, later generations will surely be allowed to take towards the witness of the apostles. They may 'touch and see'. This is exactly what we are arguing: neither the risen Lord, nor the Bible, insist on blind faith. We are allowed to let the biblical message penetrate, to consider and judge it; and in this way we come to a decision of faith.

2. The opening up of the Scriptures in us, the inner witness of the Spirit, as Calvin called it, should not be understood as a miraculous event, an illumination which must be added on to the Bible. It is not a kind of second wonder which must take place in the isolated person before he can start reading the Bible with open eyes. No, this was meant much more plainly: the discovery of design and context, of meaning and perspective, so that we begin to be enthralled by the Bible.

3. We should also beware of the misunderstanding that we can only understand, in the above-mentioned fashion, those parts of the

Scriptures which are already part of our own spirit. In that case we should only recognize our own thoughts and feelings in the mirror of the Bible. But the point is not to recognize, but to learn. In the meeting with the Bible a *strange* world opens out for us. We meet with real authority. A mighty hand stretches out towards us. We do not believe on authority, but in the Bible we do meet with authority, and we bow inwardly before it. That is what is meant by believing.

We think that from this standpoint it is possible to create a basic clarity in the somewhat confused situation between the two extremes which we indicated at the beginning of this chapter. We turn to both sides.

2. *The Bible as the Word of God*

From what has been said it must be clear that we may say with full conviction that the Bible is the Word of God. This may sound bold and we ask no one to accept it without argument; it must be clear to everyone, however, what we mean. That was the intention of this book.

It must be equally obvious from what has preceded that we have serious objections against the manner in which the thesis that the Bible is Holy Scripture has been and is used. We also object to the conclusions which are drawn from this thesis. We are fully convinced that something has gone wrong here, especially since the period of Protestant orthodoxy, to the great detriment of faith and life in the Protestant church. We hope that we have made this evident, in our first, historical chapter. If a name were wanted under which to group our objections in one concept, then we must call it rationalism, which crept unobserved into the Church and into theology. But it will not do just to search history for the blame. If we want to make clear for today why we object to the way in which the Bible is in one sense recognized as the Word of God, then we must express it as follows: *this thesis has not been taken too seriously, but too lightly.* If it is God who speaks in the Bible, then we must let him have his say, and we must let him finish. We must not think that we know beforehand what he, as God, can and cannot say. This is what is done, however, when the biblical word 'truth' is misunderstood in a rationalist manner. In the Bible, God's truth means that he is and remains faithful. He is the one 'who keeps faith forever'. One gets lost, however, with the following line of argument: God is truth and therefore we will find in the Bible, which is the Word of God, only true and trustworthy sayings, no contradictions or mistakes, nor any sagas, legends or myths, because that would mean that not everything has really taken place. Though it is easy to understand this kind of reasoning, it is nevertheless a way of rationally dominating the Word of God instead of following it obediently.

Not letting the Bible have its say is always found where people proclaim the Bible as the Word of God in order to find their own understanding of the faith, or their own pious moods or dogmas confirmed.

We hardly dare to accuse any specific church, group, sect or teacher. Who is entirely blameless? Who can be sure of himself, that he does not impose himself secretly on the Scriptures? Moreover, how many good, beautiful and profound biblical truths and insights have not been discovered in the course of history in spite of, or even because of – for the Holy Spirit has curious ways sometimes with human failings and shortcomings – this basically dominating attitude towards the Bible?

Without accusing anyone we must point out the great danger of not allowing the Bible to be God's Word, and we ask seriously if this danger is not at its greatest when we present this thesis as self-evident and completely established.

At this point we must return to the matter of the teaching on the *inspiration* of the Scriptures, and more specifically the form this teaching took in the century after the Reformation. As we have written about this in our historical section, we can be brief here.

Our main objection to this teaching is that it has an inherent tendency to bring and to keep the words of God under our domination. This teaching on inspiration reminds us of the tents which Peter suggested building for Jesus, Moses and Elijah, when he had been allowed to see the transfiguration of his Lord, 'not knowing what he said', as the Bible says significantly about this (Luke 9.33).

Again: we know how difficult it is to draw the dividing line. We do not want to doubt the personal good intentions of anyone, but we do ask whether this line of thought does not contain a basic mistake, from which many inside and outside the Church suffer.

Could we not recognize this honestly and admit it together?

Dr H. Bavinck, the clear-minded dogmatic theologian of the Free University of Amsterdam, has attempted in his broad dogmatic teaching to free orthodox teaching on inspiration from its obvious faults by suggesting a distinction between the organic and the mechanical *inspiration of the Scriptures*. This gives him ample space for the human factor in the Bible as a book. The writers have been used by the Holy Spirit as people, with their own contemporary insights and limitations, to write down the revelation. This gives him much more opportunity to allow for all kinds of human features and faults in the Bible, without having to drop inspiration as a divine tool. It is beautifully done, and if the doctrine of divine inspiration can be upheld at all, it would have to be in this form. It also shows in a very personal and human way the many difficulties which he could not ignore. And yet his explanations remain half-hearted; it is always: not this, but not quite that either. The give and take, the admission of infallibility, are not convincing. In spite of these there occurred in 1926 the well-known incident in Assen, where Dr Geelkerken was dismissed because he dared to doubt the historical meaning of Genesis 3.

Reading the Scriptures with the emphatic doctrine of inspiration as the starting point is rather like driving a car with a fixed steering wheel. Accidents are unavoidable. It was the same in 1633 when Galileo was forced by the Inquisition to retract his tenet that the earth moved, because the Bible says in Joshua 10.12 that the sun turns while the earth stands still.

Finally, to resume the consequences which the doctrine of inspiration might have, we see the following points:

1. A *legalistic use of the Bible*, which tries to force an external agreement with certain truths, which are not, however, the result of a real encounter with the Bible.

2. A certain *fanaticism* is usually a by-product of this use of the Bible.

3. *The Bible is read without any nuances*. Everything is simply God's truth and at times texts are brought out into the field like pieces of artillery. This often has the result that the finer distinctions of the Bible are not appreciated.

4. In any conflicts between the Bible and science, people are forced to bow before what is called the 'authority of the Bible', against their own intelligence. It is thought possible to ignore the questions raised by science and modern culture.

As a consequence of all this it is understandable that some may prefer not to speak any longer about the inspiration of the Bible. The term has already created too much disaster. We would like to maintain it in this book, however, because without it we risk missing something which is essential. This will only become clear in Chapter III, where we shall try to make access to the Bible itself easier by uncovering the 'key secrets'. We shall return to the concept in section B4 of that chapter, together with the other theological concept of '*the canon*'. In our view, however, the concept of inspiration definitely cannot be used to safeguard the divine authority of the Bible.

3. *The Bible as the Word of Man*

Now we must look at the other side; at the Bible as a human book. From our starting point it is very simple to find our attitude in relation to this second front. Precisely because it is God, and no other, who speaks in the Bible, we need have no fear that his Word will not be sufficiently divine. We do not need to surround it with assurances. It comes to meet us freely and openly. Thomas, see and touch. The Bible does not come to us as supernatural, secret teaching, nor as a mysterious holiness, nor as an unassailable sacred text – like the 'holy books' we know from other religions – but as an ordinary human book. This is a part of the gospel, of the glad news. For, if there is one thing which will prove to be characteristic of the God of the Bible, then it is this: that he is God-with-us, Emmanuel. God comes into the world in the man Jesus.

The Bible is a book, a collection of manuscripts for certain times and countries, and of a certain people, precisely because we believe that God speaks to us through that book. It is historical, set in time and in history. Therefore, there can and may be no objection to the careful examination of the Bible as a historical book or a literary document, and this is what the biblical criticism of the nineteenth and twentieth century set out to do. To criticize; the basic meaning of the word is *to draw distinctions*. Not to condemn, but to distinguish, to read and examine with care and the power to judge:

what is written here and what is its exact significance? There is an asking and seeking, a touching and feeling, and this is a good and wonderful thing. The congregation which confesses the Bible as the Word of God has little reason to be suspicious of this kind of biblical criticism and of this kind of scientific historical research. In this book, which comes from the Church, it is perhaps a good thing to admit openly and without holding back, that in the past, and perhaps even in the present, the Church has been unjust to the scholars by rejecting their scientific work and by judging their personal faith because of the critical approach to the Bible which these men had dared to adopt. These men have a right, not only to a cautious recognition, but to the open thanks of the congregation of Jesus Christ. Because ecclesiastical theology and the Church itself have in the past not dared to take the human side of the Bible seriously, opposed camps have come into existence, which have done much damage to both Church and faith. The two fronts, with their ramifications, are a sin which has to be confessed, too. The history of Protestantism could have been quite different.

The objection we do have against the critical-historical examination of the Bible – and that we have one is clear from the previous chapter – and some of its results, is that it has *not been scientific enough*. Real science adopts an attitude of *great reserve* towards the subject of its research. Real science asks questions rather than putting forward theses. Often the questions are more important than the answers. And the questions must be real ones, not questions which presuppose an answer. They must be questions which are related to the subject, not strange questions to which the subject *cannot* give the answers.

All this may sound difficult, but in reality it is simple. If a school wants to appoint a teacher, it can send a questionnaire to the head of a school or to a board of examiners, but not to a child of that teacher's class. But the spontaneous reactions of such a child about the teacher 'who can tell such super stories' are perhaps more to the point than the completion of official forms. The science concerned with the Bible gives the impression of only sending forms to the prophets and the apostles, forms with questions which have been framed according to the scientific ideas of the nineteenth century. The concepts have been those of historical correctness, of the time and place and date of actions, of the influences which have affected various texts and words, of the origin and originality of the words of Paul and Jesus. And so Moses, David, Mark and Peter have appeared before the examination committees, and it is not surprising that they have often given the wrong answers. They were no good at filling in forms. But were these questions the right ones? Should the Bible not be approached in another way; should it not be questioned differently from the way in which the critical-historical method does it?

Thus it comes about that, in spite of the probing researches of the scientists, one often has the impression that their analyses and their researchers have missed the real contents of the Bible. To put it in a somewhat homely image: the critical scientific approach to the Bible sometimes makes one think of trying to eat soup with a fork. What is offered in the many commentaries concerning the authenticity, the reality, the dependence on others' sources, and so on, is not so much wrong as beside the point. The same rationalism which we thought we had seen at work in orthodox theology has, in various guises, also affected the scientific research of the Bible, making it so scanty, so unfruitful, seemingly so negative, that congregations have been shocked, while the theologians and preachers often see no other way than to ignore the results of such research, or to fight against it from a negative standpoint.

In this context we can only give a short summary of this rationalism and its ramifications. The nineteenth-century mechanistic-causal way of thinking made it simply impossible for biblical scholars to do justice to the miracles in the Bible. They were either explained away as natural, or they were ascribed to pious imagination. But no one asked what the function, the significance, the message and also the reality of the different biblical miracles could be, according to the intention of the Bible itself. On the other hand, little was gained by faithfully establishing that the miracles were a historical reality because God is omnipotent (supernaturalism). In one case the miracles were not accepted, in the other case they were, but in neither did anyone ask: what does the Bible want to say with this? And this is what changes every time in the Bible. The serpent which speaks in Genesis 3 is a different sort of miracle from one of Jesus' healings.

The ethical idealism of many exponents of the Bible makes it diffi-

cult for them to do justice to the rough and realistic sections. The coarse stories of Samson were by preference declared to be legends – as they may well be – so that they could be left to one side and attention concentrated on the prophets, who were highly appreciated as preachers of a moral religion.

In the same way, existentialism deprives some modern interpreters of a view of the historical and cosmic aspects of the gospel, which play such an important part in the future expectations of Jesus and of the apostles. The whole gospel is reduced to a message, a kerygma, which summons the listener to make a personal decision (in the same way as the pietists like to do). The preaching of the coming of the Kingdom of God is dismissed as something which is of that period, something which does not belong to the essence of the gospel message.

In our previous chapter we have already pointed out that this kind of rationalism with regard to the Bible is being overcome more and more in ecclesiastical and scientific circles. More and more, the Bible itself is asked what it has to say, so that the content of the biblical message is traced more clearly. This offers new possibilities of learning to understand the Bible with the aid of concepts taken from the Scriptures and from biblical ways of thought. This is what we shall discuss in the next chapter.

III   The Bible and its Key Secrets

A Salvation is from the Jews

Every reader of the Bible knows how the 'offspring of Abraham' (Ps. 105.6) plays the main role in biblical history. It is also clear that the blessing which the God of Revelation has granted to this people, does not remain restricted to Israel. 'By you all the families of the earth will bless themselves' says the Lord who calls Abraham (Gen. 12.3). This world-wide intention and destination is expressed repeatedly in the Law and Prophets when nations and peoples are included by the men of God in their message, or when they are summoned to the praise of Israel's God in the Psalms.

> May God be gracious to us and bless us
> and make his face to shine upon us,
> that thy way may be known upon earth,
> thy saving power among all nations.
> Let the peoples praise thee, O God;
> Let all the peoples praise thee!
>
> Ps. 67

This prophetic vision is fulfilled when Jesus, the Messiah, the Christ, has come. The wise men from the East come to kneel before the child (Matt. 2.2). The devout Israelite Simeon sings of the light for the nations, when he takes the child of Joseph and Mary into his arms in the temple (Luke 2.32). In Acts, the windows and doors are opened and the gospel goes out to the nations. At first the young Christian congregation (of Jews) is still hesitant, as the story of the Gentile centurion Cornelius in Acts 10 shows. This hesitation is very understandable. It is all the more surprising when Paul turns his face westward in the direction of Europe with the determination of a pioneer. That even this courageous apostle needed a little push of the

Holy Spirit can be read in the well-known story in Acts 16.1-10. The preaching of the gospel is not very successful at first, obviously because Paul has tried to remain too near home. But the vision in the night helps him over the difficult point, and he lands on the shore of 'the new world'. The gospel begins its journey through Graeco-Roman civilization. The wonder and joy about this course of events continues to sparkle everywhere in the Gospels and Epistles: 'Remember that at one time you Gentiles in the flesh. . . . were at that time separated from Christ, alienated from the commonwealth of Israel. . . . But now in Christ Jesus you who once were far off have been brought near in the blood of Christ' (Eph. 2.11-13).

Attention should also be paid to the dynamic tension in this whole chapter. The unity of which this letter to the Ephesians speaks with such emphasis is not an existing unity based on a general ideal of mankind, but a unity which has been 'made' (v. 14). It is indeed true that all men are 'men' and 'God's offspring' (Acts 17.29), but that is not being discussed in the letter to the Ephesians. It is necessary to take off the liberal spectacles dating from the Enlightenment to discover the dynamic tension in Ephesians 2.

But however far Paul ventures into the world of the nations, and though he is almost led to consider Israel as entirely rejected through the unbelief and the hardness of heart of his own people, yet his heart is always drawn to Jerusalem, as Acts 20 so movingly describes. The method of his preaching and the structure of his message always remain the same: first the Jew, but also the Greek (Rom. 1.16).

We do not want to devote more time to the significance of the people of Israel for the gospel, nor to its place in the message of salvation in the past, today and in the future. Our concern in this context is to underline for the reader the obvious fact that *the Bible is a Jewish book*. We say emphatically Jewish and not oriental. The latter word would not be wrong, because the whole Bible is a typically oriental book, oriental in the sense of Semitic, from the Near East. The reader is reminded, for example, of the image of the universe as divided into three storeys, the heavens, the earth and the dark regions under the earth. In the story of the creation in Genesis 1 this image is the obvious presupposition. The second commandment in Ex. 20.4 also reminds us of this, and in the epistles this division can repeatedly be glimpsed between the lines, as in Phil. 2.10, and in Eph. 4.9,10. One other example out of many is the role played by a person's name in the eastern outlook on life. The name is the person; that is to say, in and through the name he is known, revealed and thus made tangible. Black magic can be exercised through the use of the name. This is exactly what is forbidden to Israel in the third commandment (Ex. 20.7). This is also what lies at the foot of Jacob's struggle beside the Jabbok (Gen. 32.22-32).

This oriental, Semitic aspect, however, does not quite capture the essence of the Bible. In the oriental world Israel occupies a special position, as Abraham is actually called *out of* Mesopotamia, and has to leave his family and his tribe, and as Israel is delivered *out of* Egypt in order to lead its own existence in the midst of the Canaanite nations and their religions. Though the Bible has a thousand connections with its closer and wider surroundings, their human history and realities, their religions and philosophies, their ambitions and actions – it does not miraculously fall out of the sky – yet it has its own special character. It is Jewish, in the midst of all the other nations. It is our belief that it is this difference, this Jewishness, which is the key to the Bible and its secrets. To start with a standard comparison of the Bible with what the world provides in good and bad, in exalted and crude, in religious and profane affairs, is like hanging the paintings of van Gogh beside some colour photographs. We wonder whether the main offence of the historical criticism of the nineteenth century was not that it overlooked this. But was it really overlooked? It was of course realized that the Bible was specially about the Jewish people, but in the context of the liberal thought of the Enlightenment, this was immediately interpreted as a national limitation. It was called particularism. The basic intention of the Bible, or at least of Christianity, was to overcome such national limitations. This typically Jewish aspect could not be taken seriously because of the basic assumptions then prevailing. In this respect the Bible was not permitted to have its say. This was the lack of reserve to which we referred at the end of Chapter II, the unscholarly attitude to what should have been scientific biblical research. It is surprising how many possibilities open up once the saying 'Salvation is from the Jews' (John 4.22) is taken really seriously.

We would like to enlarge a little on what we have already said about the Jewish character of the Bible, and for this purpose we take the distinction between *origin* and *form* on the one hand, and

essence and *content* on the other, to which we have already referred briefly. We make this distinction with reserve, because in the
Bible, above all, form and content should not be separated. But perhaps we may still be permitted to make it.

1. The form and wording, scenery and costumes in the Bible are
of course totally Jewish, even though there is a breath of Hellenism
blowing through the Gospels and Epistles. This is in accordance with
the fact that here was the point at which the windows and doors
to all the nations, especially to the 'west', were thrown open. But
in origin and climate of thought the Bible is totally Jewish. The
Bible is about Jewish people and Jewish customs, Jewish houses and
objects, about Jewish morals and imagery and particularly about the
Jewish language, Hebrew. This is made accessible today in a great
deal of literature, both professional and popular. An endless number
of examples of these typically Jewish-Israelite characteristics may
be given. A few follow here.

*The Israelite lived on the steppe, or in cultivated areas, but he did
not belong to a sea-going nation. Water, from a spring or as rain,
was therefore a precious gift to him, but the sea constituted a dreadful menace. Therefore water is the arch-enemy, a demon. The reader
is again reminded of the creation narrative in Genesis 1, in which
one of the basic points is that the waters are separated. Then there
is the Flood in Genesis 6-9, and the crossing of the Red Sea. Baptism,
representing a going under and rising out of the waters of death,
also gains in perspective against this background. The part played
by water in the Psalms also becomes much more significant. 'All
thy waves and thy billows have gone over me' (Ps. 42.7). The
powerful Psalm 93 takes on a new dimension, as does the Lord's
power over the stormy sea (Mark 4.35-41). This is not the breaking
of natural laws, but rather the subjection of demons. The concept
of natural law was unknown to the Jews. Jesus opens the way for
a view of nature as an ordered whole with laws and rules, by
liberating it from demons. When we read in Rev. 21.1 'and the sea
was no more', we should consider this partly as a victory over the
fear of elemental forces. The Jew thought in totalities, which means
that numbers are often not the result of the arithmetical addition
of units, but rather represent a group as a whole. Thus there are
still references to 'the twelve' after Judas has fallen away (John*

20.24; I Cor. 15.5). This number 'twelve' also represents the whole
nation of Israel, because of the twelve tribes. This also explains the
important place given to such numbers as 12, 144, and 144,000
in Revelation. If we begin here to count and reckon in the western
manner, instead of understanding and surveying, we shall get
irrevocably lost.

The Jews like to conduct a conversation through asking questions.
This is well known even today. Jesus did it in his discussions with
the scribes (Mark 11.27-33; Luke 10.25-37, and many other places).
How like a lively Jew is Paul when he writes: 'Are we to continue in
sin that grace may abound? By no means!' (Rom. 6.1). This manner
of answering with a question is often more than just style. It is
the essence of God's revelation. This revelation is not a quiet teaching of a set of truths, putting forward a number of theses; through
question and answer a road is travelled. God is in conversation with
man and man does not live as an isolated thinking creature; he has
to justify himself.

2. This last example already begins to show how Jewish style and
form tie in with essence and contents. This is the reason for the
many biblical words and concepts which cannot just be translated,
like removing out of the Jewish-Israelite shell a content which is
generally recognizable. This is the case with many objects for daily
use, plants, animals and things, which are and remain ordinary.
There is a word for them in Hebrew and we have a word for them,
so that we can simply translate. But in many cases this does not work.
Here is one example.

The Jew sees man as a whole. He makes no distinction between internal and external, between soul and body, spirit and matter,
though he does know very well the finer distinctions between the
various parts of the body. Heart and kidney, bowels, eye and hand,
they all have their emotional value, but man himself is one whole
and cannot be separated into two or three parts like body, soul or
spirit. When Samuel goes to Bethlehem to anoint a king from
among the sons of Jesse (I Sam. 16), we read that man looks on the
outward appearance, but that God looks on the heart. This seems
to use a distinction between what is internal and what is external,
and that is how it is mostly quickly explained. What matters is the

internal, and the body, the external should not count (v. 7). But then in verse 12 the red light seems to go on for a moment, for there we read that David was ruddy and had beautiful eyes and was handsome. It would seem that the external appearance had some importance after all! The 'heart' proves to be, not the spiritual and internal, but the centre of the personality. In contemporary terms, it is the existential being, which determines character and looks, head, eye, and stature. So Paul says, when he appeals to the brethren to present their 'bodies' as an acceptable offer to God (Rom. 12.1). We talk of giving our 'hearts' to the Lord, with a strong accent on the internal side of the phrase. But the Bible makes no distinction here, and so is basically very up-to-date. This way of experiencing man (the words 'view of man' are not right in this context) as functional and total is exactly the trend of modern philosophical ideas.

The word truth in Hebrew is the same as the word faith, and does not indicate an impersonal state of affairs, so that we can discuss what is 'true'. There is only truth in a relationship between two persons or parties. This explains why there are so many references to truth and faith in connection with the Covenant between God and his people Israel. Truth, therefore, is not a theoretical concept but a practical reality. The Dutch Bible Society translation of the Tanach mostly uses 'faith', because the word 'truth' has theoretical associations for us.

In the Gospels, however, which were written in Greek, we find the word aletheia, and this can only be translated with our 'truth'. Though this word already tends towards a more theoretical and neutral meaning (this or that is true) in the Gospel, the Jewish root is nevertheless almost always dominant. Those who do not know or sense this, at once land in difficulties, like Pilate, who can only shrug his shoulders when Jesus says that he had come 'to bear witness to the truth'. Elsewhere Jesus had also used the curious words: 'I am the truth' (John 14.6).

The same thing holds even more for the Hebrew word righteousness. This has an entirely special content, and the root also means help to the helpless by driving away the oppressor. That is what Moses does at the well of Midian (Ex. 2.17). Essentially the word is connected with help or salvation. When Psalm 98 speaks of God coming to judge the world with righteousness, the reference is not *just to a severe judgement, but even more to the coming, with wonderful power, of the Saviour. The old Dutch metrical version of this Psalm used, very suitably, the words: 'cruel violence has to yield'. Though for us the words justice and righteousness are always associated with the impartial upholding of the law and the inflicting of punishment, in short with impersonal jurisdiction, this is not by at all the meaning of the biblical 'righteousness'. It is obvious that as a result expressions like 'to fulfil God's law' acquire an entirely different connotation from that usually felt by western Christians.*

What we have just discussed is nowadays often called the Hebrew way of thought, which is then contrasted with the Greek or the western way of thought. This distinction contains a good deal of truth, though we must not exaggerate it in our understandable joy at this discovery. The characteristics of western man, reflecting and theoretical, static and analytical, have their very real significance. Later on we shall have another opportunity to reflect on this relation between Jew and Greek, between Jerusalem and Athens. But in order to do so we must first have a sharper vision of what is typically Jewish in the biblical story of salvation. Before we go on to that in Chapter III.B., we shall first introduce a historical note.

Since Paul carried the gospel of the Messiah Jesus to the countries surrounding the Mediterranean, the Jewish origin and character of God's revelation has been largely lost. The gospel entered into Graeco-Roman civilization, where great poets, thinkers, orators and lawyers set the tone of the spiritual climate. The Gospel was translated, as on Golgotha, into Greek and Latin (John 19.20). This had to happen. We must be grateful for it. Jerusalem and Athens, Sion and Rome, were spiritually married. There is some truth in the saying – in an expression coming from Jacobi – that the Church Fathers were Christians at heart, but still pagan in their heads.

They thought in an atmosphere of concepts and truths which originated in their own non-Jewish past. That salvation was from the Jews, they found truly difficult to accept. The children from this marriage, the dogmas and the Christian symbols of faith (the confessional documents) of the ancient church, not only resemble their Jewish father, but also their Graeco-Roman mother. It has long been a much discussed point in theology as to how far the doctrines of the

trinity and of the dual nature of Jesus (God and man), so clearly
of Greek philosophical origin in their wording and concepts, are
suitable to express the essence of God's revelation. Or should we
consider them as the answer of the Christian Church to the nations,
that the proclamation of salvation is from the Jews? We shall go
into this later. At the moment we are only concerned to open up the
perspective. We must thank God for the ways of history, but as
children of the Reformation who have learnt always to return to the
Scriptures, we can no longer simply accept as 'pure truth' what the
ancient Church laid down once and for all as the treasures of faith.

B And it came to pass . . .

The Bible tells a story. It is a book full of stories and narratives.
The smallest child in the Sunday school knows and enjoys this. 'And
it came to pass' is the refrain that recurs all the time. A story unfolds. For every Jew it begins with 'our father Abraham' (Acts 7.2),
and it continues via Moses and the exodus from Egypt, to Canaan,
where the people find a temporary resting place, though the stories
go on. The Judges, King David, Elijah and the prophets follow. The
exile is a dark and deep interruption, which almost seems the end,
but a new movement follows it. There is a new exodus, a new beginning. With the birth of Jesus we are back in the mainstream
of the story. The words 'and it came to pass' occur three times in the
Revised Version of Luke 2 and the appearance of Jesus is a continual
movement, a true 'walking the earth'. After Pentecost the real
trek begins, when the Jew Paul carries the name of Jesus to the
Gentiles.

The Bible is therefore an extremely dynamic book, an exciting
story, a progress through time, a bright sequence of events that
makes history.

Why do we insist on this representation of the Bible as a book
of history? Because we are convinced that these are the points at
which the tracks diverge.

For the Jew – and that implies for the Bible itself – the essence
of God's revelation is the event of God's salvation, the great deeds
of which the Psalms speak so often. 'He made known his ways to

Moses, his acts to the people of Israel' (Ps. 103.7). This story of salvation runs like a golden thread through everything else that the
Bible contains, whether songs, prayers, contemplation and wisdom,
theological knowledge and priestly service, law, praise, experience or
liturgy. It is this thread that matters, that gives firmness and design
to everything else. This is what the pious Jew lives by, what
characterizes Hebrew thought.

For the Greek – who is to a large extent the father of the western
mind – what matter ultimately are the *thoughts*, the ideas, the meaning of and behind everything that happens. The Greek mind seeks
the timeless truth in the passing events, like a white kernel in a
rough shell. 'Truth' for him is not a relation of faith between two
parties, as we met in the Hebrew use of the word, but an eternal
state, a timeless certainty. In this sense truths are the possession of
the human mind, like gleaming pearls perhaps, shining quietly
through the ages. At certain times they may shine brightly, at
others they may be obscured, but they remain untouchable, eternal,
resting in themselves. At best they may be illustrated, applied or
realized, by history, by certain events or stories, but they are and
remain true for ever. They are not in history but timeless, not
concrete but abstract.

When the Greeks accepted Christianity and the Bible it was
obvious that, with their longing for truth, they would start looking
for the deeper meaning of the biblical stories. We have already seen
how the allegorical method was victorious for over ten centuries.
At these points the wrong track was taken, the track that later came
to be known as *idealism.*

Idealism prefers to make somewhat light of the reality and to
seek for the meaning of history, for the deeper truth in the concrete event, for the eternal in the temporal, for the spirit in matter,
for the soul in the body, for the unseen in and behind the material.
Once on this track it is easy to see that *materialism* is none other than
the quarrelling twin-brother of idealism.

Since the time of the great poets and thinkers of noble Greece, this
idealism has pervaded our western civilization as ozone pervades the
air. Humanism, in its contemporary manifestation and organization,
is the spiritual child of idealism. If one knows the signs, it can be
recognized everywhere in and round the Church and Christianity.

What can be said about idealism? It would be immature, legalistic and also unbiblical to denounce it utterly. Not for nothing did the gospel go into the world as the *Greek* New Testament. The Greek mind has bestowed rich treasures on our civilization and on our Church in particular. It is right that we should feel respect and gratefulness. But in this connection and union between Jerusalem and Athens everything depends on the right sequence. We read in Revelation 21.26 that the glory and the honour of the nations will be brought into the new Jerusalem. The beauty and the imperishable value of Greek thought must also fit into the living whole of the biblical revelation; not the reverse. If we admit the latter, there will be accidents. We shall begin to read the Bible through idealistic spectacles and though we shall still be able to see the contents of the Bible, they will be distorted and obscured. The salvation story of the Scriptures would thus become a general truth. It seems as if the Bible has much less to offer than we had at first expected, as happened to Lessing when we heard him complain that historical truths can never furnish the proof of eternal intellectual truths. It seems as if the truths in the Bible are not so profound after all, as if not all the stories have such exalted meaning, and as if the norms and principles are in a strange way interwoven with customs and morals which can never be ours. Even the Christian doctrines seem less easy to prove from the Bible than some of the teachers of dogma would have us believe.

But if we make biblical thought our starting point, and take seriously the fact that God has begun a *history* with his people in this world, in which salvation unfolds, then God's profound truths spring open for us, his commandments are concrete, his praise is heard, even in the Church's dogma. But all this depends on the Pauline sequence: first the Jew and then the Greek. Now, however, we feel the need to make all this clearer through examples, in order to guard against misunderstandings.

That truth is concrete, an event, a history, may be shown with the aid of two words, love and election. In I John 4.8 we read the much-quoted words: 'God is love'. How often this is misunderstood! It is supposed to mean that God intends and does the best thing possible for all men at all times. In one sense this is true. But idealistic ears have picked it up wrongly. According to the Scriptures the fact that God is love means that he really loves, and real love is never general, but concrete. God loves specific people and a specific nation, Israel; and in Israel he loves his servants and prophets, like Moses and above all, Jesus, his beloved Son (Matt. 3.17). This is not love for each and every man as a matter of course, but love with a point. It is he! Now it should not be said too quickly that that love of God according to the Bible is a small, narrow and limited love. This is what many biblical scholars, with their idealistic spectacles, came to conclude. They might speak of Jewish particularism; happily that had been overcome in other parts by real Christian universalism; love of all people. No, the love-with-a-point is the genuine article. To take an example: picture a charity committee which sends children away for holidays. The ladies of this committee do their work with love. The more children they can send away, the better. There are hundreds of them. If one child cannot be sent, then there is always another to replace it. In principle every child is 'replaceable' because these ladies' love for children is general, a generally cherished feeling for 'the child'. Beside this we place a mother. She loves her child. The child dies. Later she has another one. Does that compensate for the loss of the first? To some extent, yes. But that first child was essentially 'irreplaceable', entirely unique. She loved that child with a passionate love. Her love was not the application of a general idea, of, let us say, love of one's neighbour (that much abused word), but her love was in itself a deed, an event, directed to this real child, this child. This is love with a concrete point. Which love is the greater, that of the ladies, or that of the mother? It is undoubtedly true that the former is wider, more universal, but the latter is incomparable. Everyone can feel that. Well, that is how the love in the Bible is. Love is not illustrated there. The love of God is not a general, given fact that has to be applied; in the Bible the love of God is carried out. God elects, and later, in Christ, this very special love goes out to the 'many', which is in the Bible often a special term for 'the nations', as in Matt. 26.28. It is the miracle of apostolic activity that this love spread from nation to nation and from man to man. Thus this love is and remains a passionate act, an event, something which happens. A curious confirmation of this is the story of the Canaanite woman (Matt. 15.21-28). At first Jesus rejects her with the well-worn words: 'I was sent only to the lost sheep of the house of Israel.' This always seems a bit embarrassing to us, as long as we read the story with idealistic spectacles. We exert ourselves in explanations why Jesus really did say this, as though he could not really mean it. Because Jesus loves everyone. True, but that is not a matter of course, a general truth that is eternally valid. It is not an idea which was at first rather lost in Israel. No, in this story we are witnessing the miracle of the door that is opened to the Gentiles, of the Saviour who turns to the nations with his blessing. He turns, it is something that happens. This is the only way of preserving the dynamic tension of the story, and of explaining to us the fact that Jesus wants to bless us, too.

The word 'election' is no more than a variant on our first example. The point of this supremely biblical word is the initiative taken by the eternal God when he turns to sinful man to elect him for communion with him; this led in the past to an idealistic misunderstanding of God's election. The word 'eternal' in particular was taken to mean timeless, unchangeable, outside history. Though people spoke of an eternal decree, this could not be an event in time, and in practice the word election called up a timeless concept. Once this misunderstanding had crept in, the precious gem of the Bible became a scandal and an offence for the idealist, so that the biblical baby was thrown away with the idealistic bathwater. The mention of this word is enough to make some people shiver and run away from theological conversation. For them, a God who has irrevocably and for all time elected some for life, leaving others in their lost state, is an impossibility. Quite right, too; but how differently the Bible puts the matter. God goes his way, electing all the time. Election is an event, a method, a way of progressing from the one to the other. I elect you, says God, and I do this in order to elect others through you. Thus I will seek men in electing love. Election and love are not two concepts between which there is a great tension, they are one. At this point we agree with the lines laid down in the synodal publication: 'De uitverkiezing' (On Election), which contains the following words: 'In election we confess that the eternal God in his grace grasps and bears our small lives. This turning towards us takes place along the road of time and history, along which the Lord God comes to meet us, electing us.'

We consider that the main point of the Bible is the history it relates. The Bible is a history book! It could be objected that the Bible contains many sections in which no stories are told and where no history is described. There are sections of wisdom and reflection, praise and liturgy. It is not all about God's 'ways and deeds'. There are many passages, texts and sections formulating a general truth, or presenting a profound wisdom of life, valid and true for all time. These are not events, but 'a being'. The same is true of God's commandments. We are thinking of the many laws and commandments in the first books of the Bible, of the wisdom in the Proverbs, of the imperishable words of prophecy. 'The grass withers, the flower fades; but the word of our God will stand for ever' (Isa. 40.8). Who is not reminded of the many sayings of Jesus which shine like pearls for all time. 'Blessed are the poor in spirit' (Matt. 5.3). 'You therefore must be perfect as your heavenly Father is perfect' (Matt. 5.48). Then there are the exhortations in the apostolic epistles. 'For he (authority) does not bear the sword in vain' (Rom. 13.4). Surely that is not history, but a general truth and a law of God? In short, it is *Torah*, wholesome doctrine, teaching, *doctrina* as Calvin would say. Can and may we not speak of deep, religious thoughts here, of eternal standards and fixed principles? Is this not where Greek thought comes into its own?

We suggest that we must not begin to quarrel over mere words. Religious truths, divine standards and biblical principles are certainly very useful words. They give a feeling of firmness, duration and divine authority, and these are good things. 'And we have the prophetic word made more sure' (II Peter 1.19). But on the other hand we ask that these truths, standards and principles should not be detached from their biblical context, and treated as independent quantities, of which we can take possession. That makes them into idealistic truths again, which do not easily fit in with the living God of the biblical revelation. We recall here for a moment the image of the thread, which we used before. We must not unravel the more general sounding truths in the Scriptures from the historical thread of the salvation story which runs through them. Only in the context of this salvation story do these words, which sound so general, acquire their true significance, their deep lustre and their divine authority. 'The fear of the Lord is the beginning of knowledge' (Prov. 1.7). This does not mean that only the believer and the devout can have a true knowledge of the Bible, but that in the Bible 'knowledge' is connected with the God of the story of salvation. Biblical truths must not be detached. They cannot be abstracted. They are not abstract, but concrete. We shall again try to show this with the help of two famous Bible passages.

The Ten Commandments are often considered to be general rules for the whole of mankind. Though this may seem obvious, on closer inspection it is not quite correct. These 'ten words' begin emphatically with a reminder of Israel's deliverance out of Egypt. Because God has saved the Israelites, they must love and trust only him. Yes, trust! That means that they must not try to find guarantees in an image, as the pagan nations did with their gods as a matter of course (the presupposition of this second commandment is that one gains power over the deity through an image). The Israelites are not to act in that way with their God, who has shown them that they can always trust him by delivering them out of Egypt. Behind all the commandments therefore we see the passion − the 'jealousy' of Ex. 20.5 − of the God who has proved his 'faith' in the liberation from Egypt. What seems an unimportant introduction recalling a historical event is in reality the nail from which all the commandments are suspended. Even the commandments of the second part, which seem so general, gain emphasis and significance in this way. 'You shall not covet' is not intended to kill every desire and longing. No, it is a sober reminder that every Israelite received his share in the promised land, and that they must not begrudge one another, because they are all allowed to live together in the land that the Lord God has given them. They must not take away one another's grace. That is the meaning of this rule, which always sounds rather too rigorous. This can be sensed in the story of Naboth and Ahab in I Kings 21: Ahab may not take the vineyard and Naboth may not give it, because 'it is the inheritance of my fathers' (v. 3). In passing, we remark that an effective reply to enthusiastic Sabbatarians can only be found in the specific introduction to the much discussed commandment concerning the Sabbath. But we shall return to this later. When we come to the point of 'application' we shall also discuss how the words of the Lord and the exhortations of the apostles are essentially very specific and directed at certain people.

Secondly, we draw attention to the first chapters of Genesis, and especially to Genesis 1. From the point of view of form, these chapters are 'stories'. That indicates that it would be too simple to deny them any historicity whatsoever. But it does not mean that they contain 'history' as we find it in our textbooks at school, real information on a real course of events, several thousand years ago. That is obviously not the intention, though the Israelite was not faced with the problems of faith and science that we know. The style of the story betrays the amount of reflection that has gone into it. There is room for all sorts of mythological material. They therefore have a function in the history of the people of Israel. They are not detached, a piece of divine information on truth, they fit into a historical framework; into a period when the people had to account for the place and significance of 'nature' over against surrounding heathendom, more specifically the wisdom of Babylonia. In these pagan surroundings, sun, moon and stars, fertility and the primeval waters, were deified. But the faith of Israel sings of and proclaims liberation from the dominion of natural forces by the living God in Genesis 1; this God has proved himself to be the sovereign of the dreaded forces of water, wind and desert in the history of Israel.

This is based not only on God's superior force, but on his deeds, 'from the beginning', in the same way as all Israel's comfort springs from God's great deeds. For the devout Israelite, these powers become the creation, ordinary nature, and are recognized as such. Thus in our century of scientific research and space flights Genesis 1 is beginning to speak to us again in a surprising manner. In this overwhelming universe we are sustained by the living God who has prepared a safe place on earth where man can praise and serve him.

What we have just said is – in our opinion – becoming more and more accepted theological coinage. It is therefore high time that people everywhere should be freed from the far too simple question whether the creation story is to be 'believed' or not, at risk of not being a good Christian. It is really too naïve to read the story of the creation under the motto: 'Where everything comes from', or 'How the world began'. Israel is not interested in this theoretical question. The first verse of Genesis 1, 'In the beginning God created the heavens and the earth', can be understood as a title for the whole of history. The story would then begin in the second verse. The terrible chaos in which man feels himself threatened and helpless then becomes the beginning from which can be sung the praise of God who creates order, rules the waters and puts man in God's good creation. But we probably do more justice, exegetically, if we do not simply deny historicity to the first verse, even if it is just a title. This is in accordance with the fact that Israel put this part of its confession in the Torah, the five books of Moses which sing the praise of God's historical and foundation-laying deeds. Exegetically, it seems to us that Israel was not content with the praise of the creation – as for instance in Job 38.4 ff and Ps. 104.5 ff – but put down the creation story in a form of literature of which the Bible does not give us another example at this point. Nevertheless, it is not a piece of natural science, but a human composition around God's deeds, to the form of which the Jewish division of the working week into six workdays and one day of rest made its contribution. In this way Genesis 1 answers one practical problem of belief.

In passing we remark that it seems to us extremely desirable, considering the context in which the first chapters of Genesis have to be read, that people should no longer always begin biblical history with 'Adam and Eve'. Biblical history begins with Abraham, where we first have historical ground under our feet. In the course of this story, reflections on nature, man, sin and the world of nations find their place. Then the first eleven chapters of Genesis can receive their proper place and treatment. It is significant that the Jew, who likes to tell a concrete story, arranging everything in the historical sequence of generations (toledoth), should put the toledoth of heaven and earth (Gen. 2.4a) at the beginning of the Torah, but this should not lead us astray.

We believe, therefore, that we can show that all through the Bible the main point is the history, the event, the continuing line of God's action with his people and with the nations. What matters is not the ideas and the profound truths, but the concreteness of God's deeds. For that matter, the name 'Testament' for both parts of the Bible is excellent. Unfortunately we no longer recognize in this word the emotions of a history between two partners, which can be heard in the word *covenant*. God stands over against the people he chooses, calls and leads, so that they answer, believe and follow.

Beside the word covenant we must, in this context, draw the modern Bible reader's attention specially to the typically biblical word *Name*. The Bible likes to sum up the concrete historical side of God's deeds in this word: the *Name* of the Lord. For us a name conjures up a label, a name-card, but the Oriental thinks of the essential, of what really matters, when one wants to get to know a person properly.

The name of God is therefore the revelation of God. It is not a summing up of divine attributes which God 'has'; at the mention of the name of God the Israelite thinks of God's deeds among the peoples of the whole creation.

> *O give thanks to the Lord, call on his name,*
> *make known his deeds among the peoples!*
> Ps. 105.1.

The name is God in action, the essence of God:

> *O Lord, our Lord,*
> *how majestic is thy name in all the earth!*

That is the refrain of the beautiful Psalm 8, which sings of God's majesty, because he has made a strange covenant with the weak son of man.

> *Our Father, who art in heaven,*
> *Hallowed be thy name,*
> *Thy kingdom come!*

The Kingdom of God is his dominion which spreads and continues through all ages. That is his 'Name'.

There are two reasons why we emphasize this Name. In the first place we are helped to see at once that these events, the things that happen, do not in any way detract from what is fixed and trustworthy. Taking off those idealist spectacles for the reading of the Bible does not make everything fluid and blurred, so that we can do nothing but wait and see, if and how God will act this time, and what will happen next in history. On the contrary: it is really through God's deeds, through his name, that the Israelite knows what his God is worth. The word 'Name' has a ring of firmness and loyalty. The Israelite prays in distress or doubt:

> *Help us, O God of our salvation,*
> *for the glory of thy name;*
> *deliver us, and forgive our sins,*
> *for thy name's sake!*
> Ps. 79.9.

In grateful trust, the Psalm of the Good Shepherd sings:

> *He restores my soul.*
> *He leads me in paths of righteousness*
> *for his name's sake. (v. 3).*

The firmness of the name, however, is not similar to that of time-less and generally valid concepts or principles (which we call eternal in ordinary language), but the firmness of the living God of Israel, the Father of Jesus Christ.

In the second place, we stress the name because we stand here on the watershed between biblical faith and religion; to put it in biblical terms: between Israel and the nations and their gods, heathendom. (To our ears, this last term has an unpleasant sound, though that is certainly not what we intend.) The difference between biblical faith and heathendom does not, however, just lie in the difference between their contents: both believe, but one believes something different from the other and they are all religions which in the end perhaps come to the same thing. No, the difference is this, that the Bible is always concerned with a real story, with an event in time. We do not mean by this that everything in the Bible has really happened, or really happened in that way – see our explanation of Genesis 1 – but we do mean that the Bible is concerned with the Name, with God's intervention, which is the origin of real history, the history of salvation.

Of this, ancient and modern heathendom know nothing. The pagan believes in the eternal existence of things, in religious truths, in eternal wisdom, reposing in itself. This is especially striking, in our opinion, in oriental religion. There we have the cycle of events. There people always have time, because real decisions can never be taken and history has no real meaning. Heathendom lives out of the eternal existence of things, under the powers which coincide with Nature or Fate. But the Bible cleaves the eternal silence of heathen-dom with the proclamation of the Name.

Once this has been grasped, the Bible comes very forcibly to life. All sorts of mistaken approaches become irrelevant and the Bible itself begins to speak, inwardly sure of itself and convincing. The Bible then stands unique among the religions of the world. In conversations with those who are outside the Church, with those who have become estranged from the Bible, inside the Church, too, this historical aspect has to be brought forward with great emphasis. It gives the Bible unexpected force. To illustrate this, a few concrete examples:

1. *Differences and contradictions in the Bible itself.* Biblical criticism in particular has opened our eyes to such points. Not only are there differences in the historical details, but also in what seem to us the essential components of our Christian faith. As long as we continue to look in the Bible for *the* truth of God, in the sense of a fixed system, timeless and general, it will disturb us that the Scriptures are written in such an obviously careless manner, with many facets and colours. That the Lord in his anger against Israel incites David *and* that Satan turns against the people in David's national census, are two 'truths' which are, of course, difficult to reconcile. Compare II Sam. 24 with I Chron. 21. One may try to harmonize, or look for the 'core' of the various stories and texts, leaving aside the details. That the core may become very reduced after the deduction of all the contradictions is something that will just have to be ignored. But how different these problems become once we get an eye for the historical line, not as a concession to modern science, but as a result of it! The history is really part of the biblical revelation. This revelation proceeds like an unfolding event, not as a clarifying process which gradually unveils the real truth as God intended it. This historical development can accommodate a great variety of things. It is the history of God with his people, always in new situations and changing surroundings. We are with Abraham in the land of Canaan or with Moses in Egypt. The Philistines and the Edomites are the opponents of the people, and then again it is the Assyrians or the Babylonians. This changes not only the frontiers and the scenery, the imagery, the language and the representation, but also the theological and moral ideas.

In the example mentioned above, the author of II Samuel 24 only knows of the opposition between God and the idols. The idols are the real temptation for the people in the period of Israel's kings. For this author there is as yet no question of the later 'monotheism'. Over against the idols he stresses God's power. In the history of David's census he sees only the hand of the Lord, even in the evil. But the author of the Chronicles, who must have belonged to the period after the exile, knows of the opposition God-Satan. He no longer talks of 'idols'. They no longer constitute a temptation for him and his people. He therefore discerns in David's sin the work of Satan, the opponent. It is after the exile that people begin to reflect on the problem of evil. It is a time of reflection, the time when the book of Job was written. So they fall back on the image, known of old among the nations, of Evil personified, the snake or the dragon. The figure of Satan makes its entry. The history of the national census is written at that time by the author of Chronicles, against this background, with a well-known result. There is no point in asking: which of the two is right, II Samuel or I Chronicles? How did it really happen? How and what should we believe? That would mean trying to find the essence behind the historical differences, while it is exactly these differences that matter. Both these sections of the Bible tell a story in a way that speaks to the children of their own generation, and we must ask what each of them wanted to say to his contemporaries. Only then will these two Bible stories have something to say to us.

These historical aspects must sometimes not only be put *after* each other, but *beside* each other. In one sense this was also the case with our example of the census. It is the same event recounted in two different ways. But the authors were far removed from each other in history. That was the point of our example: these are different points along the line of historical development. In the Gospels and Acts, however, the reader sees repeatedly how the same situation, encounter, conversation or healing is represented in totally different ways by the evangelists, who are contemporaries of each other. According to Matt. 27.5, Judas commits suicide by hanging himself, but in Acts 1.18 his end is described much more sensationally.

Biblical scholars used to like to try and cancel out as many as possible of such differences in order to track down the historical core. This was how several sayings of Jesus came to be declared 'inauthentic' and ascribed to so-called 'community theology'. We have no desire whatsoever to detract from the scientific results of this biblical criticism. But we do object to the idealistic starting point from which the search for a historical core is initiated, the search for what *really* happened, which renders all the other words and texts 'inauthentic'. Against this we would put it emphatically that these 'inauthentic' words and texts are often very 'authentic' in that they are striking. Besides, what story-teller is completely impartial? Who can recount without simultaneously colouring the story just a little? Is it not silly to pretend that this 'community theology' is negative and objectionable? Jesus emerges as Lord, alive and realistic, only in and through the information supplied by the evangelists, who had their roots in the first community, from which they send their message. This is the witness of all the evangelists. They demand faith, not in the historical Jesus, who might be accepted behind the information of the gospel, but in 'the Christ of the Scriptures'.

We must therefore be grateful for the differences and even for the contradictions in the gospels, which each supply in their own rendering their perspective on what is essential for the proclamation of Christ. This is what matters, the concrete and special details. As long as we think of a general truth, which exists by itself, we shall still be inclined to look for the 'main point'. Then we take away all the particular detail, so that we end up with a few main points about Jesus who preaches 'forgiveness' or 'God's love', or 'a message of healing' or 'the approaching end of the world'. We reduce the Bible and the gospel to a few principal truths. But in that way the Bible loses its flavour, its interesting peculiarity. Reading the Bible will lose much of its charm, because we know beforehand more or less what we are going to find. How often this has caused the biblical message to shrivel up or to go stale! Again and again one ends up with the same edifying conclusion. In reality, however, reading the Bible is like visiting a picture gallery. We would never ask for the 'main point' of the 'Nightwatch', or for a summary of the work of Picasso.

We believe that in the practice of preaching and living with the Scriptures this concrete aspect is always sought again, and made use of; but on the other hand there is always a conflicting group of people who think that they have the essentials buttoned up in their spiritual pockets, so that the Bible with its special contribution is no longer important. This trend has detracted much from the adventure of living with the Bible, and it has also done much to bring it into discredit. Therefore we emphasize again: *the truth of the Bible is concrete*; biblical truth lives in its details, like the beauty

of a painted portrait. This is the only way in which the Bible can
bless us.

*As an example of this we would like to point to the incomparably
beautiful pericope of John 7.53-8.11, which has been declared inauthentic as a result of textual criticism. It is the story of Jesus and
the adulteress. It could be said that here forgiveness, in the sense of
the general principle, is applied to this woman by Jesus. Here we
find, not the law, but grace. And, of course, she receives forgiveness.
But wait, look carefully. Jesus is not ready at once with his word of
forgiveness; he first acknowledges the 'law'. She has sinned, and she
must be punished. But he establishes the law just a little bit higher
than his opponents usually do. 'Let him who is without sin among you
be the first to throw a stone at her.' And then silence falls among the
accusers. Through the silences which the Lord creates in the conversation, he drives them all to a deeper understanding of the law.
Then the judges withdraw and the right moment has come. And Jesus
says with full authority: neither do I condemn you. This is where
the forgiveness takes place. It is not just kept on hand, but arises
in the occasion. It is a concrete event for this woman. The law is not
just pushed aside. It is rather 'fulfilled', brought to fruition so that
the forgiveness grows out of it. Elsewhere forgiveness is brought
about in another way. This is how one has to pay attention to the
special details when reading the gospels, in order to taste the real
flavour.*

2. At this point we must say something about the point which is
always topical in church, namely the *relation between the 'Old' and
the 'New' Testament, between the* Tanach *and the Gospel.*

As long as we still think in terms of eternal truth and concrete
application, the relationship between the Testaments remains a
difficult one. Having obtained the definite truth of God in Christ,
why should we still need the Law and the Prophets? Whatever
contrasts and patterns are brought in to help, it remains a somewhat forced relationship. Law (in the sense of God's commandments)
and Gospel, prophecy *and* fulfilment, shadow *and* reality, law *and*
grace, the God of revenge *and* the God of love, the expectation of
Christ *and* his real coming, these are among the many possibilities
which have been suggested at some time or other in the history of

the Christian Church. They are all more or less right biblically, but they retain a degrading element for the *Tanach*, which, as we saw at the beginning, is impossible for Jesus and the apostles.

The mistake lies in the fact that the thought here is still in terms of 'Christian truth', which was revealed fully in Jesus, a reposing, fixed truth, which earlier was still in the dark, hidden or not fully realized. 'The new reveals what is hidden in the old' (Augustine). One might consider this truth as religious 'values', which Jesus proclaimed in their most comprehensible form. Or it might be seen as being dogmatic theses about Christ, and his work of salvation. It does not make much difference. In both cases the truth has almost imperceptibly been made into a system, because what matters now when reading the Law and Prophets, is to discover this truth already, to see as far as possible indications pointing to Christ or to Christian truths. But in that case, the use of the *Tanach* will always have the character of a superfluous good work for the Church. Is not the truth completely contained in the Gospels? Why is the 'Old' Testament still needed?

At this point we must choose between two roads: either we try consistently to find something of the 'Christ-proclamation' in the Old Testament, often reading more into the text than was really meant; or we allow the Old Testament to speak for itself with the honest presupposition that for us, who have the New, it cannot have much to say on certain points. The first-year textbooks are superfluous, because we have now passed our finals. Indeed, but the photos of the primary school child are just as real for the parents as the pictures of the grown boy. The infant is not the preparation or the foreshadowing of the real man, he is complete, he is himself.

Well, Israel is the child (Hos. 11.1) and Jesus is the mature man (Eph. 4.13), but God loves them both, for here we are not concerned with truths which have to be learned from the Testaments, as from schoolbooks, but with realities, with the historical events of God's deeds, and there everything is in principle equally important, each part can acquire a tender and irreplaceable importance, even though there are special moments and junctions. In the growth of the child into a man, including the dreadful years of the adolescence of Israel – if the reader will forgive this image – the revelation as a historical event is complete. It is always the same child. The living child must not be cut into two parts, as the wise Solomon knew so

well, nor should the one living Bible be hacked into two. The
scripture cannot be broken (John 10.35). Idealistic eyes do not see
this, but for those who understand the Scriptures as one whole it
cannot be otherwise.

The image of a play can also be used here. All the acts and
scenes belong to the whole, even though the climax only comes in
the last act. Perhaps this climax can be gradually foreseen, even in the
early parts, but that is no reason to say that the message this
play perhaps brings lies already hidden in these early parts. Everything must be left quietly in its place. Abraham and Joseph, Balaam
and Samuel, David and Elijah, they must all have their own say.
They are not just the 'preparation' which we could dispense with
if necessary. No, they have their part to play, they have a message.
Not a truth that will become entirely clear later, but their lives
and what the Scriptures write about them are part of God's salvation. Without division, without separation, without confusion,
without change, as the famous formula of the Council of Chalcedon
defined the two natures of Christ; the same terms are valid for the
two Testaments. Who would publish or stage the last act of a play
separately?

As an example we refer to Gen. 22.1-19, the offering of Isaac.
Traditionally people like to see in Isaac, or in the ram, a shadow
of the offering on Golgotha. However beautiful this is, and however
much that offering may be an extension of this story, it cannot be
right to consider Isaac as a 'prefigurement' of Christ's offer. Biblical
criticism favoured another approach, distinguishing several 'layers'
in this story. It has been read as a protest against the horror of child-
sacrifice, from the days of Manasseh, 'who burned his son as an
offering' (II Kings 21.6). But originally it was supposed to have
been an aetiological myth, explaining the name of Moriah (v. 2),
the mountain top on which, according to II Chron. 3.1, Solomon built
the temple. The play of words on the verb 'to see' (v. 14, RSV
margin) points strongly in that direction. These scholarly remarks
are probably not wrong, but they do not explain more than the
information on the amount of paint used would explain a painting by
Van Gogh.

The core and the point of this story, which has been written with
much literary skill and great soberness, obviously lies in the testing

of Abraham's faith. Will he pass the test?, the reader asks himself with suspended breath. This story is indeed a testimony of the essence of belief, of faith and obedience to God, of utter dependence on God's word and promise. So Abraham became the Father of all believers (Rom. 4). Without constraint, from this point we can draw the line which connects with Christ. Hebrews calls Jesus 'the pioneer and perfecter of our faith' (Heb. 12.2). At the level of faith Jesus has passed the test perfectly and remained true, which created the appearance that the work of God had failed completely on Golgotha. In this story, it is not so much Isaac, but Abraham who, if we insist, is an 'image' of Christ. Or, perhaps even better, they are this together. But why should we insist on seeing an image of Christ? The story by itself appeals sufficiently to our faith, even though we are certainly not Abraham, nor are we in his situation. We find ourselves at an entirely different point in the history of God with his people and with the nations. We would not and could not dispense with it as part of the scriptural revelation. It is irreplaceable and unique.

3. With these last examples, the reader will have already sensed that we are approaching the tricky point of *application*. The Bible has something to say to us, but that is not all; it has *authority* for us, says the Church. But, how does this work? At first glance, there is no difficulty, we let the Bible proclaim idealistic, general truths. It is obvious that these are timeless, so that they are also valid for us. If they are dressed in historical garb, it is only necessary for us to strip them of this, and to apply them to ourselves. The difficulties only begin when it appears that it is not always too easy to find these general truths, because they have aged, because they contradict each other, or because they have become obscured, while there are also many obviously historical and narrative parts, from which no general truth can be unearthed with the best will in the world. There are the coarse stories in Judges, the many Jewish laws, the prophetic words, which seem to have been irrelevant for centuries, pronouncements which are quite clearly connected with the time and the world-view of those days. Are they no longer valid for us? In the end we shall be left with rather a thin Bible, which proves to be different for each person.

When we understand God's truth really historically, however, and not idealistically, everything acquires and retains its place in the context of this history which has been unfolding since Abraham. But other questions then arise. What has all this to do with us now? Abraham was called to leave his country (Gen. 12), but that was Abraham. Surely not every Christian has to leave his country? Paul was stopped on his way to Damascus, and converted, but that was Paul! This does not happen to every Christian, nor does it need to, though many sermons seem to suggest just that! In short, the question about what the Bible has to say to us has become a new question, in the real sense of the word.

We intend to focus more sharply on this matter of application in Chapter IV. At this point we only want to say this, that it is best, with regard to application to our time and situation, not to work towards the general, but mainly on the contrary, to let the historical, the concrete, the special, speak as much as possible. In that way one discovers more and more surprising turns, shades of meaning and particularities, which offer their own perspectives, also in our contemporary situation. To put it more sharply: the application comes more easily the less we search for it. The Bible should be left to speak for itself, without being told beforehand what we would like to hear . . . or would rather not hear. That is why it is such a terrible sin for ministers to formulate their subject first, and then to write the exegesis of the text or Bible portion. That can never become a good sermon.

Many discussions on parts of the Christian faith are often so fruitless because the Bible is short-sightedly measured against one's own standards. Certain words of the Bible are then rejected, or employed, but in neither case is the Bible allowed to finish what it has to say. Words or sayings are detached from the concrete and definite context in which they belong, and then generalized into *the* biblical truth, often by ignoring other parts of the Bible in which the same matter acts in a quite different way. As an example, we think of the oppositions which exist in the (Reformed) church concerning the confession of the *resurrection of Jesus*.

It is clear that according to the Gospel the Risen One appears with a body. It is equally clear that on the basis of the scientific and medical presuppositions of the nineteenth century (whether these are still as unshakable in the second half of the twentieth century, we are not quite sure) it is impossible for a dead person to come back to life. The result has been that the news of Easter has been explained symbolically, psychologically, parapsychologically or spiritually. It is impossible for the authors of these explanations to form any image of the resurrection of a body. On the opposite side, there are many who insist on an unconditional recognition that Jesus was resurrected in the flesh. The opponent is more or less forced into believing, at pistol point. What can one say of such a discussion? The reader should certainly not look down on this, with a smile or with contempt. Those who insist on the confession of the bodily resurrection of the Lord feel quite rightly that the Christian faith itself depends on the Easter message. Hence their vehemence: '. . . if Christ has not been raised, then our preaching is in vain and your faith is in vain' (I Cor. 15.14). Nevertheless, the level and the approach of the problem by either party, as we have pictured it, does not do justice to the Bible. We cannot give a full biblical and dogmatic exposition of this point here, but we put forward a few points of view which must not be neglected in a biblical discussion of the Resurrection.

(a) It must first be understood that the resurrection does present a real problem.

(b) According to the Bible, 'to believe' is not to accept an uncomprehended fact, or a curious event; it is a living relationship to a person, to the living Lord. It is possible to believe correctly in 'the resurrection', and yet at the same time not to believe in the living Lord.

(c) This living Lord comes to meet us in various Easter stories which each have their own accent, nuance or point. These stories should not be made to fit one general truth, but we should ask the Bible what it has to say to us through each separate piece of information. The story of Thomas is different from the story of the men walking to Emmaus. The latter did not so much have difficulty with the news of Easter, which only confused them, but rather with the fact of the crucifixion. That bothered them. The Lord does not persuade them to believe in a miracle, but rather helps them to understand the suffering of the Messiah. And so Easter becomes a certainty, too.

(d) A real characteristic of all doubt connected with the miracle of Easter is that the Scriptures are opened (John 20.9 and I Cor. 15.3, 4). These Scriptures are the Law and the Prophets. Now it is true that there are a very few resurrections there, but it is absolutely clear that that is not what is meant. The real point is that the historical line of salvation becomes visible. The servants of God always reach bliss through suffering – Joseph, Moses, Elijah, Jeremiah, the people of Israel themselves, who go into exile and then return to live again (Ezek. 37). This puts the Easter stories into a much wider context. They do not describe an incredible miracle, but the culmination and conclusion of a method and a way in God's purposes of salvation which can be seen and touched by everyone who exposes himself to the Scriptures.

(e) For the Jew, at least for the Pharisee (not for the Sadducee), the resurrection was the proof of the dawning of the messianic era. This is so in Matt. 27.52 and 53, where the evangelist notes that, after the death of Jesus, many of the dead rose from their tombs and appeared in Jerusalem. It is the Gospel of Matthew, written for a Jewish audience, which has this curious detail. Resurrection needs no proof, but is itself the proof that Jesus is the Messiah, in spite of the crucifixion. The same train of thought is found in Acts 2.24 and 36. 'Let all the house of Israel therefore know assuredly that God has made him both Lord and Christ, this Jesus whom you crucified.' Compare also Rom. 1.4. We do not maintain that our difficulties have been solved by this Jewish-messianic train of thought, but only that we must not lose sight of it in our thinking about the resurrection.

(f) The miracle of Easter should not be confined to the few relevant stories in the gospels. Gospels and Acts, Jesus' words and deeds, indeed his whole ministry, the miracle of the Christian congregation, all this is one proof – in the sense of a pledge – the first decisive beginning (Acts 17.31) of the reality of the resurrection. Paul thinks in the same wide context, speaking of Israel: 'For if their rejection means the reconciliation of the world, what will their acceptance mean but life from the dead?' (Rom. 11.15). With the Messiah Jesus, God gives the new beginning into this world. That is the resurrection of the dead. The question about the consequences of this revolutionary act of God for the body of Jesus himself, and for our bodies, is only a detail of this, even if it is a detail closely connected with the rest.

(g) We have already said that in the Bible, the body has a different significance from that which we usually ascribe to it. Body *can mean the man himself, his 'I', his being. According to Matt. 6.22, the eye is the lamp of the body.*

(h) The corporeal nature of the appearances excludes any docetic misunderstanding. This term is used in theology to convey the fact that the corporeal is not just apparent. The gospel is not a doctrine or an idea, but a reality and an event which affects our whole existence.

(i) This corporeal body cannot be touched by us. Jesus comes and disappears through closed doors. Our own tangible world and reality remain intact, but they are shot through by the new thing which comes from God.

(j) The typical character of the intangible and yet real miracle of Easter is stressed by Paul, when he speaks so strangely of the spiritual body in I Cor. 15. Here we see into the core of the reality of the resurrection. It is not elusive because it is so mysterious and dark, but because it is in itself as radiantly light as the sun. There is no dark patch in the proclamation of our salvation, but such a patch of strong light that all our imaginings are beside the point. The Easter witness should be left to stand, as the basis of everything else, as Paul does in I Cor. 15. It should really be the basis, and not one of the many subsidiary things which we have to believe (or not believe).

(k) According to the Gospels, there really is a difference between the resurrection of Lazarus and that of Jesus the Lord. Lazarus dies again, the Lord does not! It is difficult to grasp this difference, but it should be noted.

(l) In discussion, the resurrection of the body is often a stumbling block, but in preaching, in the Easter sermon, when the preacher has to let the facts of the text speak for themselves in their own context, the corporeal nature of the resurrection may open up quite naturally.

4. Once we have grasped that the real point of the Bible is a history – indicated in the Name as a coherent totality of acts of that God who remains true to himself – then we also reach a point high enough to get a view of the two concepts used in theology, namely those of inspiration and the canon of the Scripture. (Cf. also Chapters I.A.2; I.B.1; II.2.)

In the word 'inspiration', we should detect an idea of the speed, the whirlwind in which the Spirit of God masters man. '. . . men moved by the Holy Spirit', as is said of prophecy in II Peter 1.21, can be applied both to the spoken and the written word. Inspiration here is an event.

The word 'canon', used of the Bible, conveys the sense of coherence in God's acts, his fixity of purpose, which is laid down in the sixty-six books of the Bible. In the Scriptures, that is to say, in the canonical books, the Name is preserved and established for us. 'And we have the prophetic word made more sure . . .', the unknown author of II Peter 1.19 writes when he underlines the coherence and the connection of the prophetic writings with the appearance of Jesus the Messiah.

The words 'inspiration' and 'canon' therefore belong together. As these are often sensitive points in theological or ecclesiastical discussions, we feel obliged to elaborate somewhat here.

'The wind blows where it wills, and you hear the sound of it, but you do not know whence it comes or whither it goes; so it is with everyone who is born of the Spirit', Jesus says in his conversation with Nicodemus (John 3.8). This expressive saying of Jesus could also be applied to the Bible. Here we have written books. By themselves they possess no characteristics of holiness, divinity or infallibility. But as we read the Bible, we feel in it the pulse of urgent happenings. The history of God with his people and with the nations is in progress. It is dynamic and active. God speaks and acts and men are driven, with good or bad — as for instance Jonah — grace along his surprising ways. Here is inspiration, here is the blowing of God's wind. Here is living God, God in action, called the Spirit of God in the Bible, God's breath which brings life and which calls men and things into existence as God's partners. 'When thou sendest forth thy Spirit, they are created; and thou renewest the face of the ground'; see Ps. 104.27-30. 'It is the spirit that gives life' (John 6.63). There is also the beautiful passage in Gen. 2.7, 'Then the Lord God formed man of dust from the ground, and breathed into his nostrils the breath of life; and man became a living being.' Inspiration runs right through the Bible in this way, as truly as the whole Bible is about the history of the living God with his creation, with his people and with the nations. Inspiration here is the word used to indicate the exciting event which we are witnessing in the Bible.

Now, however, we must go one step further. In this event, we *sometimes – certainly not often – catch the Holy Spirit recording the words and deeds of God. In Exodus 24.4 we read suddenly in the middle of the story of the proclamation of the words of God: 'And Moses wrote all the words of the Lord', and in v. 12 we even hear the Lord speaking of 'the law and the commandment, which I have written for their instruction'. We shall miss the essential point if we ask how this writing down took place. The point is that at that moment in Israel's tradition the written word is beginning to play a part. We experience this especially in Jeremiah 36, concerning Jeremiah and his secretary Baruch. Here 'the scroll' is a decisive factor in the dispute between God and the people of Judah, with its rebellious King Jehoiakim. In the same way in the Gospel we see the mercurial apostle Paul busy, not only with sandals and his staff, but also with his quill and parchment. A wonderful example of this is the mildly ironic letter to a certain Philemon on behalf of an escaped slave. In Gal. 6.11 we read, 'See with what large letters I am writing to you with my own hand.' What would our Bible be without the apostolic letters? It therefore becomes clear, quite naturally, that the Bible does not just give an impartial account of what happened between God and his people, but that in that event the Bible itself has a place, as the written word. Particularly for the Jews after the Exile, the 'Scriptures' begin to play an important role, as is quite evident from the gospels. Here we find constant references to the Scriptures. In Luke 4.16-21 it is obvious that the 'Scriptures' have unquestionable authority for Jesus and for his audience. The tension felt here is due to the question of whether the son of the carpenter of Nazareth is right to place himself in the direct line of that authority.*

This is the point at which we can take the last step. The Scriptures have to play a separate and decisive role in the living events of the salvation-story, because in that way the authority and the power, the faithfulness and the steadfastness of God as partner of his people are mirrored and laid down. Without the written description, the events would run into each other and become to later generations a confused and everchanging stream without coherence and connection. But in the Scriptures, Israel and the congregation of Jesus Christ can recognize, distinguish and appropriate the Name. The faithfulness of God can be discovered. In what happens between God and man, therefore, the Scriptures acquire that typical authority which is described

theologically as the canon. *The collection of books is the authoritative source and norm in the living encounter between God and his
people.* It is entirely in agreement with this that in the Gospels and
Epistles we repeatedly find turns of phrase which ascribe or give
authority and power to the apostles in a specific manner: Rom. 1.1, 5;
I Cor. 9.1f.; John 20.23. The word apostolate, which is used nowadays
for the missionary task of the congregation, would be better reserved
for the typical place of authority and the task of the apostles in the
Bible. In the early church a manuscript had to be apostolic in order
to be admitted to the canon.

To sum up:

(a) Without the concept of the canon, the concept of inspiration
causes the Revelation of God to be buried in a never-ending stream
of events. There are no borders or limits anywhere. We wonder if
this is (or was) not the case in Roman Catholic theology, where
tradition is always growing new offshoots and where the Church
is its own standard in this ever-continuing explanation of tradition.

(b) Without the concept of inspiration, the concept of the canon
makes the Scriptures into a rigid authority, which rises motionless and
timeless above the life of the Church as a divine revelation, without
any well-defined reason. In that case, the Scriptures are no longer a
living part of what happens between God and us, intended through
proclamation to reach even the man of today. The living aspect,
the event, the Spirit, is no longer there. Our question here is whether
this is (or was) not the case with Protestant theology since the time
of orthodox theology (cf. Chapter I.B).

(c) It is essential that the canon should consist of a limited
number of books, though it is mere accident that this number should
be sixty-six. There might have been more or less, and for a long
time there was uncertainty in the Church about the exact limit
of the Scriptures. The Roman Catholic Church of the Middle Ages
included the so-called apocryphal books, but under the name 'Apocrypha' (that is to say, not equivalent to the canonical books). In
this case, the Reformation fixed the borderline. In our opinion these
differences of delimitation are of no real theological value. But it
is important to realize why certain books should be part of the Holy
Scriptures.

From what has been written, this must be quite obvious, when we
reflect that what matters in the Bible is an event, a history of a

certain time and place, then and there. In the Bible, the witnesses of these events speak to us. The origin of the books of the Bible is interwoven with this history. Very striking in this context is the Pauline tradition of the Last Supper in I Cor. 11.23. 'For I received from the Lord, what I also delivered to you. . . .' As we watch the witnesses pass the word from one to the other, the authority grows. What Saul had heard from the 'careful congregation' (which carefully preserved what it had received), he sees at the same time as a revelation of Jesus the Lord. There is therefore no contradiction here between what Jesus says and what the congregation 'lives'. It is the same thing as with a traffic accident or a crime. The judge has to listen to the spectators and other people involved. In this interrogation the notable witnesses are those who speak to the point and who inspire confidence. These are the witnesses the judge retains. In the same way, Israel and the Church have set apart those books, among the many writings in circulation, in which the matter was presented to them in a convincing manner. The contents are not true because the Bible is true; the Bible is true and inspires confidence, because what happens in the Bible is convincing. In this book we ask no one to accept the canon beforehand, but we do ask that they join us in the study of the Bible and then decide whether the sixty-six books occupy this strange authoritative position with good reason.

(d) The canon, the Holy Scriptures, that is to say this strange collection, functions as a standard. The word reigns: the Name has authority. In Chapter IV we intend to discuss in more detail the way this authority gains power over us.

(e) When we consider the authoritative way in which the Bible deals with the events it witnesses, we sense the impossibility of playing off the Bible against the holy writings of the nations. Some may ask why we should uphold the Bible, and not the Vedas of Hinduism or the books of mature Chinese wisdom. Do they not all speak in their own way of higher or divine affairs? Indeed, but that is not the point. General religious truths and insights can be found anywhere, but in the Bible we have a concrete history with certain unrepeatable decisions. Ask the witnesses, read the Bible! We think that then the special character of the Bible will manifest itself. The Bible says, with Jesus, in John 7.16,17: 'My teaching is not mine, but his who sent me; if any man's will is to do his will, he shall know *whether the teaching is from God or whether I am speaking on my own authority.'*

5. In what has been said so far, the question of the significance of the Church's teaching has repeatedly come up. We use this more or less inclusive term to describe early Catholic dogma and various other theological doctrines, including those of the Reformed confessional writings, which are sometimes called confessions.

The dogma of the early Church is the development of the teaching of the ancient Church, as it was laid down in the seven ecumenical councils of the first eight centuries. The core of this dogmatic development is the confession of the triune God and of the dual nature of the Redeemer. All the rest is mainly elaboration or reflection on this. The Eastern Orthodox Churches do not go beyond this dogma of the ancient Church; they consider that the development of dogma is now complete. The term theological doctrine *refers to reflections on various parts of the teaching of the Church, as it has taken place in the course of church history. The teaching on sin and grace, on the incarnation and the work of Jesus Christ, the doctrine of the Church and of the sacraments, of creation and of salvation – these are found in the theological works of the teachers of the Church of all centuries. Rome has consolidated this development in the doctrinal pronouncements of councils or popes. We find this element of teaching again in the confessional documents of the Reformed Churches, in a certain context and situation – the Dutch Confession, for instance, was composed in a time of persecution and inquisition – not as just the voice of one teacher, but with the authority of the community of a certain Church behind it.*

There is great division in the Churches on the matter of the place and the authority, the contents and the limits of the doctrine of the Church. The growth of the Church towards unity in the ecumenical movement is seriously hindered by this much disputed point.

Among the Churches of the Reformation the matter of 'doctrine' continues to be a seed of discord, particularly in the Netherlands Reformed Church. It has been glorified and reviled, misrepresented and misjudged. It is tragic to see how the doctrines of the Church which ought to be a meeting point, a symbol of recognition, have become a token of division. Mockers have spoken of the 'articles of disunity'.

In this book we have so far stressed strongly, in Chapter II.B, that the revelation in the Bible is an event, a history. We have done this because of the ever-recurring danger that the Scriptures would be understood as a sum total of general truths, which could then be organized idealistically in a system of doctrine, in a general system. What matters now is to establish that our position is not so fixed that there can be no room for doctrine. On the contrary, to take the historical character of the revelation seriously implies that doctrine attains its proper place. For the purpose of clarification we conclude with a few pointers.

(a) When a story of salvation unfolds in the Bible, centred on the deeds of God and the response of man, the simple implication is that we are here concerned with reality, with the concrete and objective affairs with which the story confronts us.

> *He has sent deliverance to his people*
> *and established his covenant for ever.*
> *Holy is his name, to be feared.*
>
> *To fear the Lord is the beginning of wisdom;*
> *all who do so prove themselves wise.*
> *His praise shall last for ever!*
> Ps. 111.9,10 from: The Psalms: *A New Translation.*

It is true, however, that revelation does not just consist in deeds, which are done wordlessly. Along with the *acts of redemption* go the *words of redemption*, which illuminate the acts and make clear their mutual coherence. The words from the cross in the events on Golgotha should be called to mind here. Such words also belong to the established and objective order. The teaching announces itself, and man reflects on it, as in Ps. 119. In this teaching his mind is occupied with God as he has revealed himself in his deeds.

> *Great are the works of the Lord;*
> *to be pondered by all who love them.*
> *Majestic and glorious is his work.*
> Ps. 110.2,3

Man knows, of course, that God in his majesty exceeds the teaching, but he only knows God as he has made himself known in his revelation. In the acts of God and in the explanation which goes with them – in the Bible the word is also the act – he meets his God.

If it is true, then, that in the Bible itself acts and words, events and teaching (*Torah*) belong together, then it is obvious that anyone who is concerned with the Bible will also leave a place for reflection and the formulation of the faith. In this way the Church became concerned with dogma and confession, theology and dogmatics, each in their own way holy matters. For the nuances contained in these reflections we refer to Chapter IV.B 3. How wonderful it would be if people in all sorts of Christian circles, inside and outside the Church, could overcome their fear and contempt for dogma and thorough theology! The basic theological words of the Christian faith, such as creation, election, reconciliation and sanctification – one can still hear how these words were originally verbs, events in time – are at the same time words which come to us from God, illuminating the cohesion of the acts of God. This can be illustrated with two examples from the Bible.

First of all an example taken from the field of reflection on the being of God. The Jew confessed, as in Deut. 6.4, that God, the Lord, is one. This word 'one' had for him the meaning that the God of his fathers had, in the history of the exodus out of Egypt and the entry into Canaan, distinguished himself from all the other gods by these acts. His God is entirely apart. But in addition, this confession contains an element of teaching. The Jew's God is unique. Compared with him, the other gods are no gods. This teaching element, though one of the climaxes in Israel's confession, is not, however, its end. God has more to say about himself. Later – we are thinking of I Cor. 12.4-6 and of the end of II Corinthians – this uniqueness of God is recognized and confessed in the complete uniqueness of Jesus the Lord and in the gifts of the spirit which he inspires. The secret of the Trinity is given a biblical background here, and the self-revelation of God opens up more and more in history. The teaching lights up and accompanies the procession of acts.

Another example concerns the norm for living. The proclamation of the 'Ten Words' is preceded by the act of deliverance out of Egypt. The introduction recalls this emphatically. But then follows instruction for the life following this act of deliverance. It is obvious that there is no uncertainty about the standard by which this liberating God will measure his people from now on. And this teaching is also continued in history. The Lord Jesus goes from one synagogue to the other, teaching all the while, as was the Jewish custom. He sits on the mountain in order to teach (Matt. 5.1-2), a clear parallel with Moses, who also gave the law from the mountain. The Lord is going to pass on the Law, and it is not difficult to recognize the structure of the Tanach behind all the other elements of the Sermon on the Mount (Matt. 5-7). This line is picked up again later by the apostles in their exhortations, especially in rules for the household (Col. 3.18-4.6). Here again we have a teaching element which is passed on and which belongs to the biblical revelation itself.

(b) Only when teaching and action are seen as one, does it become clear that the historical coherence is not just a matter of one thing after another, an arbitrary succession of blind facts, of which we have to give a theological explanation afterwards, but that it has already been provided in the Bible itself. That Jesus himself has the greatest respect for this coherence can be seen in the story of the walk to Emmaus (Luke 24), where the Risen One opens the Scriptures and shows how the lines of suffering and glory already had their beginning in the Law and the Prophets. The Messiah reveals himself in the context of the authoritative prophecies.

It is this coherence which marks the history of Israel among the nations, biblical history as a history of salvation. Using this unity of teaching and action as a vantage point, we can obtain a good view of two dangers which threaten Christian thought and life.

On the one hand, there is the danger that the teaching may be detached from the deeds and made into an absolute. The teaching then suddenly ceases to be teaching in the real biblical sense of *Torah*, holy teaching, law, news of salvation. It becomes a law in our western meaning of the word, a system of dogmatic truths, which are at our disposal, an idealistic system of thought. This leaves the road clear for an unbridled confessionalism, which is all the more dangerous when it is thought that no dogma or confession is professed. The folk who proclaim loudest that they do not want any dogmatic Christianity are often those who are most rigid and dogmatic.

On the other hand there is, particularly nowadays, the danger of too much reliance on the one fact of what happened, the acts of

God in the history of salvation which culminate in the one act of Jesus the Messiah. The *meeting* between God and man comes to occupy such a central place that the teaching is forced into the background and is considered unimportant. Dogma and theological teaching are at best interesting symbols from the past, which only serve to show the long way the church has travelled in history. In the past one often heard the expression: not the teaching, but the Lord (*niet de leer, maar de Heer*). The intention may have been good, but it was dangerous. It is precisely this teaching which has to make clear how the Lord exists for us. Today the word *existential* is used by preference in this context. Here, too, the intention may be right, but one runs the risk of reducing the meeting-in-faith with Christ to an intangible inward and religious event. It is the teaching, the coherence and order of the deeds of God, dogma and theological reflection which are needed in order to see how God comes to us in the salvation-story.

In the answer to question 21 of the Heidelberg Catechism we can still detect how the Reformers turned intuitively away from both these pitfalls: 'A true faith is not only a certain knowledge whereby I hold for truth all that God has revealed to us in his Word, but also a hearty trust . . . that not only to others, but to me also, forgiveness of sins, everlasting righteousness and blessedness are given by God.' The teaching is certainly not left out. Here we see clearly the character of biblical faith: it is falling in with the decisions which come to us from God, and consenting to the truth which is revealed to us.

(c) This is also an opportunity to say something of that much used set of concepts: objective and subjective. These are popular terms in certain church circles. The issue is often put like this: the objectiveness of the (theoretical) truth is in itself very beautiful, but it is insufficient. Something has to be added from the side of the subject, the person who has to make this objective truth his own. The objective lacks the complement of the subjective. This thesis in itself is already a clear proof that the objectivity spoken of here is not the liberating objectivity of the Bible. For the Bible confronts man as such with salvation. When Jesus calls Zacchaeus in Luke 19, Zacchaeus does not have to begin by applying the truth of Jesus' words to himself. Salvation happens at the moment when the Lord speaks the words: 'Today salvation has come to this house.' Only

God's supreme power bears witness, and it is this Christ who surrounds us with his mercy. The objective and subjective are merged into one.

By what we have just said we do not mean to imply that in our thinking about the Bible we cannot use these words at all. They can serve us well in making it clear that the truth of God is absolutely not dependent on our faith. He comes to us objectively and all-powerfully in the history of the Bible. To this truth, the story of these events, we subjects, we people, may listen. And if we refuse to do so, then God's salvation nevertheless remains true, even without us. In that case the proclamation and the events go to others, as Paul has to experience so often in Acts, to his great sorrow, when the people of his own nation refuse to listen to the message that in Jesus the Messiah God's salvation-story has reached its culmination (Acts 13.13-49). In this tremendous narrative we see how God's redemption moves through history, objectively and subjectively.

In the same way, we have seen in Chapter I, the Church walking through history as it were on two legs – objectivity and subjectivity, stressing the objectivity when God's truth threatens to be lost in what man experiences of it inwardly, yet stressing the subjectivity in a period of scholastic and barren objectifying of the truth. One cannot walk on one leg. It really is a miracle, a miracle of the Holy Spirit, when people who live with the Bible use both their legs well, in a natural manner. 'When the Spirit of truth comes, he will guide you into all the truth; for he will not speak on his own authority, but whatever he hears he will speak, and he will declare to you the things that are to come' (John 16.13). How clearly we see the change in accent in a saying like this: objective and subjective, but together they are *one*, 'all the truth'.

C And God said . . .

On the first page of the Bible we immediately meet a God who speaks.

> And God said . . . 'let there be light
> . . . let there be a firmament'.

This refrain, which makes the story of the creation, when read as a whole, such a suggestive one, occurs seven times.

On the last pages of the Bible there are also many voices to be heard. 'And I heard a great voice from the throne saying, "Behold, the dwelling of God is with men . . ."' (Rev. 21.3) 'He who testifies to these things says, "Surely I am coming soon"' (Rev. 22.20).

Right through the Bible we find the same thing. Continually there is speaking and calling, asking and answering, proclaiming and singing, praying and praising, sometimes also writing or committing to paper, teaching or admonishing, but always there is the spoken *word*.

It sometimes happens, however, that the speaking is in the background. In the Torah we find in the books Leviticus, Numbers and Deuteronomy many regulations and rules – the Bible calls them 'decrees' – which, it is felt, have little to say to us. There are parts in the Prophets in which the narrative, the events, feats of arms, palace revolutions and political intrigues, demand all the attention. There are lists of generations of officials which, to our feeling, at times disturb the reading of the Bible. Some of the books of the Bible of later origin give visions in which it seems as if we have gone 'past the word', e.g. Ezek. 47, Zech. 1-6, Dan. 7-12 and the Book of Revelation. But in these parts there is nevertheless sometimes a glimpse of a 'word', a 'thus says the Lord' which reminds us that even all this takes place within the context of the history between God and his people. It is an event, as we have tried to underline so emphatically in Chapter III.B. But these events are not just dumb happenings, an automatic unrolling of facts, nor are they the accidental process of powers and forces, nor yet a drama of good and evil controlled by God. According to the Bible, these events are at the same time an encounter, a dialogue, a conversation. The event is word at the same time. The *word came*, as we read so often in the Prophets.

Perhaps the reader is asking himself why we are emphasizing ideas which every reader of the Bible already knows quite obviously. Of course there is a great deal of talking in the Bible, by God and by people. The Bible is the Word of God, as many will be prepared to concede in advance. But we think that there is a hidden problem here, because modern man has little feeling left for the mystery of the word. (Perhaps it is better to speak of man in so far as he still lives in the climate of thought of the nineteenth century. That was when modern science began to develop, the exact thinking which is still celebrating its great triumphs today. How a man thinks, his intellect and his logical insight, these show their worth specially in the applied sciences.)

We have no desire at all to make acid remarks here about the idolization of the human understanding, from a Christian standpoint, or anything like that. As Christians we applaud new developments wholeheartedly, and we have the greatest admiration for the achievements of the natural sciences and technology. We follow with interest on the television the astronauts' journeys into space.

But it is a fact that this development has as a matter of course made an absolute rationalist of every one of us. As we already saw in Chapter I.B.1, rationalism has its roots in the time of the Renaissance and of the seventeenth century. The name of the philosopher Descartes is the best known example. Indeed, this rationalism is really as old as the origin of our Western civilization in the thinking of the Greek philosophers. But since the last century it has really become the climate in which we all live and breathe. For that is when the intellect, the *ratio*, became married to the world of things around us, the *empirical* world. With very few exceptions, earlier generations of thinkers had not done this. They reasoned and concluded, but in the nineteenth century people begin to *experiment*. The searching intellect attacks reality in order to get a grip on the world of dead and living matter. This empirical rationalism has given us all a businesslike attitude. With everything we ask: does this tally with the facts? What is the truth? We test our reasoning on the facts, and conversely, we X-ray the facts with our reasoning intellect. We thus want to capture and measure everything with and against our reason. In itself, we hasten to add, this is very healthy. It may and should happen. We do not feel at all attracted to the idea of putting our minds out to grass, even where the Bible is concerned. But it is a different matter if rationalism robs us of an eye for the truths and realities, the areas and forms of life which in their nature cannot be encompassed by reasoning, let alone by computers as, for instance, love or the arts.

In our opinion, what we have just said is also valid for the miracle of language. Wherever words are spoken, a world opens up which has its own separate character and being. This is the point where the Bible, the book of the spoken word, can become the victim of unlimited misunderstanding, if we have not become suspicious of our own (empirical) rationalism.

For rationalism has the tendency to appreciate a word or a conversation purely on its businesslike truth content. We ask at once: what are the facts behind this word? Is what is said there true? Is there a tangible, a factual reality behind these words? In that case, we only see the word as the means of conveying the content of thought. What is being said is detached from the manner in which it is said. *We are only concerned with the contents.*

It is obvious that no man 'who uses his reason' will approach a painting by Renoir, a suite by Grieg, a poem by Vondel, or even a letter from a soldier to his girl in this way. It is not just the content that is important, but the manner in which an atmosphere is created, a mood interpreted, a drama described or love expressed. *Form and content are one.*

Unfortunately our rationalist generation does approach the Bible in such an 'unreasonable' way, both inside and outside the Church. Wherever this happens people are lost, hopeless. The Bible at once becomes a strange and inaccessible book. With a few exceptions – the famous 'beautiful and simple passages' – large parts of the Bible remain inaccessible and strange to us, and we have the greatest difficulty in 'believing all the same' in many things.

But the whole picture changes when we do not ask at once rationally how this or that has to be imagined – for instance how God speaks to the prophets – but first look at the form into which the words of the Bible have been put. Strictly speaking, our talk of form and content is already wrong, the fruit of our rationalist attitude. It would be better first to take delight in 'the many and various ways' (Heb. 1.1.) in which God speaks in the Scriptures, and in which men speak among each other there. We have already pointed this out in passing, but now we stop to point it out emphatically.

The lofty words of God to prophet or man of God, nation or individual, can be overpowering, as in the book of Job. Man is silent or falls upon his face (Ezek. 1.28). But the words of God are also often intimate, friendly, confidential, as in the stories of the patriarchs. God speaks to Moses as a man speaks to his friend

(Ex. 33.11). To Adam and Cain he speaks provokingly: 'Where are you?' (Gen. 3.9); 'Where is Abel your brother?' (Gen. 4.9). It would be the height of rationalism here to bring up the problem why the Lord God asks these questions, because as the All-knowing he must know the answer already. This question is really intended both to seek out and to elect, and is closely connected with the biblical connotations of 'to see', as in Luke 19.5, where Jesus 'sees' Zacchaeus and makes him come out of the tree.

Sometimes the words of God or the conversations between men are fierce and direct. Jeremiah spoke the truth to the face of both king and people (Jer. 7.2ff.). But often the prophets also make use of a symbol, like the false prophet Zedekiah in the realistic story in I Kings 22, where he makes himself horns of iron in order to demonstrate and guarantee convincingly the striking-force of the Israelite army. In the same chapter Micaiah, the son of Imlah, on the other hand, makes use of an ironic story to speak God's truth to the two kings in a most challenging manner.

Often the word does not just come indirectly, but disguised, as with Nathan, who tells David the story of the rich man and the poor man with his ewe lamb (II Sam. 12.1-4). David is unmasked by this much more efficiently than he would have been by a direct accusation. This indirect and even disguised way of speaking is very popular in the East, and everyone knows what a great part the parable or *mashal* plays in the Bible. It is made use of for all sorts of different purposes, and it would be another rational impoverishment to think that parables only serve to give the truth of the gospel an easily understood form. Sometimes this is the case, but by no means always.

In some instances, to speak through or in the name of God is an authoritative announcement of salvation or judgement, as in the famous passage in Isa. 40.1: 'Comfort, comfort my people, says your God.' At other times such speaking carries the reader or listener with it in the train of thought, as we so often find in Paul: 'What shall we say then? Is there injustice on God's part? By no means!' (Rom. 9.14,19 and 30). The famous chapters 9-11 in the Letter to the Romans are not really a dogmatic argument by the apostle about election and rejection; they are a conversation, a conversation with a Jew and a Gentile Christian, with the prophets and with God himself. In the course of this conversation new perspectives open up, the truth begins to dawn, even though much remains hidden in God's unsearchable wisdom, which is confessed with praise in the beautiful ending (Rom. 11.33-36).

In the gospels we are at the climax, the fulfilment, of biblical speaking. The way in which Jesus handled the word astonished people from the beginning. 'For he taught them as one who had authority, and not as the scribes' (Mark 1.22). Because the gospel stories are so well known to us, we often no longer have an eye for the very varied and special forms in which the gospels pass the word of Christ on to us. It is by no means an imaginary danger that we may believe so unquestioningly in the absoluteness of the divine words of the Redeemer from the start that the finer nuances, the ordinary human, historical and psychological contours of the situation in which Jesus is speaking, escape us.

If we want to be obedient to the Bible, we shall have to pay attention to the special character of each Gospel, the special way in which each evokes Christ for us. The high and exalted words of Christ in the Gospel of John are totally different from the more ordinary language of the three other evangelists. But the direct, hasty and fierce tone of Matthew and particularly of Mark is entirely different from the mild and charitable manner of Luke, who takes his time to show us Jesus in his compassion for the erring and the lost. In all the gospels we must pay attention to the special character of each pericope (clearly defined portion of scripture) by itself.

What we would like to underline in this context is the uniqueness of the *conversations* of Jesus. The way in which he carries on a conversation with disciples or opponents, with tax-gatherers and accidental spectators, is entirely unique and does not occur anywhere else in world history. Jesus' irony is not eclipsed by that of Socrates and in revealing dialogue even Sartre is not superior. His words are at once sharp and merciful – the conversation at the house of Simon the Pharisee is probably the most telling example (Luke 7.36-50). It is well known how wittily he replies every time to the scribes who want to ensnare him, inspiring respect and amazement (Mark 11.27-33; 12.13-17). What strikes us in John 18.19-24 is how Jesus combines an open, self-giving attitude with royal dignity. Here he confronts the high priest with self-confidence, and does not accept the blow on the cheek without answering back.

Passion sermons, as well as passion music, sometimes give a very one-sided picture of 'the suffering Lord'. Jesus' attitude to all who are confronted with him in their distress is one of pastoral compassion, helping and serving, but at the same time he respects human dignity. The most beautiful example of this is perhaps the wonderful way in which Jesus protects the adulteress from her accusers, both with his words and with his silence, as we pointed out in Chapter III.B.

It is a delight to acquire an eye in this way for the enthralling power which comes over us through the *word* of Jesus. What is proclaimed by him is interwoven with the manner in which he speaks, and his very speech is a liberating salvation. In our over-rationalistic world, in which the word has become a quick and soulless means of communication in the realm of big business – witness the many abbreviations which we need – a confrontation between a man and Jesus who speaks may become a real encounter, an encounter in the true sense of the word, in which one person really meets another and opens his being to him. This can be a liberation from the loneliness from which may suffer consciously or unconsciously. Once the rationalist misunderstanding of words and language has been put aside, it becomes possible to understand how John the evangelist can call Jesus 'The Word' in the famous opening of his gospel, John 1.1-14. This does not have to be profound philosophy or dogmatic speculation. Jesus is the speaking of God, through which a new world opens up miraculously.

It is now time for one final illustration that the words of Jesus must not be divorced from the situation in which they were spoken, nor from the speaker or the person addressed, in order to establish rationally and as soon as possible *what* has really been said. We must give rather more detailed attention to the parable of the good Samaritan, Luke 10.25-37.

This famous parable has gone down in history as a cry in distress to a neighbour for mercy. As such it has had a tremendous influence. The words 'Go and do likewise', with which this section closes, always have a tremendous power. All the same we feel that, read in the traditional manner, this parable keeps its essential secret hidden. It is usually overlooked that this parable is part of a conversation between Jesus and 'a lawyer' (v. 25): the 'encounter'.

It is not difficult to sense that in the short conversation of vv. 25-29 Jesus has driven the lawyer into a corner which he had wanted to avoid – and this was done with agility and delicate irony. Jesus throws him back on to 'the Law', while he had wanted to make Jesus admit that his merciful attitude towards tax-gatherers and simple and poor people did not do justice to the severe law which was the condition of the Kingdom of God. As this man is obviously trying to save his face in v. 29, it seems likely that the spectators listened to the discussion with a certain amount of malicious pleasure. If one assumes that among the spectators were also priests and Levites, then one can sense something of the subtle stage-management of the parable which follows. When in v. 30 'a man' travels from Jerusalem to Jericho, it seems as if this could hardly be anything but an allusion to 'the lawyer' with whom Jesus is in conversation. The Greek word tis (someone) which occurs both in v. 25 and in v. 30 often has the meaning of an allusion. See for instance Luke 19.12. Unfortunately this feature can no longer be found in the RSV, though it is clear in the AV. Thus, the good lawyer is forced to take part, willy-nilly, in a play in which the listeners, priests and Levites, are also involved en passant. This play forces the lawyer to see clearly that to love your neighbour ceases to be a problem when one has first been saved by the neighbour from great distress, even if the neighbour is a despised Samaritan. For it is very striking that the question in v. 36 is not – as the traditional explanation always implies – which of the three passers-by really loved the neighbour, but which of the three was the neighbour, to whom the man by the side of the road was of course deeply grateful. This all fits in exactly with the play as we believe we can see it here. The lawyer was not just troubled by the question who was his neighbour, whom he should love; he had never realized how wonderful it is when mercy is shown simply to the poor, the despised and the sinner. All this is suddenly clarified for him because he is placed in the part of the one who suffers.

The point, the accent of this parable is, therefore, no longer the well-meaning and Christian help in distress of another person (though this is also part of the story), but that one should be humbly prepared to accept mercy and then to give love in return. That is why the commandment of love is placed in the most important biblical context, which after the Exodus from Egypt is the framework of the law. God began by showing mercy to the enslaved people. According to the Torah, love on the side of Israel is in essence always basically love out of gratitude. The Pharisees of Jesus' day had forgotten this. From Jesus, however, this seldom comes as the content of direct information; it is not a moral programme or dogmatic pronouncement. He illumines it with his whole being and in all his words, as he does here for the lawyer. Therefore, what that parable was for the lawyer, the whole witness of the gospel is for us. His truth only becomes alive for us when we have to, or want to, act in the play ourselves. There is no place for spectators.

The point of the Bible, therefore, is that which is said, the encounter between God and his people. For us, who are involved in this meeting, the Bible is the Word of God that wants to enlist and convince man.

We end this section with a few remarks and conclusions.

1. In the encounters between God and man it is not a question of two equal partners who answer each other at the same level. In the Bible, God really has the first and also, of course, the last word, unless one believes that the praise and adoration of the redeemed creature is the final conclusion of this encounter. But in any case, God is the great Other who takes the initiative and keeps it. Our reply is to follow, to obey, to believe. Nevertheless it remains a *meeting*. The Word of God comes with superior power, it is true, but it does not force our human liberty. In a real encounter one party tries to convince the other, but not force it. That is why the ultimate possibility here is the 'no' of unbelief and rejection by God (Matt. 25.31-46). That is where judgement finds its place in the history of God and his people. We are here touching on some difficult dogmatic matters, which we cannot go into further at the moment. The point we want to make, however, is that the insight that everything takes place within the framework of the dialogue between God and man, helps to clarify things considerably.

2. If it is true that the Bible is essentially a speaking of God, and if this speaking of God is essentially an encounter, then the Bible will always be new and up to date. We cannot imagine that a time should arrive when the Church could say: now we know everything. The implication of this would be that what is and should remain an essentially living word had congealed into a fixed

truth. The whole Scriptures are rather like the parable of the Pharisee and the tax-gatherer in Luke 18.9-14. As soon as people assume that they know how to pray and know what to ask for in order to find the humble attitude of the tax-gatherer, then they are already again like the Pharisee. Since Jesus told this parable, all Pharisees have prayed like the tax-gatherer, as Luther so wittily remarked. In appealing to the Bible, therefore, it is always as well to assume an attitude of great caution, especially when one believes oneself to be in verbal agreement with it. This is called a 'legalistic' appeal to the word of the Bible. Leaving the situation and its intention to one side, a word or a commandment is taken and put forward as a generally valid rule. That this word might acquire a new significance in a new situation has been excluded in advance. An example of this is the famous passage on divorce in Mark 10.2-12. 'What therefore God has joined together, let not man put asunder' (v. 9). Does this mean that divorce is always a breaking of God's law? From the corresponding passage in Matt. 19 it is clear that exceptions are possible. Verse 9 is probably an addition, so that we already have a case of casuistry here: a special rule is put forward, but exceptions are made for certain cases. This, however, is always a very unconvincing course of action. It is better to admit that here, too, Jesus does not give a general rule, but speaks in a situation, in an encounter. The situation is the eastern form of society in which the married woman is without rights against the arbitrariness of her husband. This can be seen from the way the question is put in v. 3 : 'Is it lawful to divorce one's wife for any cause?' (The AV reads: '. . . to *put away* one's wife'). The law of Moses had already protected the woman against such arbitrariness, and Jesus continues in the same principle. When, however, through the legalistic usage of this word of Jesus in our society a man or woman is forever tied to the arbitrariness of a partner with whom life has perhaps already become hell, the intention of Jesus' word is turned into its reverse. Then the letter kills!

3. The Reformation made the marvellous rediscovery that the Bible is a word that liberates; a word that lives, and that creates life, even apart from its contents (which are as varied as the Bible itself). In our conversation with Rome we may always, with cheerful confidence, rely on the fact that a theology of the word is bound to win. It is also a cause for joy and generous gratitude to see that Rome

today is emphatically prepared to let the Scriptures have their say. It is obvious, however, that we do not emphasize the Scriptures because we believe them to contain 'all the truths of God'. That would make the Bible into a lawbook containing God's revealed truth, which could, if desired, be arranged into a well-ordered theological system which one would have to 'believe'. It must be recognized that this approach pushes everything out of place. Unfortunately such a distortion did take place in the Church and in church history. (Chapter I). Under such conditions it is not surprising if there remains little to be said that makes any impression on the Roman Catholic Church, in which somehow the source of the revelation acquired a place beside the Bible.

4. It is also clear that, on the basis of what we have said, the sermon, the proclamation of the word, has a central place in the church service. The Bible in the pulpit! But if that is so, the Bible must really be permitted to speak in the sermon, and not the pious mind or the needs of personal experience. Nor should the sermon be (exclusively) a dogmatic or moralistic exposition; it should rather be experienced and accepted as a conversation, which is the meaning of the Greek word 'homily'. It should be a conversation in which, in the nature of the encounter with God, God meets us with the superior power of the Holy Spirit in the word of the Scriptures, summoning us to make a decision. 'Repent, for the kingdom of heaven is at hand' (Matt. 4.17).

5. Finally, whatever the exultation with which the sermon is praised in a reformed theology of the word, it will be impossible to safeguard it from rationalistic misunderstanding unless it is placed within the framework of the whole service as encounter between God and his congregation. A church service is basically not a meeting where one can listen to a convincing speaker, but a coming together of the Lord and his Church. We remind the reader of the 'tent of meeting' which plays such a large part for Israel in the stories about the desert. That is why a real theology of the word will be happy about the renewed interest in the communion and the revived liturgical interest. A new appreciation of singing, which is speaking in an exalted tone, is also important in the encounter with God and his Word. The fact that congregations sometimes sing so soullessly and in such an old-fashioned way, indicates that the Word has not yet been properly discovered as a living and effective power. It is not

an accident that congregational singing developed precisely in the Reformation period.

D Our Father . . .

We believe that we are not far from the truth when we assume that many people unconsciously alter the opening words of 'Our Father'. They keep themselves apart from any Christian communal life, and believe and pray by themselves. Therefore they really pray: 'My Father, who art in heaven'. But because they imagine that many others in *their* inner room are also praying, the adding up of many isolated people makes it possible to go on praying: 'Our Father'.

Speaking of the inner room, in Matt. 6.5-15, where Jesus instructs the disciples in the right way to pray, the 'room' which Jesus indicates is not intended as a rejection of the community, but much more as a protest against the show, against the self-conscious prayer of the 'hypocrites'. This can be seen from the fact that the Lord's Prayer is not put in the first person singular but in the 'we' form. The congregation, the together-ness, is presupposed, even when a person is praying alone in Psalms, Gospels or Epistles. Jesus prays alone in Gethsemane, but he asks his disciples to watch with him (Matt. 26.36-46).

This relatively arbitrary example of the Lord's Prayer may serve to make us aware that *individualism* might raise serious obstacles to the reading of the Bible for us modern people. It may be useful, before we consider this further, to explain more carefully what we mean by the word individualism. Here we introduced it rather in a tone of disapproval. It is not, however, our intention to deny the valuable and positive content which this word has had through history. As far as that goes, the situation here is exactly the same as with the words liberalism, idealism and rationalism, against which we objected in the earlier parts of this chapter. By individualism, for instance, one might understand the rights and duties of the individual to examine independently, free from group prejudices, in order to come to a personal conviction about life. In ancient classical

times and in the late Middle Ages and the Renaissance, those who
dared to be individualists were not unimportant men: they included Socrates, Galileo, Erasmus. Since those days individualism
has become common property in our Western European culture.
Who would want to do away with it now? The Reformation also
made its positive contribution here. Luther dared to defy, alone,
the Pope, the Council, tradition and the Diet, in order to venture
forth, alone, with the Word of God. But the emphasis of the
Reformation is just that little bit different from that of the Renaissance and humanism. For the two latter, man becomes the norm.
He has to examine and determine everything for himself. For the
Reformation it is God who calls man to the decision of faith through
the Gospel, and in this decision he can have no recourse to the
authority of church or tradition. This decision of faith undoubtedly
brings with it personal freedom, but it has its origin in and remains
connected with God who speaks. All the same it can be said that
the Renaissance and the Reformation together have ensured an
enduring place for individualism in our civilization. Over against
collective experience and thought, which accords no place to the
independent decision of man by himself, individualism will always
be judged positively. This collectivism is seen in such movements as
fascism and communism, but it also runs through the whole of
everyday life, where impersonal forces and developments cause the
feeling that one is swept along in a stream against which no resistance
is possible. Technology, advertising, means of communication, political and economic forces, in short the well-known picture of our time,
looms up before our eyes here.

   This collective mode of existence, which in a manner of speaking
already goes beyond individualism, has to be distinguished from those
civilizations and peoples who have not yet reached individualism. In
an unfortunate phrase, those people are sometimes called 'primitive'.
For them the isolated person is still entirely tied up with and hidden
in the greater unit of the family, the clan, or the nation. These are no
impersonal massive groups, but communities in which each person has
his place as a matter of course, without as yet being able to distinguish
the individual consciously from the community.

   In the oriental world to which the Bible introduces us, this collective way of thought is universal, with the qualification that in
the Bible itself the communal way of thought has entirely its own

character. We hope to be able to show this later. Now we want to put forward the definition that today we understand individualism to refer to that attitude to life in which man is considered in principle as an isolated, independent person, and experienced as such. The fact that he nevertheless takes part in larger connections and communities is considered to be an accidental detail, often a necessary evil. Particularly in religious matters, this is considered to be the latest wisdom. Here is the well-known attitude that 'everyone has to make up his own mind, one must not talk people into things.' Undoubtedly this individualism has worked as a solvent in Protestantism, while, on the other hand, the Roman Catholic Church, out of fear for individualism, did not dare to make room for the personal responsibility of each person, which was certainly to its own detriment.

How is all this dealt with in the Bible? As we have said, in the oriental world which we enter when we open the Bible, man lives in natural connection with larger groupings; household (which is somewhat larger than our 'family') and generation, tribe and nation. Outside this context, the isolated person is a 'stranger', like Abraham, when he had to leave his tribal background (Gen. 12.1). The biblical idea of community does not coincide with primitive collective consciousness. Nevertheless, a man who for some reason or other finds himself outside the community, is wretched, like the poet who sends up his complaint in Psalm 42 :

> *These things I remember,*
> *as I pour out my soul:*
> *how I went with the throng,*
> *and led them in procession to the house of God,*
> *with glad shouts and songs of thanksgiving,*
> *a multitude keeping festival.*
>
> Ps. 42.4

The isolated person, the exile, is not only without protection, he is really also without any chance of life. A man can only live and act in the greater context of the community.

The language of the Bible has a separate word for this 'whole', which is not an adjective, but a noun. In Hebrew this is *kol*, the wholeness, the totality of something. This is not the result of an addition, but a basic word that occurs countless times in the Law and the Prophets. All the people, *all* the children of Israel, *every* day. In the story of Christmas we meet it again, when the angel announces 'a great joy which will come to all the people' (Luke 2.10).

To what extent this way of thought, which is based on the 'whole', determines everything, so that it raises difficulties for our individual way of thought and feeling, can be shown from an example which underlines it sharply.

In Joshua 7 we find the story of Achan who took some of the devoted things, i.e. things put under a ban. This is the whole of the spoil, which had to be burned or delivered up, just as after the conquest of Jericho all the inhabitants had to be killed. Jericho is considered to be one whole, with everything in it. But there is one Israelite who acts egoistically, and therefore individualistically (though an individualist is not necessarily an egoist). He keeps part of the spoil back. When he commits this deed, we hear in verse 1 that the *Israelites* broke faith in regard to 'the things under the ban'. That something has indeed gone wrong for and with the whole people is shown in a curious fashion by an unexpected defeat from the small town of Ai. That is how Joshua discovers that there is something wrong somewhere. Verses 11 to 13 refer again to 'the things under the ban', which have put Israel under the ban as well. By casting lots the trouble spot is discovered, in a search of the smaller units, the tribes and the families. Finally it becomes clear that it is Achan, the son of Carmi, of the family of Zerah, of the tribe of Judah, who was at the root of the trouble. In spite of his honest confession, Achan is stoned, not just with his spoil, but also with his sons and daughters and all his possessions. The heap of stones in the Valley of Achor remains as a warning for future generations.

What are we supposed to do with such a story? We can offer the following remarks:

1. It is clear that we have to do here with a manifestation of oriental collective consciousness, which in its results and application in this specific case wounds our moral awareness. We must not try to reason this out of existence, but simply accept it. In this atmosphere, in this cultural pattern, the eastern nations, including Israel of that day, thought and lived. It is a similar case to that of the polygamy of the patriarchs. These are the relations, this is the climate of life in which the history of God and his people Israel takes place.

What matters is the history, and it is not advisable to unwrap it from the packing of the oriental collective attitude to life, even though this collective approach can no longer be ours, nor does the Bible insist that it should be. Does this mean, then, that we are exclusively committed to our Western individualist attitude to life? No, because . . .

2. Though this collective approach can and may no longer be ours, all the same we must not throw away the baby with the bathwater. In the story of Achan we detect something real about human relationships in guilt and fate, which can only be ignored as a result of a superficial individualism. In the profound situations of life – we are thinking of our experiences as an occupied nation – it becomes clear that we only live and experience in a really human manner, as and because we stand in a larger context. Is this not the reason that death is so terrible for man, because in death he is absolutely alone? And is the simple fact of marriage and family not a clear contradiction of the individualist pattern of life? Do so many marriages break up these days because the partners seek an individualist interpretation of marriage? There is the well-known joke about the man in the life-boat who suddenly seized a saw and began to make a hole in the bottom of the boat. To the protests of his fellow-passengers he answered: what has it got to do with you? I am only sawing under my own seat! The best people of our generation are certainly those who realize that modern man cannot live by individualism alone. The agonized cry of the poet Marsman has almost become a cliché:

> I stand alone, neither God, nor society
> involve my existence in any inspired community.
>   *Tempel en Kruis* (Temple and Cross)

Life as the 'lonely adventure' is viewed with loathing.

3. In the story of Achan, the point is not just a collective approach to life, which contains a reality even according to the ordinary depth-experience of man. What this story is really about is that the people of Israel are God's holy people. YHWH who delivered the people out of Egypt has made it into this curious unity and wholeness. Here is not the natural collectivity of a tribe or people; the God of the salvation story has given this striking awareness of community to Israel. This is the secret which also underlies the story

of Achan. It becomes very clear from the complaint of Joshua in vv. 7-9. It is so terrible that Israel is beaten, because God's name (his acts of salvation) is at stake. 'What wilt thou do for thy great name?' (v. 9). That is why the whole thing is so important!

There is a striking parallel to this in the story of Ananias and Sapphira in Acts 5. Here, too, the punishment is extraordinarily severe because the wholeness has been damaged. The Holy Spirit has been deceived (v. 3), the Holy Spirit which, since Pentecost, has been so powerfully at work in 'the whole church' (v. 11). The trouble spot is radically removed. The congregation is not, of course, a natural collective unit, but a creation of the God of salvation. That is why it is so sensitive.

We now come to a conclusion: in the Bible we find a collective way of thought, which in its external appearances lies closer to a primitive oriental awareness of life than our western individualism. There are, however, gradations and variations in this respect in the Scriptures. The prophet Ezekiel, for instance, lays great stress on personal responsibility. 'The soul that sins shall die' (Ezek. 18.4). But the difference from the general oriental collective approach is that it is characteristic of the Bible that the community depends on the God of the Covenant, the God of the salvation history, who creates his people (Ps. 95.6, 7) and who founds his congregation in order to rule over it as Lord. 'None of us lives to himself. . . . If we live, we live to the Lord, and if we die, we die to the Lord; so then, whether we live or whether we die, we are the Lord's' (Rom. 14.7, 8). This *we* should therefore be taken very literally. It is a totality, and not the sum total of pious individuals! This Jewish variation of eastern collective thought has altered it into something personal which is not merely a natural fact. The God of salvation who acts and speaks, demands an answer of faith: conversion and obedience. In the story of the meeting between Jesus and Zacchaeus in Luke 19.1-10, Zacchaeus is called personally, but how clearly this conversion is contained in the framework of the community: 'Today salvation has come to this *house*, since he also is *a son of Abraham*' (v. 9)! He can take his place again among the whole nation of God.

In order to enlarge on this biblical concept of community, we make two additional remarks. (a) The man of the Bible does not only live in the context of the whole of the present generation, but also in the perspective of the generations of history. Hebrew has two words for generation: *dor* (generation) and *mishpahah* (family, as lineage). In Israel there was a strong consciousness of the living connection between the generations of the past and of today. At the Passover the father of the family was supposed to say to his children: 'It is because of what the Lord did for me when I came out of Egypt' (Ex. 13.8 and 14). The patriarchs are not just the tribal ancestors, who stand at the beginning of the line; the future history of the people is in some way already contained in their lives. They are the trunk, the root, the rock from which future generations have been hewn (Isa. 51.1, 2). They did not remain alone. This living awareness of the connection between and identity of the ancestors and the later generations is sometimes called 'the root-idea'. Once one has noticed this, one is struck by it repeatedly. 'There shall come forth a shoot from the stump of Jesse, and a branch shall grow out of his roots' (Isa. 11.1).

The sons of Jacob are at the same time the tribes of Israel, just as the name of the people and of the tribal ancestor is the same (Jacob-Israel). When Jacob blesses his sons in Gen. 49, it is difficult to distinguish whether these blessings are intended for each son, or for the later tribe. Some biblical scholars assume that some of the vicissitudes and situations of the tribe were later put into the mouth of Jacob. This may seem shocking to those who simply believe in the Bible; but the difficulty in distinguishing between the tribe and the tribal ancestor is really the essence of the affair, and very significant.

The stories of the patriarchs also already contain much that is told later in the history of the whole nation. Abraham has to go to Egypt (Gen. 12.10-20). His descendants later also have to go to Egypt because of famine (Gen. 45 ff.). All kinds of themes thus return in the Law and the Prophets – the theme of 'the exodus', of 'the desert', of 'being a sojourner' and of 'the return'. Jacob returns from Paddan-aram (Gen. 32) and the people of Israel return from exile. We read in Gen. 15.17 and 18 that the Lord makes his covenant with Abraham by the light of a firepot and a flaming torch, but the covenant with the whole people of Israel is made by the fire and smoke of Sinai (Ex. 19.17-20).

It is known that the Israelite feels himself to be strongly connected with the generations which come after him. He lives in his descendants. This explains why to have no children is felt as being cut off from the living connection of God's people. The many stories of wives who (at first) are not blessed with children are an obvious proof of the important part which this 'root-idea' plays in the Bible. Therefore the long lists of generations in the Bible, which seem dull to us, are for the Jew as interesting as the births, marriages and deaths columns in a local paper. The lists in Matthew 1 and Luke 3 are also part of 'the good news'.

In the centuries before our era the Jews realized correctly that this communal way of thought did not need to be limited to the people of Israel. What is experienced by their own people is also essentially valid for the whole of mankind, however much it may be obscured there. In Adam (man *and* humanity) all men form one whole. These concepts are clearly behind Paul's speech in the Areopagus. 'And he made from one every nation of men' as Acts 17.26 says literally. In Romans 5 Paul makes grateful use of this 'root-idea' in order to place the proclamation of Christ in a world-wide context.

It is not easy for us to place ourselves in these trains of thought. Because we are used to thinking individually, this 'root-thinking' seems unreal to us. What should we think of the idea that my life was already contained in that of my ancestors, or that my life and deeds should again become reality in the line of the generations after me? But perhaps we can sense something of these connections in the decisive moments of our existence; members of the Resistance died during the war in the conviction that only in this way could they preserve their real life, which would be absolutely lost in an individualistic concentration on the preservation of it. Perhaps, for this kind of existence in the depths of the historic generations only acquires urgency and force when it is realized that the living God of the revelation of salvation connects the generations in the eternal now of his steadfastness.

> He is mindful of his covenant for ever,
> of the word that he commanded, for a thousand generations,
> the covenant which he made with Abraham.
>
> Ps. 105.8, 9

A pious Jew during the occupation, whose son had just been

deported to Mauthausen, replied with intense self-assurance to a minister who tried to console him: 'Oh, we have experienced a great deal in the course of the centuries.' This is communal thought, both in breadth and in depth. One could not be more specific.

Once we have succeeded in restraining our western individualism a little, and opened our minds to this communal thinking in terms of generations, the Bible has many surprises in store for us. Dull passages begin to glow. We begin to sense how the famous dry lists of generations might perhaps form a real part of the gospel. The well-known list of witnesses of the faith in Hebrews 11 becomes much more than a row of famous 'examples', because we are really connected with them. This is said quite clearly at the end of the chapter: '. . . *apart from us* they should not be made perfect' (v. 40). The image of a relay race helps most to show the point here. For the Jewish community it is no mystery that Moses and Elijah appear when Jesus experiences a moment of exaltation (Matt. 17.1-8). Where the God of Israel reveals his glory, all generations stand before his face in one totality. One should not ask how this is possible. This is the way in which the Bible experiences and describes the connection between the generations as a reality.

This communal thinking, beginning from the roots and working up, is especially helpful in throwing a generous light on the relation between the 'Testaments', which is always a tricky point. We have already referred to this in Chapter III.B. The word 'fulfilment', which is so characteristic of the relation between 'Old' and 'New', can be understood excellently with the aid of the 'root-idea' – the main point here is not the fulfilment of the prophecies, nor the development of moral or religious ideas, though that comes into it, too. The writers of the Gospels and Epistles, however, pointed to a living link between the past and the present, in which the earlier things become fully expressed in the latter, are 'fulfilled' in the latter: the plant which begins to flower, rhyming words in a poem, spirals of a staircase. But every image falls short, unless one has already accepted this 'root-thinking' from the Bible itself as a valuable key which unlocks the living unity of Law and Gospel.

Through the tradition of the Church, the famous concept of original sin has become a fixed part even of contemporary Christianity. This concept is bound to be alien and offensive, as long as we think in-

dividualistically. How can I inherit sin through nature, as it were, when sin is a moral matter? How can Paul write that 'by one man's disobedience many were made sinners' (Rom. 5.19)? This is changed entirely when we begin to get an eye for the communal thought of the Bible. The words original sin, with their associations of sexual propagation, which in itself would pass on an element of sin (the phrase in Ps. 51.5 'and in sin did my mother conceive me', wrongly understood in this sense, has given many generations a false per- spective) could be dropped – the matter itself is very pressing. It is true that the word 'sin' has many shades of meaning in the Bible, and we cannot go into them all here, but it always has a personally moral accent. Sin is a deed, for which one or more persons are re- sponsible. At the same time, however – and this is what is made so difficult by our individualist approach – sin affects the community. Not only in its consequences, as experience has taught us sufficiently – crime, addiction to smoking or drink, sexual freedom – but also in a way which cannot be explained rationally, there is a partnership in responsibility and guilt. The best people among the German nation were ashamed of the guilt of the most wicked. And the very best in Europe took a share of the load of sin which the German nation had piled upon its shoulders. It may even be that the very denial of such a solidarity is the worst sin of all, as the story of Cain can teach us in the well-known words: 'Am I my brother's keeper?' (Gen. 4.9). Again, we think that it is the biblical 'root- idea' of the community which can remove, not the personal vexation, but the rational absurdity of this solidarity. That is why we find the most impressive and intense confessions of solidarity in guilt and responsibility at the highest (rather than deepest) points in the Bible. We are thinking of the prophet Jeremiah, of the dark and glorious passage in Isa. 53 and of the prayer of Daniel in Dan. 9.4ff. The prayer begins with 'I', to continue with 'we', in which are in- cluded kings, rulers and fathers and also 'all Israel' (v. 7). The de- vout Daniel associates himself absolutely with the guilt of the whole. This, however, brings us to the point at which we must indicate the other striking characteristic of the communal thought of the Bible.

(b) Contemporary biblical scholars have pointed out that in the biblical setting, the community in which life is lived and experienced is not an impersonal fact, but a living entity, a 'corporate personality'.

The totality of the larger community can function in a few members, and one person can take the place of the whole. In itself this is no strange thought for us, because for us, too, 'the nation', or 'the church' or our own family are not impersonal collective units. They all have their own soul, their personal character, their own spirit, while any one person out of the greater context can represent the whole. We remind the reader, for instance, of the function of the Queen in and for our nation. At the risk of over-emphasizing the point, we must also put the question whether our individualism and our contemporary democratic attitude have not eroded the awareness to which we were referring just now. We always make the separate individual the starting point of our thoughts; these individuals together transfer a certain responsibility or task to other persons, who in their turn will be relieved by others. They occupy a certain position by the consent of the majority. The Queen only reigns by the grace of God in our country, but it must be said that her place in the life of the nation is strongly symbolic. In reality, the ministers are responsible. We come closest to the Israelite pattern of the one with and for the many in the way in which we participate in sporting achievements. The whole nation glories in the victories of an athletics or football team. That is a *national* victory.

This curious function of a part or of an individual in the whole is a striking feature of the biblical atmosphere of thought which should not be overlooked. The most suggestive example of it is perhaps the story of David and Goliath in I Sam. 17. Goliath acts as the champion in the sense that his victory will be the victory of his whole people (v. 9). This is quite unthinkable for us in a war, but for the Philistines and the Israelites it was very real. Thus a dimension of solidarity and responsibility, of connectedness and community appears in the Bible, which we have lost entirely.

In the context of this pattern of thought, many words in the Bible take on importance.

The *elders* represent the inhabitants of a town or a region. This is not intended in our modern democratic sense, as a conscious transfer of responsibility – as with a society and its committee – but the elders are the whole. They act representatively. See, for instance, the charming scene at the gate in Ruth 4. Here there are several references to 'the elders *and* (that is to say) all the people' (vv. 9,11). Of course all the inhabitants are not present at the gate, but the ten men of the elders whom Boaz takes as witnesses are the whole of the people. In our translation the identity of both is not so clear, but in the Hebrew text that is certainly what is intended.

The word *first-born* is highly significant in the Bible. In him Yahweh lays his hand upon the whole family. The first-born (who opens the womb) is the special possession of Yahweh. It is he. In the stories of the patriarchs this word plays an important part, as is well known. In Ex. 4.22 Yahweh calls Israel his first-born son (in Hebrew *bechor*), and the sentimental value of this word would be difficult to overestimate. The whole blaze of God's electing love is contained in it. But it would be totally wrong to ask why God did not elect other nations. No, the other nations have been chosen through the elected one. In the *bechor* the other children are present. The concept of the 'corporate personality' presupposes that election is not exclusive but always inclusive. This suddenly lights up a detail of the gospel, when we read in Luke 2.7 that Mary gave birth to her first-born son. In Heb. 12.23 the (triumphant?) Church is called the assembly of the first-born, and Jesus himself 'the first-born among many brethren' in Rom. 8.29.

The *Levites*, who later take on the role of the first-born, as is carefully recorded in Num. 3.12 (see also Num. 8.16), are not just the helpers in the priestly service, but in them all Israel takes part in this service. The same also goes for the *priests*, who fulfil in the whole nation the role of the father in a family. '. . . be to me a father and (that is to say) a priest', a certain Micah says in Judg. 17.10 to a Levite whom he installs as priest in his private sanctuary.

The *first-fruits* are well known from harvest and sacrificial cults, and they crop up in the apostolic letters as the 'first-fruits of the Spirit' (Rom. 8.23), or as the first Christians in a certain region. In Rom. 16.5 (AV), Paul calls his well-beloved Epaenetus 'the first-fruit of Asia unto Christ', and in I Cor. 16.15 he calls Stephanas 'the first fruit of Achaia'. Behind these names we sense at once a whole congregation or a whole regional church. James calls the Christians 'a kind of first-fruit of God's creatures' in 1.18, and all this is, of course, based on the fact that Christ is called the first-fruit in the tremendous resurrection passage in I Cor. 15.20 and 23. It is therefore important to pay special attention to the perspective opened up by such words. Again, these words are not exclusive, but inclusive.

The *king* in Israel is, of course, a representative or a substitute figure *par excellence*. There are many other associations with this figure, some of which are distinctive of Israel. We shall not go into them at the moment; at this point we are concerned with the function of acting in and for the whole nation.

The later prophets introduced the strange concept of the *remnant*. The nation as such was or would be lost, but 'a remnant returns', as the name of one of the sons of Isaiah recalls: *Shearjashub* (Isa. 7.3 and Isa. 10.20, 21). This does not just mean that a few will escape from the exile and the judgement, but also that in them the whole nation will be allowed to make a new start. Thus Paul can say in the course of his argument in Rom. 9-11 that a part of Israel has hardened its heart, but that all the same 'all Israel will be saved' (11.26).

The seven thousand of Elijah's time, who did not bow the knee to Baal (I Kings 19.18), the three hundred men of Gideon's army (Judg. 7.7), the twelve disciples which were chosen by Jesus (Mark 3.14), all these instances undoubtedly contain the concept of a person representing the whole. That the high-priest Caiaphas made a forceful appeal to this biblical idea with 'one for many' is known to every reader of the Bible. 'It is expedient for you that one man should die for the people, and that the whole nation should not perish' (John 11.50).

Paul sums all this up in the image of the *body* and the *members* (I Cor. 12.12-27). Everyone has his special place and function. The eye is not the same as the hand nor the head as the foot, and yet they all form one whole together. There is no trace of a crude collectivism, nor, however, are there the bad aspects of an individualism which detaches each person from the whole, giving him an isolated position.

Would it be too much to say that this communal philosophy of the Bible, with its delicate shades of meaning, could bring healing to our contemporary generation? Those who do not reject it in advance, but who are prepared to take a receptive attitude towards it, will undoubtedly experience the strong persuasive force of this biblical way of living and feeling. The Bible could give this back to us. We consider this communal approach, with its delicate gradations, to be one of the key secrets which can help to throw light on the basic points of the Christian faith. Just one of them may be indicated.

The person and work of Jesus *occupy a central position in the Christian faith. Our salvation is in him. 'He is the expiation for our sins' (I John 2.2). This centrality, this absoluteness of the figure of Jesus, has become more and more of a problem for modern man. This is not surprising, considering the thought-climate of western man after the Renaissance and the Enlightenment. Many people can no longer accept the proclamation of Christ in the significant and absolute accents of the Christian confession, because they no longer have any inner access to it. For some this indeed proves to be a cross. This is often evident in personal conversations or pastoral care. In this situation, which does not date from today or yesterday, many people in and outside the Church have increasingly taken to accepting only the profound and imperishable thoughts and truths which Jesus is supposed to have proclaimed, or of which he has given examples in his life. The line of argument runs as follows: essentially Jesus cannot have been of decisive significance for another person, because ultimately every man is responsible for himself. Substitution and sacrifice are impossible from the individualist point of view. It will do no good here for the Church to proclaim Christ's reconciliation straight from the Bible. One then runs the risk of imposing burdens which are too heavy for an individualist generation. The only way to help here is to create an understanding, through the whole biblical proclamation, of that remarkable existence in community which the Bible transmits to us. The message of Jesus the Messiah can only acquire significance and urgency within the larger context of the whole pattern of biblical thought and experience. Only in that way can a man reach the position of decision, for or against Jesus. We cannot save ourselves or modern man from the stumbling block which is contained for every man, Jew or Gentile, in the preaching of Christ on the cross, in the words of Paul (I Cor. 1.23), but we can take away the absurdity, the inner and essential preposterousness which it contains in the eyes of many. According to I Cor. 1.24, the preaching of Christ is also the wisdom of God. For the one who has been called, these things open up. He begins to see and to confess how it can be a liberating fact that we can be* human in such a manner that One stands as a substitute for the many, and so saves and reconciles them. Of course new questions will be asked, but the point here is the perspective, the inclusiveness which alone can make Christ and the teaching of reconciliation a reality.

A second point which we would like to mention here is the question of the Church and the ministry. It will be quite obvious that this insight into the communal thinking of the Bible makes the Church much more than the institution which holds services and practises community. The present individualist generation considers the Church solely as an institution for the needs of the free and self-sufficient individual, as every church visitor is told constantly. But it cannot be expected to realize its error unless it gains access to the relevant biblical thinking. In the churches, however, and especially in the ecumenical movement of our day, questions concerning the ministry play an important part. For the Roman Catholic Church, salvation depends entirely on the presence of the priest, who alone is allowed to dispense the sacraments. It is the priest who by his consecration has received the full powers to distribute the grace which Christ and his apostles have entrusted to the Church, among the recipients of the sacraments. The Churches of the Reformation see these things differently. But what then is the real significance of the ordained ministry? According to the Dutch Confession, articles 30 and 31, the ministers are there to govern the church, to nourish true godliness and to explain the Word of God. But we find little else there concerning the real place and function of those who are ordained. Are they just administrators or functionaries of a religious society? Could a Church manage, at a pinch, without an ordained ministry? Or is every church member perhaps a minister? When the question of the admission of women to the ministry became an acute one in the Netherlands Reformed Church, one minister began his introduction to this subject like this: 'What is the ministry? What is a woman?' Yes, what is the ministry? We cannot go into the details of this question, which is so important in the present ecumenical situation. We can only state the problem, and as our small contribution, we would like to offer the following remarks.

It is quite obvious that in the Bible we meet ministries and ministers. Not so much the actual words, perhaps, but we hear of

apostles and prophets, overseers, deacons, bishops and elders, evangelists, pastors and teachers, in short, members of the Church who
have been allotted a special task and who are equipped with special
gifts. They have to perform a certain service (ministry) in the name
of the Lord, in and for the Church. This is mentioned repeatedly,
especially in the so-called Pastoral Epistles (I and II Tim. and Titus),
but it is also referred to quite often in other places (Eph. 4.11).
Some of them quite clearly have a certain authority and power,
in the first place the disciples themselves (John 20.23). What the
implication of all this is for our present ecclesiastical organization and
the Christian situation is another matter. These are practical questions which we want to consider in Chapter IV. What we put forward here, for reflection, is the question whether our modern individualist patterns of thought do not make it particularly difficult
to do full justice to the given biblical facts. We believe that this
may force us into two opposite directions at once.

(a) In the Gospels and Epistles we see outstanding figures who
stand alone and who are charged with special force and power. The
Lord of the Church gave them their positions, and they have come
down to us through history and tradition. It is of course possible
to appeal to a few biblical texts for these special authorities, but for
an individualist generation it becomes increasingly difficult to understand why the salvation of all should depend on this or that person,
put apart by a special consecration. In order to maintain their position in the growing tide of individualism, these people have to be
surrounded by more and more assurances from Scripture and tradition. The structure of the Roman Catholic hierarchy is becoming
gradually more pronounced, and it is not a coincidence that it was
in the second half of the nineteenth century (1870) that the Roman
Catholics had to announce the dogma of the infallibility of the Pope.
Was this a sign of certainty or of uncertainty? Basically, the devil –
we beg the reader to forgive this far too loaded word – of individualism
has to be driven out by the same individualism. Ordained clergy
become high and unassailable personages who carry the whole
Church alone, or among each other. Latterly a change has set in in
the Roman Catholic Church. We say no more about that here. The
tendency to stem the tide of growing individualism with a greater
emphasis in the churches on the ordained ministry and the persons
appointed with power and invested with authority is not restricted

to the Roman Catholic Churches. Other churches, too, have 'catholic' movements.

(b) It is also possible to take up arms for individualism plain and simple, and then there is really no longer any place in the Churches for offices and ministers. In that case, it is pointed out that in the gospel every Christian is called to witness. It is feared that certain offices and ministries have made things too easy for the others, by usurping their task, and complaints are raised about an institutionalized Church which suffers from too many officials. These complaints are not unfounded. The clear instructions in the Gospels and Epistles concerning the ministry are then in part neglected, just as the other side lays too great a burden of proof on these passages.

It seems that the way out of this ecumenical problem is to return to the nuances of the communal thought of the Scriptures. Of course there are in the congregation certain services, tasks and offices, but this is not at the cost of the whole, but rather in the name of and for the whole. Ordained men do not need to be given a place apart as holy persons, but they have been instituted in order that the congregation can carry out its task in the world and for God. They do not kill the activities of the other members, but they lead and stimulate by carrying out their special service as representatives. In the congregation we learn from the Bible that we can help each other out. Only in the context of biblical communal thinking do the offices of the Church acquire their natural but real significance.

IV   The Bible Today

Introduction

Because of their sharp insight into the human psyche, the Books
of Samuel give an almost modern portrayal of the history of the
two kings of Israel, Saul and David. One of the most striking passages
in them is the conversation in II Sam. 12.1-14 between Nathan and
David. The latter, though pictured as the Messianic king, the servant of God, who 'walked with integrity of heart and uprightness'
(I Kings 9.4), can still not resist the temptation to misbehave like an
eastern tyrant when he is at the height of his royal power. Instead
of protecting the lives of his subjects, as Ps. 72.2 proclaims of the
just king, he rules over them with the greatest arbitrariness. He lets
his faithful officer Uriah perish on the battlefield so that he can
marry his wife Bathsheba, with whom he has committed adultery.
These dark events in the life of David are described with great
honesty in II Sam. 11.

Then the prophet Nathan comes to announce God's judgement.
One would almost say that this is done with great subtlety; he tells
the story of a rich exploiter, a 'wicked man' whom 'violence covers
as a garment' (Ps. 73.6).

This man, Nathan recounts, had taken the only sheep from his
poor neighbour, and served it to his guest. Of course such a thing
is only possible in a society where the strong can prevail over the
weak. David, the king of Jerusalem, the city of God, feels personally
affected by this story. In his realm such a thing cannot be
allowed to pass. His reaction is therefore sharp. 'As the Lord
lives, the man deserves to die' (II Sam. 12.5). But then arrives the
moment at which David really becomes involved in the story. Nathan
speaks the truth straight into David's face: 'You are that man.'

This story may serve as an illustration of the meeting between the

Bible and us. Seated on the throne of our reasonable, moral and religious insights, we read the Bible with interest. We study it as a historical document, we read it as a source of moral or religious thoughts, or we bow our heads reverently to the revelation of the truths of God, passed on to us by the prophets and the apostles. The stories and the texts will teach us more or less, depending on their contents, but on the whole they have something 'to say' to us. But mark you, we remain on our throne, graciously granting the Bible an audience.

In the history of Christianity people have often listened to the Bible in this fashion. How could we do otherwise, starting from our own standpoint? That is to say, in the preceding chapters we also studied the Bible in this fashion, in order to try to let it say what it has to say. But this has led us to the discovery that the Bible itself, from its own standpoint, breaks through this contemplative attitude of listener and reader. It happens at times that the finger of the prophet seems to point straight at us from the pages of the Bible: you are that man! We came nearest to this 'speaking' character of the Bible in Chapter III.C.

Consciously or unconsciously, the Church has always confessed and witnessed that this pointing and 'personal' aspect of the Bible is its real character and life. The authority emanating from the Bible was recognized and that was one of the reasons why the Church acknowledged the books of the Bible to be 'Holy Scripture', the sole power which could insist on obedience, as we have described, in Chapter I.A.2, 'The Bible in the Early Church'. This is why the Bible is the 'Word of God'. We are deprived of our more or less uncommitted attitude and hear: 'Thus says the Lord'.

In the decisive moments of the history of the Church this has often been a tangible reality. We are thinking especially of Luther's life and of the years of the Reformation. But in smaller settings, too, an element of this direct man-to-man prophecy remains a special quality of the Bible, both in the constant preaching in the Churches, and in the personal use of the Bible. The reader who is at home in ecclesiastical Jerusalem understands that here we have arrived at the matter of 'application'. It used to be a popular practice of some preachers first to hold a long historical and dogmatic peroration in connection with the text, in order to finish up with the personal application. Even the most obstinate sleepers had to wake up then, because that was the really important bit!

We want to devote this chapter to questions which present themselves quite naturally:

How is this authority exercised?

Is it possible and permissible to appeal to the Bible?

What is the effect of the distance in time between the period of the Bible and the reader today?

Can everything in the Bible be applied to our own time?

How does this application work, both personally for the believer, and on a large scale for questions concerning the Church, the nation and society?

What follows is divided into two parts: the sequence of A and B – note the headings – is intended to express that this authority *is* really authoritative. The Bible has and keeps the initiative – like Nathan.

A The Bible in Conversation with Us

1. *The Authority of the Bible is All-embracing*

We put this thesis first because the example of the prophet Nathan might tempt us into thinking that the application only becomes serious when the *moral conscience* of man is involved. This will indeed often play a real part in the meeting with the Bible. Jesus, speaking of the coming of the Holy Spirit, says, according to John 16.8, '. . . And when he comes, he will convince the world of sin and of righteousness and of judgement.' From a saying like this we understand that sin and the admission of guilt play a part in listening to the Bible, when it really comes to life for us, through the power of the Spirit, so that we get the feeling: this is something from which I cannot escape. This is it. Perhaps this also helps those readers who find difficulty in forming any kind of concrete image for themselves when the words 'Holy Spirit' are used in church. One should remember the pointing finger of Nathan.

The point here, however, is that the truth of the Bible is fuller and broader than just this morality. Not just the judgement, but also the *comfort* of the gospel comes to us with authority. This was, after all, the great discovery of Luther, when the good news of justification through faith alone opened up for him.

It is also true, however, that a biblical *insight*, a certain vision of man or of the world, of history or the cosmos, comes to us with authority. It is for instance a luminous discovery of present-day biblical scholarship that according to the Scriptures man does not consist of a mortal body as a dwelling place for the immortal soul, but that he is, as man, one whole, an indivisible wholeness of many physical organs which all live together through the breath of God, which has been bestowed on man as a gift, 'breathed in' (Gen. 2.7, Ps. 104.29). In the Bible this aliveness of the body is called *soul*. Thus man lives as a mortal and finite creature before God's face.

Concerning the *way of salvation*, in particular the essential aspects of God's saving actions, there is sometimes a knowledge granted to us, which confronts us with that authority. We are thinking of the triumphant and certain words of Paul, 'For I am sure . . .' at the close of Rom. 8, which echo through the ages with a clear and ringing tone.

A similar clear and decisive knowledge has sometimes been given to the Church on her way through the centuries. There have been bright moments when the authority of the Word rose up. At those times the Church had to *confess*, and beside all that was human and relative there was also an element of power, of authority, especially in the field of dogma and teaching.

During the first centuries of the Christian Church, it was a great temptation to 'spiritualize' the gospel, as we have already seen. The Gnostics considered the gospel as a liberation of the immortal soul from the reality of the lower, material order. Over against this the Church confessed in the Apostles' Creed: I believe in God the Father, Maker of heaven and earth. This cut off for ever one path which Christian speculation might have followed, though later many strayed on to this forbidden way.

In the fourth century, battle was joined over the essence and being of Jesus the Saviour. We do not want to suggest that the Church emerged from this battle without any tear in its biblical garments, but since then it has been an authoritative dogma, established with

intuitive certainty over against Arius, that in Jesus of Nazareth
God himself intervenes and saves decisively (Nicaea 325). In the
days of the Church Father Augustine it was firmly established,
once and for all, against Pelagius, that according to the Bible the
grace of God is not just a detail, or the beginning of man's salvation,
but that it is the essence of it.

Would it be too bold to say that we believe that in our twentieth
century the Church has been given the insight that Israel occupies
a key position in the way of God's salvation for the world? It is
humiliating but true that it took the most terrible persecution of
Jews of all time to put us, the Christian Church, back on to the
track of Israel. This has been made clear to us with authority. We
refer to Chapter III.A of this book.

This last point brings us to an example of cases where the Bible
tipped the balance in momentous decisions which individuals had
to face. During the war years it happened that one Saturday evening someone withdrew a promise to hide a Jewish fugitive. The
next day, Sunday, Daniel 1 was discussed from the pulpit, where
'the chief of the eunuchs' (v. 9) takes a great risk for the sake of
the Jews. Suddenly the person concerned, who was in the church,
knew with great conviction that he must help that Jew, and gave
him the needed protection, with great confidence and tranquillity.
The authority of the Bible also has a liberating effect. It creates a
Christian liberty in every direction. Mind and heart, senses and
hands, in short the whole existence of man, may be touched by it.
In the example above it was the first chapter of Daniel that tipped
the balance. But it could have been any other passage of the Bible.
It is better not to begin with a separation into more and less important things. In this sense, too, it is true that the authority of the
Bible covers everything. At this point, however, we must hasten
to make our second point, or there will be misunderstandings.

2. The Authority of the Bible is Spiritual

What we have just said will at once raise the question as to how
we know when and where the Bible speaks or has spoken with
authority. Where is the proof that a certain confession is really the
will of God? How can we be sure that a certain dogma really formu-
lates God's salvation? These are the kind of questions which often

caused the fiercest battles in the history of the Church. In the differences between Rome and the Reformed Churches this is a well-known bottleneck. Who is the authority which lays down what *the* truth is?

Rome considers that this authority lies in the tradition of the Church, since 1870 more closely defined in the infallible dogmatic pronouncements of the Pope when he speaks from the papal chair – ex cathedra – as the bearer of authority on matters concerning faith and morals. Here is an objective power which can say: this is how it is! The Churches of the Reformation, on the other hand, appeal solely to the Bible, which makes them vulnerable to the objection that explaining the Bible is always a very personal matter. Who can say that this or that is what the Bible says? Is it not true that any appeal to the Bible must be highly subjective? Conversely, Roman Catholic theology has never laid down, even at the Council of Trent (1545-1563) (although the opposite has often been implied), that the tradition of the Church and the papal pronouncements could add new truths to the biblical source; what was meant was that tradition and Pope could only unfold biblical truth, and that dogmatic pronouncements of the Church must in any case be in accordance with the Scriptures. Here, however, we are back at the question of how one can be sure that they are in agreement, considering the obvious imperfections and one-sidedness, not to mention the mistakes and errors in the pronouncements of the Church in the past. Here we find we have gone right round in a circle; Rome and the Reformers together are faced with the question of an authoritative explanation of the Scriptures.

There is a broad current in the Church and in Christendom which evades this difficulty by following an ostrich policy. 'Everything in the Scriptures is the Word of God and has to be accepted as truth.' 'I accept the whole Bible, from cover to cover.' Nowadays this attitude is often somewhat condescendingly called *fundamentalism.*

Fundamentalism is a movement which originated in America in the second half of the last century. Its aim was to defend itself against Darwinism, and the insights in the field of the Bible and of the natural sciences, by falling back on the never-failing Bible. Some doctrines, such as the divinity of Christ, the virgin birth and the reconciling sacrifice of the cross, were made into central points. These were the foundations of the faith, hence the name fundamentalism. It was otherwise specially interested in the call to conversion and the sanctification of life. It liked to lay down certain rules which a true Christian would never break, in any circumstances. A moralistic intellectualism is characteristic of this movement, which can easily be recognized in many Christian and semi-Christian revival movements. When we employ the word fundamentalism in the following pages, we are thinking of the fundamentalist use of the Bible.

Through the centuries, this fundamentalism has been a recurring and, we must admit, understandable attitude. Especially since the Reformation, when the authority of the Bible was brought into the field against Rome, fundamentalism, in stricter or milder form, has been in vogue. 'It says so in the Bible, and therefore it must be true.' The Bible is used as the book containing all the truths of God. It is characteristic of fundamentalism to advance texts indiscriminately. In sectarian circles this is even more prevalent. Everyone knows the zealous propagandists who defend their movement with a whole arsenal of texts which often leave one helpless.

We believe that there is still a great deal of muddled thinking on this point among all of us. It was one of the main objectives of this book to help clarify matters, as we explained in Chapter II.

It is easy to produce all kinds of objections against fundamentalism. It is seldom consistent. Sometimes it insists on a literal explanation, but other parts are suddenly explained in a spiritual manner. It makes an arbitrary distinction between one biblical word and another. It has a legalistic flavour, and it is biased. It acts with fanaticism which does not build up and help, but which divides and hinders.

Yet it is of little use to ponder long on the weaknesses of fundamentalism, because the root of the trouble is not touched; these reproaches from others, most frequently from the Church and the theologians, remain largely on the level of the pot calling the kettle black. Who, for instance, is completely impartial in his appeal to the Scriptures? Is it also not quite obvious that sometimes a Bible passage is intended 'literally' and historically, but that in other cases

only a spiritual and symbolic explanation can do justice to a text?
And as for fanaticism, is it really possible always to handle the
Scriptures coolly, peacefully and liberally, without ever succumbing
to the famous 'fighting spirit of the theologians'? Many Church
Fathers have witnessed with great passion to *one* particular truth . . .
and they have been blessed!

This is why we feel that we can only reach clarity in the matter of
fundamentalism by learning to use the keys which we tried to pass on
in the last chapter. More specifically we are now thinking of what
was discussed in detail in Chapter III.B, namely that the Bible is
an event, a history. This is the flexible thread which connects all the
dogmatic, spiritual, ethical and inner truths together. Fundamentalism, of both old-fashioned and modern style, starts on the other
hand from the presupposition that in the Scriptures we find piles
and piles of Christian truths. There are bits of biblical teaching
on God and man, creation and sin, reconciliation and redemption,
judgement and the second coming of Jesus, Sabbath and Sunday, baptism and healing, sanctification of life, laws and everything else
besides. This is all indeed very true, but as such it is beside the point.
If we think that way, we will get hopelessly entangled in the
fundamentalist complex. What *is* the point, however, is that in the
Bible we are witnessing a history, a saving event between God and
his people which terminates in Jesus, the Messiah, the King of the
Jews and which then fans out again in the proclamation of the
gospel by the apostles to all the nations on earth. This is finally how
we as Christians have been brought into 'the Truth' from among
the nations; not through a teaching which has been accepted by us,
though that may happen as well, but through an event which
reaches us.

> Through the world there runs a word
> That drives men onward, ever on.
> 'Strike your tents,' it says, 'and go
> To the land which I will show.'
> To your voice we listen, Lord,
> We are strangers in our home.
> Bring us, with all those who roam,
> To the new Jerusalem.

Through the world there moves a throng
of those who have defied the ban.
Here no longer I belong;
of this earth on which I live
I no more am citizen.

Jan Wit

This Israelite tone, full of dynamism, full of promise and faith, is the tone of the words of Jesus at the close of the Gospel according to Matthew, where he shows his disciples the way into the future: 'Go therefore and make disciples of all nations, baptizing them in the name of the Father and of the Son and of the Holy Spirit, teaching them to observe all that I have commanded you; and lo, I am with you always, to the close of the age' (Matt. 28.19f.).

If we keep this *historical character* of the Bible fixed before our eyes, then, and then only, does it become suddenly clear that we cannot pull the words and texts of the Bible towards us in the fundamentalist way, as if they were truths valid to everyone for all time. 'It says so in the Bible, therefore . . .' That would be like a man who finds a prescription by a famous doctor, and who says: 'He is a famous doctor, his prescription is sure to be good, so I will use it for myself.' It is indeed true that the prescription is good; that is a fixed truth, but all the same . . . one had better be careful.

The conclusion to be drawn from this is obvious. When we read the Bible today, there will always be distance between them and now. This and this is what God said to Abraham. But what does it mean *for us* today? Paul wrote such and such to the church in Corinth, for example that women should keep silent in the churches (I Cor. 14.34), and that any speaking in tongues should be interpreted, or else they should keep silent (v. 28). But what does that mean for *our* congregational life? This creates a certain gap, a distance which makes it impossible for us to accept ready-made and fixed truths. At one time this distance will be much greater than at another. No fundamentalist today will put into practice the command in Deut. 21.18-21 that a rebellious son should be brought before the elders and be stoned. But with the words in Deut. 6.13 and 10.20 'You shall fear the Lord your God' the distance has shrunk to a minimum. The name, the holy teaching, reaches easily across the distance of centuries. Jesus holds his own with this word in the hour of temptation (Matt. 4.10). But some distance must remain, on principle. We cannot skip the question as to how this or that word from those days can be applied now, with the simple retort: the Bible says, therefore . . . !

This difficulty has, of course, always been felt, and one obvious and much used solution is to distinguish between those truths which are 'temporal', of a certain period, and those which are 'eternal'. This and that is no longer valid for us, but such and such is. Naturally this leads to the question of which pronouncements are purely historical, and which are still 'valid' today. At this point it is easily felt that this distinction between 'temporal' and 'eternal' truths is no real solution. But one inevitably ends up in this alley when the key of the historic character of the whole Bible is lost from sight, so that one begins to use it as a book of general truths. Our first point in the present chapter was also aimed at this distinction between what is 'temporal' and what is 'essential'. The authority of the Bible is valid all along the line and . . . the whole Bible has authority. At this point in our considerations, however, we must add to this that *the whole Bible is historical*, a book that speaks to us today of the days of the past. Even with the clearest and most striking words of the prophets and the apostles and also of Jesus himself there is a distance between then and now. It is there with the 'Ten Words', e.g., 'Thou shalt not steal' and 'Thou shalt not kill' there with the command of Jesus that we must love our enemies, with the apostolic exhortations to be humble and meek, and also with the Pauline explanations of the reconciliation and salvation wrought by Christ, of the death on the cross and the resurrection.

We believe that this narrowing of the road brings us a great benefit, because it forces us to slow down when we are trying to race through the Bible at too great a speed. This imposes the necessity on us to realize that *if the Bible really gains authority over us, this is indeed a personal authority*. At the point where the road narrows, there is at the same time an inspection of our papers, as it were. This distance always demands a translation, an interpretation, a decision for today. We ourselves have *to risk* the application. Such and such means, for us today . . . *this*.

Does this make the application less reliable? Does it become subjective? Does this mean that the Bible loses some of its effective authority? This may appear to be the case, but we believe that the opposite is in fact true. The authority with which the words of the Bible come towards us is not *legalistic*, but *spiritual*. It appeals to our own decision, instead of presenting us with anything that is ready-made. The authority of the Bible does not force us, it does not drive us into a corner, but it comes to us in a spiritual way. This is what makes it a real, personal and certain authority. It aims to convince, and that is why it is right that there is room for decision on the part of listening man. In this way the latter is not elevated to be the measure of all things, but God's Word is given the chance to speak to us through the Holy Spirit and through faith. It is not in our hands to bring it about that this authority asserts itself or convinces; that is something that the Holy Spirit will do at the right time and in the right manner. 'I have yet many things to say to you, but you cannot bear them now. When the Spirit of truth comes, he will guide you into all the truth; for he will not speak on his own authority, but whatever he hears he will speak, and he will declare to you the things that are to come. He will glorify me, for he will take what is mine and declare it to you' (John 16.12-14). This is how Jesus says good-bye. His word will ever again be new and alive among us, until the history of God's salvation is complete (Matt. 28.19).

We believe that in this way the spiritual authority of the Bible is solid, objective and fixed. An authority which is imposed upon me does not really convince me. It remains arbitrary. It does not speak to me. But an authority which appeals to me, and asks me: 'You say what you should do in your situation, when the Bible says this' – such an authority can win me over with a certainty and a conviction which are not easy to prove, but which are all the more convincing spiritually. 'Judge for yourselves', Paul says repeatedly to the members of his congregation, who do not want to accept his apostolic authority just like that (I Cor. 10.15 and 11.13).

The moment has come to give one single example of this subtle but clear spiritual authority of the Bible, which wants to enter into conversation with us.

The many appeals made by the evangelists and the apostles to words in the Law and the Prophets which are being fulfilled may sometimes seem arbitrary to us. In his speech in Acts 2.24-28, Peter appeals to Ps. 16.8-11 concerning the resurrection. John 17.12 says of the betrayal by Judas: '. . . that the Scriptures might be fulfilled', and there are many other places where the appeal to the Tanach seems to us at first sight little to the point. Paul, for example, in his letter to the Galatians, makes an emphatic appeal to the stories of Abraham and Isaac, Sarah and Hagar, Isaac and Ishmael. When he then says in Gal. 4.28 to his Gentile-Christian audience: 'Now you brethren, like Isaac, are children of promise', this seems to us a strange leap. But is that really the case? What would we like to do with the story of Isaac then? When the Lord promises a son to Abraham, does this mean a promise to all the childless couples of our time? Of course not. But in that case, what is the meaning of this episode in the stories of the patriarchs? Surely it is this, that God has started there to build up a history, solely on miracles and surprises. If Abraham receives a son from Sarah, the implication is that God's people, who originate from this son, know that their existance is due to grace. So it goes on for this people. It is very clear after the Babylonian exile, when unexpectedly the totally deserted city of Jerusalem is populated again.

'Rejoice, O barren one that dost not bear . . .' (Gal. 4.27, quoting Isa. 54.1).

The apostle asks: is this element of surprise, of grace, so different for the Christian Church of the Gentiles? That the gospel has reached us, and that we may take our place in the history of the God of Israel, is that not grace? Is it not true, then, that we are, like Isaac, children of promise, having our origin solely in miracle and grace? Is the Church, seen culturally and socially, not a somewhat quaint 'afterthought' which at times causes an ironic smile among the worldly powers of nation, state and society, just as Isaac evoked mockery from Ishmael who had been begotten after the flesh? The Church cannot be explained fully by sociological and historical rules. Her secret, too, is the promise, the grace, of God's undertaking. And this is over against Ishmael, whose existence was not a biological miracle at all. We will not go into this more deeply here. We do believe, however, that Paul saw the great depths in the story of Isaac, and that he gives, on his own responsibility, an application for his own time, when the Jews and the Jewish Christians who wanted to uphold the Law would not or would barely recognize the existence of the congregations from among the Gentiles. Paul

*intervenes for the liberty of the Gentile Christians, and with an
appeal to the Law and the Prophets. Is this not the way it will always
go when we appeal to the Scriptures? Not as a short cut, to make
the Bible prove us right, but in order to allow the Bible to speak with
us, thus giving it the chance to reveal its spiritual authority to us.
This at any rate is what the evangelists and the apostles did. The
great liberty with which the apostles explain the Scriptures can be
seen by everyone who compares Paul with James. In Rom. 4.3 Paul
quotes the example of Abraham – Gen. 15.6 – to teach that the
Law also teaches justification by faith. James appeals in 2.21-24 to
exactly the same verse to underline 'works'. Does this mean that
they contradict each other, and that their appeal to the Scriptures
is arbitrary? We could answer with Paul in Rom. 3.31: 'By no means!
We uphold the Law'. Both these apostles have let the Scriptures
speak in a spiritual manner, and very much to the point, one against
a dead faith, the other against dead works.*

*We know that the Reformer Luther, in explaining the passage in
the Epistle to the Romans where Paul himself quotes from Hab. 2.4
– 'He who through faith is righteous shall live' (Rom. 1.17) –
added the word 'alone'. Sola fide. By faith alone! This 'alone' had
no basis in the text, and it has been attacked. But who today, even
among Roman Catholic theologians, is not convinced that this high-
handed addition brought out the essence of Paul's message particularly well? This came to the Reformer with spiritual authority, and
it has convinced many.*

3. The Authority of the Bible is Concrete

This proposition belongs with the previous one, as concave belongs
with convex. Precisely because the authority of the Bible is spiritual,
it is at the same time concrete. All the same, we sense the necessity
to emphasize this again, because the idea can so easily take root that
spiritual equals intangible, inward, vague, floating and without
obligation. At any rate, this is how the word 'spiritual' is so often
handled. The spiritual care of the armed forces is entrusted to
chaplains who are only allowed to speak of religious things, while
it is assumed that the hard facts of armaments, strategy and politics
are on an entirely different level. This opposition, which recurs
in all sorts of variations, is, however, quite definitely unbiblical.
That is to say, in these pages the word 'spiritual' makes us think

at once of the Holy Spirit, which in the faith touches those very concrete realities with force and power, which is even capable of putting them out of joint. Remember the saying of Jesus that true faith can move mountains (Matt. 21.21). The authority of the Bible, therefore, is concrete; it can be pointed out in reality, as the finger of Nathan pointed to David. You are that man!

Having arrived at this point, we expect an objection from the reader, who has probably already felt it ever since we so emphatically put forward our previous proposition that the Bible as a whole is 'historical', even in the general-sounding words of the apostles, prophets and Jesus himself. Are the Ten Commandments then not general moral laws? Are the words of Christ about loving one's enemy not for all people? Our answer must undoubtedly be 'yes', but we attach the greatest importance to the motives which accompany this 'yes'. In our opinion, it follows from its historical character that the Bible has the same concreteness, the same direct application to an individual, as Nathan demonstrated, and this was felt by the people who at the time heard the words of the prophets, the apostles or Jesus.

Amos addresses his prophecies of judgement emphatically to certain nations by name. Even if in other cases the message is intended for all the nations it still remains a message aimed at a specific audience. At times this specific, special and concrete character will be more obvious than at others, but it is always contained within a concrete framework. It is always: 'Adam, where are you?' (Gen. 3.9). Abraham is called, and not some other Babylonian. The nation of Israel is freed from Egypt and is the receiver of the 'laws and institutions' which are specially intended for this people, because they have been liberated. To his disciples Jesus says: 'You are the salt of the earth; you are the light of the world' (Matt. 5.13-16). This emphatic 'you' which stands at the beginning of the sentence, corresponds of course to the even more emphatic 'I' with which Jesus begins the Sermon on the Mount in which he shows the disciples the way to the Kingdom: 'I say to you . . .' and then follow the well-known words about loving the enemy, going the second mile and turning the other cheek, which are definitely meaningless as general rules; they are, however, true for the disciples because they have acquired the possibility of being the salt of the earth and the light of the world through their Lord who has 'come to

fulfil' (Matt. 5.17). The words of the Sermon on the Mount only
have their force and appeal within the light-circle of the Gospel. They
are *concrete* to a high degree because they can only be said to people
who hear the gospel of the liberating Lord. Indeed, these words *are*
the gospel, pointed for his disciples, in their situation.

*This is a good occasion for introducing a specific example to illustrate
how the words of the Sermon on the Mount (Matt. 5-7) in particular
have often been the victim of a somewhat premature generalization.
In 5.38 we read: 'You have heard that it was said, "an eye for an
eye, and a tooth for a tooth". But I say to you, do not resist one
who is evil. But if anyone strikes you on the right cheek, turn to
him the other also.' First of all it should be noted that this 'eye for
an eye' was not said in disapproval of primitive revenge, but as a
quotation of Ex. 21.24, where it functions as a limitation for
unbridled revenge. The measure of punishment must correspond to
the injustice suffered. This is in itself a good rule, of which Jesus
certainly did not disapprove. It occurs in the Law and Jesus appeals
constantly to the Law. But for his disciples Jesus opens up another
possibility, which is given with the fulfilment of the Law (v. 17).
The deepest intention of Moses cannot have been to say to the
Israelites that they must always go to the law and appeal to the
judge. No, there is another way of defeating the opponent, and that
is the method of 'the other cheek'. To strike the cheek (Greek:
rapizein) may indeed hurt badly, but if you hit the right cheek,
then the intention is obviously to humiliate by slapping with the
back of the hand the cheek of a man who is facing you. He is then
humiliated in the presence of onlookers. He could then hit back (as
we do in a slanging match), but that amounts to admitting that he
has been hit. If he turns the other cheek, however, he indicates that
he is master of the situation, that he is not giving in and he puts
the other party at a disadvantage! Through the adoption of a
disciplined attitude the possibility is thus created that the other will
review the situation and that his rage may cool off. Note well, however, it has to be a disciplined attitude. This is not the morality of
slaves (Nietzsche), but on the contrary an aristocratic attitude, without pride, born of the real liberty which Jesus gives his disciples. This
is not the principle of non-violence (Tolstoy), though in certain cases
this can certainly be a very good principle, but a life based on the*

gift of liberty. This is shown incomparably in the majesty, the glory, with which Jesus, especially in the Gospel of John, accepts his suffering and humiliation. When he is struck in the face before Annas, his controlled reply is: 'If I have spoken wrongly, bear witness to the wrong, but if I have spoken rightly, why do you strike me?' (John 18.23). Dr Martin Luther King applied this in his own way to the situation of the American Negroes in the twentieth century. With his co-workers, he could struggle for the liberty of the Negroes, because that liberty has already been granted them: not by the laws of the United States, but by Christ!

If the reader will bear with us in a second example of the concreteness of the commandments, we choose the section about 'not being anxious' in Matt. 6.25-34. This is always taken as an exhortation of the gospel to put aside all unnecessary cares for material needs, because the Lord will look after us. Every preacher usually hastens to add that this must not lead to improvidence. But what the right attitude is, is left rather vague for the man in the pew. He will have to do some work, he is not a bird or a lily! This often-quoted passage becomes much more realistic when we listen to the teaching of the biblical scholar K. Bornhäuser, in his book on the Sermon on the Mount. Bornhäuser points out that the Greek word to care (merimnan) *does not mean in the first place 'to worry', but rather* to work hard, to carry out hard labour. *Now Matt. 6.25 is spoken to the disciples. They must no longer spend their time in fishing or other work to provide for their livelihood. They must proclaim the Kingdom of God and its righteousness (v. 33), and then what they need for food and clothing will surely be given to them. This is what the congregations which have been formed by their word must do. 'The labourer deserves his food' (Matt. 10.10). Jesus himself kept on receiving hospitality, even though he had no place to put his head. The specific application of the passage for the contemporary congregation is as obvious as it is surprising: the members of the congregation must work in order to ensure a financially untroubled existence for the minister and the workers in God's Kingdom. They must bring their contribution to the church and the mission up to a proper level, in order that the gospel may be proclaimed! Only after we have this context clear, can we detect the liberating message concerning the hard work for the ministers of the gospel and the 'ordinary members of the congregation'. All this hard work may be 'cast on the Lord' (I Peter 5.7), which is rather different from refraining from it altogether!*

All this may help us to realize that the spiritual authority of the Bible does not undermine the foundations of the concrete authority. On the contrary, precisely because everything in the Bible is specific, aimed at certain people and placed in certain situations, it speaks to us personally. Isaiah, Paul, Jesus himself say this and this word, in such and such circumstances. We hear it, while we find ourselves in an entirely different situation. What would the Lord ask from *us*, now, or what would he like to say to *us* now? Is there anyone who does not feel how much openness this demands from us, how much care and prudence, but also how much courage and willingness? In the second section of this chapter (Our conversation with the Bible), we shall try to find what our attitude should be, how and with the aid of what means this interpretation and application should be done, not so that everyone in arbitrary fashion interprets anything to mean anything, but so that the Bible alone is permitted to speak. In the course of this book we have already given several instances, but at this point we would like to give one more example of what we have in mind when we speak of the spiritual and therefore the concrete authority of the Bible.

In Genesis 48 we find the curious, but also very attractive story of old Jacob blessing the two sons of Joseph. It is told in great detail, though it would appear that the vv. 8ff. do not connect logically with the first seven verses. But we will leave that aside here. The point is that Joseph, the high official, very correctly places the elder boy at Jacob's right hand, and the younger, Ephraim, at the left hand. To his surprise the old man crosses his arms, so that Israel (Jacob) blesses the younger with his right hand, and the elder son, Manasseh, with his left hand. Jacob does not even allow himself to be put out by the bewildered protests of Joseph, who was so sure of himself. The younger Ephraim gets the blessing of the first-born, that is to say the most important blessing. Jacob has blessed them with crossed arms.

What are we to think of this typical story? Are we simply to accept it as interesting information, because it no longer concerns us westerners? But it is in the Bible, and the Christian Church tries to listen to that as the Word of God. Therefore, one Sunday it will be given as the text for the sermon. What is the application? In the first place there is the way of the allegorical method. Jacob blesses with crossed arms, and the Christian knows that God's blessing comes indeed to him by the way of the cross. Differently from what we expected, right across our expectation, God sends his blessing, the blessing of the cross. Surprising as this may be, who does not feel that this is an arbitrary way of handling the text? This cannot be a compelling explanation, though it may contain some comfort.

It is much more to the point to reflect that the surprising act of giving the younger son the precedence is a recurring theme, not only in the stories of the patriarchs, but also in the gospels. Several of Jesus' parables suddenly begin to raise an echo. Those who do not expect mercy still receive it: the prodigal son, the tax-collector in the temple, the prostitutes, the sinners. In this way one can undoubtedly penetrate into the heart of the gospel, in a quite proper manner. This is certainly contained in the passage. But this application remains too general all the same. The electing love of God, the gospel of the Kingdom of God for the poor sinner is certainly the central point, but should it not always be specifically pointing at someone? If one always returns to this theme, it becomes a general truth, and not a concrete proclamation.

For that reason we want to take a closer look at this story. Ephraim and Manasseh are not just any, isolated persons, who are receiving the blessing, but they represent the tribes, and the contents of the blessing is just this, that Ephraim's descendants will become a multitude of nations (v. 19). This story is therefore not about individuals, but about nations, about the great contours of God's salvation in Israel, where the tribe of Ephraim will occupy a prominent place, even though he was the younger brother. Here we take the leap into our own situation. In the large family of nations, there are certain nations who are the 'first-born'. In the first place is Israel itself, but via Jesus the Messiah, and in him, this right of the first-born goes to the Gentile nations, in the first place to Europe. Are we in Europe not a tribe, people or nation to whom the blessing of the gospel went in the first place? But the Lord obviously likes surprises. Will we, as 'Christian' nations of the West, always retain *this first place? God could cross his arms again and bless the Asiatic or the African nations, nations which are much 'younger' and which in our narrow and respectable view have not observed it, at least not in the first place. They still need some supervision. But could it not be that the time has come that other nations take our place? The signs in the world indicate this. Could it not be the appeal and the message of this old Bible passage that 'Joseph and Manasseh' have to be content with the blessing which it still pleases God to give them, or leave them?*

This is an explanation which we put forward on our own authority. It could be considered as a pretence at an explanation. Nothing has been proved. But does it not contain some real appeal? Is not the road of the gospel through the world of nations the actual situation of our day? Are we still allowed to be Ephraim, or has the time come that we must be content with the place of Manasseh?

This last example has taken us right back to exegesis (explanation) as it has to be practised every week in each manse, in order that the proclamation may really have authority on Sunday, in the midst of the congregation. This leads us, at the close of this section, to stop and consider the *forms* in which the concrete authority of the Bible may come to us.

4. The Authority of the Bible demands Proclamation

Law and prophets, Epistles and Gospels, are essentially and intentionally *information*. As we have already seen repeatedly, this is how they have been presented by their authors and composers, to their environment and to posterity.

> *He established a testimony in Jacob,*
> *and appointed a law in Israel,*
> *which he commanded our fathers*
> *to teach to their children;*
> *that the next generation might know them,*
> *the children yet unborn,*
> *and arise and tell them to their children,*
> *so that they should set their hope in God,*
> *and not forget the works of God,*
> *but keep his commandments.*
>
> Ps. 78.5-7

People hear, an event is reported, tidings are spread and the commandments are kept to be passed on. This is where the word *proclamation* should come in. This is the gospel, the good news, what people today like to call the *kerygma*. The Bible is kerygmatic in its entire design and structure. It is not a register of laws and rules, in which specific cases can be looked up – as the theologians of Jesus' day liked to do only too well – nor a book of life in which 'beautiful' texts can be found, nor is it an ore from which a Christian attitude to life or religious teaching can be smelted, nor the illustration of a pious way of life. We are not saying this is an impossible approach, nor that this approach is sometimes not the right one, but it can only be taken in order to serve the real purpose, which is to do full justice to the Scriptures as the book of proclamation. Anything else that may be necessary is already contained in this.

What is our purpose in emphasizing the word proclamation, *kerygma*? Simply this, that the Bible is a book out of which one should *preach*. 'Preach' is a loaded word – used colloquially it has overtones of unwelcome or unnecessary moral or religious advice – but here we should like to plead for a restoration of the sermon to a place of honour, as the Bible is essentially proclamation.

For this restoration, it is of course first necessary that the Church and the ministers admit wholeheartedly that they have often been the cause for the discrediting of the sermon. Lengthy expositives, laborious explanations, incoherent stories, pious commonplaces and unctuous sentimentalities all did and do occur, and will go on recurring in the future. To give a sermon shape is no simple matter, though a good sermon seems such a simple affair. But the main thing for us is that at this point we can see so clearly what a sermon should consist of. It should be a continuation of the design of God's salvation story to the man of today. To the man of today! Beginning with the Bible, towards us, not in the opposite direction. The latter is often the temptation of both the preacher and the man in the pew. The latter likes to hear something 'that answers his needs', and if that is not forthcoming, he is 'dissatisfied', he 'misses' something. The preachers in their turn, in their proper zeal to address the man of today, are often very much 'with it'. Newspapers, plays, bestsellers, or just 'life' often constitute the starting point of their sermon, for which they have found a suitable text in the Bible.

But is that really the way to let the Bible speak? Is the Bible then not just a mirror of our own thoughts? Far be it from us, however, to lay down a precise pattern here. A sermon may begin with today's news, while it is essentially determined by the text which forms the basis of it. On the other hand, it is not very inspiring when the preacher gives an elaborate explanation of a text, without making it clear to the congregation what all this has to do with our situation today.

In spite of all these errors, which continually threaten, we may yet boldly continue to hold that the authority of the Bible demands *proclamation*. With this word proclamation we want to suggest three elements which the sermon ought to contain.

In the first place, the *starting point: the Bible* itself, the Scriptures, the Word of God. In the second place, the element of *authority*. It is really a matter of speaking, of coming towards us with authority. Thus says the Lord! 'As the Father has sent me, even so I send you,' the Risen Lord says to his disciples (John 20.21). In the third place, the *specific element*, the 'up-to-date-ness'. The man of today can and must be touched. A real sermon is incomplete if one of these elements is missing. In that case it is a 'sermon' in the wrong sense of the word, even if it is 'beautiful'.

For the preacher, the 'servant of the Word', it is a responsible, but always absorbing task to let the Bible speak to him, asking himself in what way the message of a given text should be passed on to the congregation. Here the minister must at a certain moment be prepared to risk a decision. He has to interpret, to translate it into the language and the circumstances of the people who are listening. Sometimes he will have to have the courage to say specifically: this, or this, is what the Lord is saying, or asking of you, even though it is not written literally in the text. The spiritual authority of the text implies this.

For the people who come to church, listening to a sermon is far from being a passive hearing without tension. If things are as they should be, the listener *experiences* the encounter between the Word of God and himself. To achieve this he should learn to ask for the text, rather than for the preacher. He should go to church with the thought: what surprise will the Lord have in store for me today? How will this text come to life? 'O that today you would hearken to his voice!' (Ps. 95.7).

In order to avoid the wrong appearance of partiality, we hasten to add a few remarks to this plea for 'the sermon'.

1. The Bible has a place in the Christian congregation, even apart from the sermon. The congregation prays, sings, and praises when using the Psalms. In the Scripture readings from the *Tanach* and Gospel, the panorama of God's deeds is spread before our wondering eyes. In the promises of grace God's forgiveness comes to us in the compact form of one text, without explanation. In family prayers (the house church), the reading of the Scriptures will serve more specially to make the contents of the Bible familiar. This is also the purpose of the catechism class, and of Bible stories in the children's service, or in the schools. In private meditation on the Bible, the aim is mostly to gain intimacy with the things belonging to God's salvation. In all the different ways of using the Bible mentioned here, the proclamation *may* at some moment strike us, but that is not necessary. In preaching, however, this is the basic purpose.

2. The authority which is hidden in the proclamation may take different forms. It does not need to be severe and high, as it is in the story of Nathan, but even so it is real authority. As well as judgement there is comfort; besides the summons to duty, there is encouragement. Sometimes treasures are discovered which delight the soul, but they may possibly startle it. A sermon may be a meditation, but it may also be a direct appeal; it may tell a story, or it may teach. In short, sermons may differ as richly in form and content as the Bible itself. A minister will do well not to confine himself too much to one particular form. He should be adaptable to the style, tone, and nature of the specific text which he has to 'serve'. However – and this is the point here – the authority must break through in some way or other. A sermon is not an uncommitted religious speech, but the passing on of a message from a high authority. Thus says the Lord!

3. The Bible is also the book of mission, precisely because it addresses itself so specifically to the person. The message may be passed on. This trait comes very much to the fore in the gospel; after the Torah had been 'preserved' in Israel, Paul carried the proclamation of the Scriptures to the nations. This implies that we are

certainly not Christians just so that we may draw rations from the Bible for our journey through life – though this, too, may happen repeatedly – but in order that we may together as a congregation put the lamp on the stand (Matt. 5.15) so that it may shine for all who are in the house. According to Rev. 2.1 and 5, these lamps are the congregations themselves, and the house is the image of the world of nations. The salvation of Christ is a 'light for revelation to the Gentiles', as the Israelite Simeon remembers when he sees the child Jesus (Luke 2.32).

This last remark leads up to the special attention we must still give to one form of proclamation which has been much discussed in the years since the last war.

5. *The Authority of the Bible and the Pronouncements of the Church*

What takes place in the weekly proclamation in the congregation may, and must, at certain moments assume larger proportions. If it is true that the authority of the Bible is a concrete one, then we cannot escape the fact that the Church, which stands in the centre of the world like the lamp in the house, must in certain situations express 'witness over against government and nation', as the Constitution of the Netherlands Reformed Church puts it specifically in Article III. It is essential that such a witness should have a very specific point to it. That was the case in the days of the prophets. They were charged to make known the Word of God concerning quite specific people – they received 'a burden', as the AV puts it in Isa. 13.1 and 15.1 and many other places. Jeremiah had to address himself to king and people, so that he was devoured by his charge when he wanted to keep silent – as Jer. 20.7-10 shows so movingly – while he was physically destroyed when he did speak. Jeremiah really was a 'suffering servant of the Lord'.

The Bible, therefore, has something public, a larger national and also especially a supra-national dimension. It is a proclamation 'for the nations'. According to Matt. 10.18 the disciples will be taken 'before governors and kings . . . to bear testimony before them and the Gentiles.' When we come to realize this, we sense that we narrow the Bible down seriously when we explain it solely in terms of the salvation of the personal soul and the redemption of individuals. The gospel is indeed personal, but it is not private. It has a broad and 'royal' approach. That is why the proclamation of the gospel, as

we see it taking plac   oday, has such
profound effects o   se the Christian
Church can be   .

In our Wes   proclamation of the
gospel took sl   forms of the social and political
life. We reali   k how far our so-called Western civilization – to put it carefully – has 'also' been affected by the proclamation of the gospel in Europe, when our Western cultural
patterns are compared with those of Eastern countries, as in A. T.
van Leeuwen's *Christianity and World History*, published in 1964.
Even those people who have cut any ties they might have had
with the church and the Bible, or who only recognize these ties
vaguely, still have their roots in this soil which has been saturated
(as it were), with the Gospel; they breathe in a climate permeated
by the Bible, or so it seems to us. Anyone who would like to raise
objections to this could no doubt find arguments, but we do not
want to quarrel about facts, whether they are historical, cultural or
sociological in nature. We just want to make the point that the
Bible, as the book of proclamation, addresses itself with authority not
just to the individual, but also to the nations. How much of that has
so far affected history is another matter.

This brings us back to the original point for which we were
claiming attention, namely the *pronouncements of the Church* in
larger context than the meeting of the congregation for the sermon.
In the twentieth century in particular, people in the Reformed
Church began to realize that the Church as such should be able
to make statements, should have a voice, as it was put in the years
before the Second World War, in circles concerned with the 'reconstruction of the Church'. The period of the occupation and the confusing years that followed convinced the Reformed Church of the
necessity to speak, aware of a communal responsibility, and the
direction of the Holy Spirit. Particularly during the last twenty
years, the General Synod has made statements on several matters,
matters in fact of a very varied nature.

*Sometimes the Church addressed itself more particularly to its
own members, on certain biblical or ecclesiastical matters, such as
the report on Infant Baptism in 1947. Mostly, however, the Synod
had the wider circle of the nation and the government in mind.*

Sometimes it was an appeal for intercession in a critical situation, at other times it might be a pronouncement on a specific problem on which public opinion was strongly divided, such as the pastoral letter on capital punishment in 1947. The witness of the Church received general approval and sympathy during the occupation, in particular the protests against the degrading and anti-Christian measures against the Jews. The words of the Church coincided with national sentiment. This changed, however, when the Church, after the war, demanded attention for its witness in political matters.

The greatest sensation was perhaps created by the pamphlet on the 'Problem of Nuclear Armaments', which the Synod offered 'for reflection' in the autumn of 1962, as a supplement to an earlier document on the question of war and peace (1952). The fierce discussions for and against were an indication of the great extent to which such public statements by the Church are surrounded by all kinds of problems. There was in particular the question whether a Church may pronounce an opinion on such a complicated matter, on the basis of the Bible. How far does the authority of the Bible stretch in such matters, and how far can a Church risk an interpretation of this authority, on its own decision? Other synodal letters have appeared which have created much less discussion, and the authority of which was accepted with much less opposition, among them the pastoral letters concerning the Roman Catholic Church and Marriage, and the document on the teaching of the Holy Scripture.

As we have already indicated, it remains a difficult point how far a Church can prove that it is backed by the authority of the Bible when it addresses itself to its members and to the nation. It seems to us beyond dispute that the Church not only may, but definitely must, pronounce on important and critical situations of the moment; this must be so because of the nature of the Bible: its authority demands proclamation and it extends along the whole line, being both spiritual and specific. Why should the Church not be allowed to be concerned with politics, while it has to address itself to the whole man, on the basis of the word of the Bible? Why should the local church proclaim through its pastor, but keep silent in the larger context for the ears of the nations and the world? No, the nineteenth century division between 'Church' and 'politics' has worn really threadbare now, though it is understandable that some people should urge moderation in view of the denominational groups developed in the last century.

In our opinion, the shoe really pinches here on the question of biblical authority. It is, moreover, curious that in the ordinary sermon in the Christian congregation hardly anyone is concerned about this authority. People go to church for their own edification, but very few trouble themselves with the question of whether the preacher really made the Bible speak to them. The only question, most often, is whether the sermon 'meant anything to them'. Among Protestants it is usually the person of the preacher who is decisive in this matter. People go to church for 'the sermon', which in fact means for 'the minister'. For that matter, the lists of names of preachers with which the church services are announced in the ecclesiastical as well as in the public press, make one think of 'the sins of Jeroboam, the son of Nebat' from which even such keen servants of the Lord as Jehu and Jehoash could not depart, because the people insisted on 'these high places' (I Kings 12.31; II Kings 12.3 and many other texts from these stories). What church council in our situation dares to announce the Sunday service without the name of the preacher, but with the text and the liturgy for that Sunday? Do we really go to church, assuming we do go, in order to put ourselves under the glorious and holy authority of the Word of God, or . . . in order to hear a sermon to our taste and judgement?

When, however, the Church preaches to the whole nation through the mouthpiece of the Synod, totally different reactions are roused, at least in some cases. Then it is suddenly felt much more clearly that a sermon is a specific word in the situation, on the basis of the Scriptures. Opponents in particular then ask whether this or that point can really be said on the basis of Scripture. We are aware that people sometimes voice their approval or disapproval on quite different grounds, but in general it is felt much more acutely that the point here is the authority of the Bible. Has this authority been transmitted rightly and without mistakes in this situation? This is the question that is put, consciously or unconsciously. Nobody has yet said that 'the sermon' about New Guinea or about nuclear armaments or about the Dutch Society for Sexual Reform was 'edifying'; they feel that something has been said to them, they are touched, encouraged, hurt, and they ask: is this really the way in which this

must be expressed, on the basis of the Bible? Has the Synod spoken
'biblically'?

How are we to find an answer to this question? How can we
know whether a word on a particular question was really a 'biblical'
word?

The whole aim of this book so far has been to sharpen the mind
so that we can see more clearly, distinguish more sharply and arrive
more directly at spiritual certainty. But in order to apply this practically in the confusion of opinions and ideas, in fierce debates with
obdurate opposition, we shall now try to indicate a few roads along
which we can travel together, in order that the authority of the
Bible may be acknowledged more honestly than before and the
Bible itself be given a chance to convince its opponents. That is the
reason for the second part of this chapter: Our conversation with
the Bible.

B Our Conversation with the Bible

We must ask the reader to forgive us if we point out yet again what
the order of the two sections of this chapter is. If the Bible has
authority, then it really *possesses* that authority. We do not need to
give it, nor can we prove or defend its existence. Such authority
will make itself felt. That is the reason for its spiritual and concrete
nature, like the pointing finger of Nathan. The Bible in conversation with us! The Bible is not, however, a tyrant. Precisely because
its authority is spiritual, it asks us to take part, to use our own
judgement, to make our own decision, and to risk its application.
That is why it is right and reasonable that we on our side ask the
Bible questions, and participate very seriously from our side in the
conversation with the Bible. This explains 'our conversation with the
Bible'. But we are only too often tyrants, especially pious tyrants. We
are so anxious to impose our own opinion. We so much want to
exercise an unspiritual authority, and we apply the greatest skill in
using the Bible for this purpose, harnessing it in front of our own
little cart. This is one of the basic sins against which the third commandment is directed. 'Thou shalt not take the name of the Lord
in vain' (i.e. bear it triumphantly before you as a religious power)
(Ex. 20.7). That is why we remind the reader again that section A

precedes section B, that the Bible comes first, and that we are allowed to join in. We can join in the conversation which God has started. But we must join in wholeheartedly. We ask our questions, very specific and urgent ones, and we put to the Bible all sorts of things that worry us, things about which we differ in opinion, things that occupy our minds today. We ask whether and how we can unite as churches, what truth and unity are. Should we sacrifice truth to unity? Or the other way round? Perhaps there is a third way? We ask whether in the church of Christ women may be called to the ministry and whether spiritual healing is still possible today; whether 'real' miracles can still happen. We ask what our attitude should be towards totalitarian ideologies and whether Communism is in itself the same thing as National Socialism. We ask whether we may and should use nuclear armaments in the last resort, or whether here we should give an unconditional 'no' in answer, and whether this implies that we must be conscientious objectors. We ask what the Christian attitude to the developing countries should be, where one revolution after another seems to undo all the good intentions. We ask about a new marriage morality, and whether sexual intercourse outside or before marriage is permissible. We ask what reading matter should or should not be printed in a free country, and what we should put into the hands of our children. We ask what our attitude should be towards homosexuality, and about the way in which we should, or must, use our prosperity and our money. Of course we also ask whether there are not many questions on which we really cannot expect to receive light from the Bible, and whether we must really bring the Bible and the Christian faith into everything and, if so, how this should be done. We ask whether the state and our society can frame their own standards and rules, with the light and insight they possess, or whether the Lord God perhaps also has something to say in these matters. That is why we try to understand the Bible as well as possible, and that is the reason why the churches need not be ashamed to try and apply God's Word also to the concrete questions of life. If in particular this last problem has been tackled in a defective or much criticized manner in the various statements and writings of the Synod of the Netherlands Reformed Church, then let the well-known saying of Augustine be our comfort: that it is better to limp along the right road, than to walk beside that road.

Now we would like to put forward some practical points of view and rules which ought, in our opinion, to be observed if we are to participate properly in conversation with the Bible, without quenching the Holy Spirit (I Thess. 5.19) and without hindering the authority of the Bible itself.

1. A *Living Relationship with the Bible*

One is sometimes struck by the profound wisdom which simple people have acquired through years of companionship with the Bible. They surprise us by quoting or comparing texts, which suddenly begin to speak to us. They have an intuitive feeling for the roads and boundaries of biblical territory, which is often such confusing country, even though they have no expert technical knowledge. They know the pitch of particular biblical words and passages, so that they can make them harmonize in all sorts of settings, while they also have a very good ear for anyone who hits just the wrong note. The biblical example of this is the unknown poet of Ps. 119, who sings of the glory of God's Torah. 'In the way of thy testimonies I delight as much as in all riches' (v. 14). We meet here with real scriptural feeling. In Roman Catholic circles people sometimes refer to a *sensus catholicus*, to indicate a correct sense of the cohesion of the teaching system of the Church, a 'Roman Catholic' sense of life; similarly we would speak here of a *sensus scripturalis*, the right sense of the cohesion of the Scriptures. We hold that an appeal to the Bible to confirm a particular opinion is pointless unless one can prove to have hit the tone of the Bible as a whole. Specific texts must derive their power to convince from the wider context of the Bible; otherwise one should not produce them as 'proofs'.

It therefore also has little meaning to take a random passage for a Bible study group composed of a random selection of people, and then to proceed to discuss this together. The feeling for the Scriptures referred to above, which is a fundamental knowledge of biblical cohesion, has to be the basic presupposition if one wants to begin a really fruitful conversation with the Bible.

In the time of orthodox theology (see Chapter I.B.1) scholars spoke of the rule 'compare Scripture with Scripture', specially in the case of difficult texts. Their assumption, quite rightly, was that the Bible should explain itself, and not be explained by an outside authority. They liked to use the phrase *analogia fidei et caritatis* for what we referred to just now with the words *sensus scripturalis*. With this they formulated the same thought that we had in mind, that texts and words must not be carried in from here and there like wandering stones, but that – in analogy with the Christian Faith (and Christian love) – fixed lines and contours should be distinguished in the many-coloured variety of the Bible.

A brilliant example of this feeling for the Scriptures which may be mentioned here, is the teaching of the Reformers themselves, on justification by faith alone. This does not indicate just one part of our Christian confession, but the entire structure. Man over against God is dependent on his favour (Favor Dei), as partner in the covenant with God, as the child to his father. The whole relation between God and his people, between the Creator and his creature, and between Christ and his followers, is one of dependence and trust, of 'belief'. Only in and through this relation can there be any talk of a life for God, in penitence or praise, in gratitude or intimate companionship, in prayer or complaint, indeed even in dispute and rebellion. This is what Luther read in the Psalms as the basic relationship which can have many variations, but which is in essence always again the justification by faith alone. To think of these words as applying only to the relationship of sin and grace, denying it its central position, is to diminish the essence of Reformed teaching.

If this basic relationship is overlooked, one lapses into pagan patterns, in which the deity and man are pictured in the position of 'fair exchange is no robbery'. 'I give in order that thou givest' (do ut des) was a basic rule in Roman sacrifices. This relationship can be varied in many different ways, but essentially it remains the same: a businesslike relation in which the partners keep the balance by offers and favours, an attitude of mutual guarantees. The first of the Ten Commandments of Israel warns against this entirely pagan attitude. Israel had to learn to live in an open, dependent and basically defenceless and unguaranteed attitude of faith and mercy with God, its liberator, who was so entirely different from the other gods! This relationship also leaves full room for punishments and rewards, merits and sacrifices, without damaging in the least the basic relation of 'justification by faith alone'. This is the light in which the Reformers read the Bible, even when there are references to 'good works' and 'sanctification', to 'judgement and punishment', to 'merit and reward'. All the same, it is perhaps a historic fact that the Reformers, and their heirs, in defending themselves against Rome, did not dare to speak with sufficient freedom – with these basic suppositions as a starting point – about good works and sanctification. Conversely, it is curious that in our own age the teaching of justification by faith is again recognized by leading theologians as the basic biblical relation which Rome has never really relinquished or limited. Here new possibilities in the conversation with Rome open up.

A living companionship with the Bible, beside showing the broad cohesion and the biblical outlines, will, however, also create an awareness of the special, separate character of particular parts of the Bible. One should not be too ready to compare everything with everything else. One mistake which is often made in telling the gospel stories is to combine the details given by one evangelist with those given by another, and make one story which does not occur at all as such in the Bible. The remarkableness, the pointedness of one particular story in that one gospel is lost in this way. Because we have already referred to this, in Chapter III.B, we will not go further into it now. We have recalled it, however, because to 'compare Scripture with Scripture' only goes right when an intimate companionship with the Bible has created the right feeling for what belongs together in the Scriptures, which makes it possible, not only to combine, but also to distinguish.

Moreover, we must guard against romanticizing this 'feeling' for the Scriptures, making it sound as if only initiates were capable of explaining the Bible aright. Too often there have been accidents here, in the course of church history. The devout poet of Psalm 119, who searches the Scriptures with such joy, also admits: 'I have seen a limit to all perfection, but thy commandment is exceedingly broad' (v. 96). The Bible always has surprises in store for us, and who is proof against mistakes, short-circuits, or partialities? The only thing we want to plead for, quite soberly, is that a real knowledge of the Bible, from inside, is necessary in order that a section or a word from the Bible may really come alive to us, really turn the scales for another person. For a more exact description of this we refer to the 'key-secrets' in Chapter III, in which the first 'secret' is the key to the following. It is our conviction that the whole

Bible, *Tanach* and *Gospel*, must be read from the Israelite position. Salvation is from the Jews. The Israelite keynote of the whole of the Bible should not escape us. This is the only way in which the Bible can really speak to us. That means that the *sensus scripturalis* should be understood as a *sensus israeliticus* (the feeling of Israel in one's finger-tips). If we have not learnt this through intimate companionship with the Bible, then we shall remain strangers to the Bible, and whole sections of the Scriptures will remain strange and incomprehensible to us. A real conversation will never develop, and it will be impossible for the Bible ever to have authority over us. Once again, we give a single illustration of this point.

In the famous high-priestly prayer of John 17, Jesus says the well-known prayer for unity. 'I do not pray for these only, but also for those who are to believe in me through their word, that they may all be one; even as thou, Father, art in me, and I in thee, that they also may be in us, so that the world may believe that thou hast sent me. The glory which thou hast given to me I have given to them, that they may be one even as we are one, I in them and thou in me, that they may become perfectly one, so that the world may know that thou hast sent me and hast loved them even as thou hast loved me' (vv. 20-23).

This is the extremely well-known passage on which the Churches base their ecumenical aspiration. Most often this prayer is said to mean that when all the Churches are united, the world will be convinced of the truth of the gospel. An appeal to strive after unity is read out of this passage, though it never seems to have acquired any force or urgency in the Churches, in spite of our joy at the ecumenical awakening. But can this explanation of the Scriptures really achieve a hold on us? Does it not inevitably remain powerless, because the Israelite keynote is absent? Did Jesus really have our hopeless divisions among the Churches (of the Gentiles) in mind? It is really stupid that we should always take that for granted. How differently these words begin to speak to us, however, when we recognize in that so often repeated word 'one', the 'one' of Deut. 6.4: 'Hear, O Israel: the Lord our God is one Lord.' This was the basic confession of faith of every Jew, and therefore for Jesus: only one nation, one congregation could belong to this one and unique God (the Hebrew word ehad [one] is difficult to render in *its full significance for us; it contains the sense of single, unique, as well as of intimate).* The great sorrow which Jesus had to bear is precisely this, that his own people did not recognize him as the one sent by that one God. That is exactly what his cross consisted of. That is why he went to Golgotha. In this prayer he adjures his heavenly Father and his followers to preserve this Israelite one-ness. They must show that their teacher, Jesus, was no sectarian, but that he belonged with all his heart and being, fervently, to the one God of Israel, and that he spoke in his Name. In that way the Jewish people who rejected Jesus will yet believe that he had been sent by the Father. The word 'world' (cosmos), in our opinion, often has in John's Gospel the meaning 'the Jewish world'; enclosed in a piety of its own, it is not open to receive its Messiah. See also Chapter IV.B.4.

Unfortunately, however, the Christians who came to believe in Jesus through the word of the apostles have generally speaking not recognized this Israelite tone of the word one, and the Christian Church has not been much concerned with being one with Israel. No wonder that this prayer has never yet been answered, and that Israel still does not recognize its Messiah in the preaching of the Churches from among the Gentiles. If only the World Council of Churches would re-read this high-priestly prayer with the *sensus israeliticus*, with a feeling for Israel.

2. *Learning Aids*

At the present time, Church and Christianity will certainly have to combine the living relationship with the Bible with an eager use of whatever results and insights scientific research affords. Here we are thinking of the various branches of learning which are developed to the advantage of theology, both at the universities and at the colleges, as well as of the many more popular publications which put these advances within reach of many people.

We do not deny that the scientific study of the Scriptures has in the course of church history led to deviations and erring from the main road, but after our Chapters I and II we do not need to go into this again. Now we only want to show in what way scholarship has served the Church, and still continues to serve it.

In the very first place, knowledge of the *original languages* in which the Bible was written is indispensable. Hebrew (and, for a small part, Aramaic) is the language in which the Tanach was written. Though the script and oriental mode of expression are strange to us Westerners, this is in essence and structure a simple language. Much more difficult and refined is Greek. That is the language in which the writers of the gospels and the apostles wrote down the witness of the Messiah Jesus. For this they used the popular form of Greek current in that period in the countries round the Eastern end of the Mediterranean Sea. It could be compared with the Malay language of the Indonesian Archipelago. This *koine*-Greek (*koinos* = common or general) is certainly a much simpler language than the literary Greek used by the poets, philosophers and historians of ancient Greece, but with some of the writers of the 'New Testament' it can still be felt that they are not writing in their mother-tongue. The First Letter of Peter and the Letter to the Hebrews contain very good Greek. But in all of them one finds numerous Hebraisms, pointing to the language, the style and the way of thought of the *Tanach*, which is usually quoted in the Greek translation, *the Septuagint*, by Paul and others. Obviously, it is better to be aware of this Hebrew background to the Greek part of the Bible.

In John 20.1, for instance, we read that Mary Magdalene went to the tomb 'on the first day of the week', but what is really written is: 'on day one'. Now this is exactly the way in which the Jewish authors of the Bible used the numeral, especially in Gen. 1.5: 'And there was evening and there was morning, one day'. Consciously or unconsciously the writer of John here makes a connection between the day of the resurrection and the first day of the creation.

The parchments and scrolls written by the writers of the Bible have all been lost, or at least they have not so far been found; but in their stead a great number of copies, and copies of these copies, have found their way into the ancient Jewish and Christian world, and an almost incalculable number of these have been preserved, or have later been found again, in fragments. The spectacular discoveries of the Qumran texts, in the caves near the Dead Sea, should also be mentioned here. These, however, were in the main not biblical scrolls. The scholars who prepare, decipher and evaluate these manuscripts render invaluable services to theology.

It is self-evident that, in part through these new scientific advances and discoveries, the question of a new translation of the Bible became more and more urgent. We have already seen in Chapter I that in the period of the Reformation the learning of the Humanists was of great service to the renewed interest in the Scriptures. The world-famous translation by Luther (which dated from the Wartburg period) the Dutch *Statenvertaling* and the English Authorized (King James) version were in their time works of responsible scholarship, in particular aiming to do justice to the basic text. Our generation, however, has seen several fruits of more recent research into various translations of the Bible, in many different languages.

An annoying misunderstanding in some circles is that these new translations constitute a 'new' Bible. The reverse is rather the case : their intention is to give us the original Bible as faithfully as possible. On the other hand, there are those who rather naïvely expect the new translations to provide solutions for difficult theological questions or ecclesiastical differences. This is only very rarely the case. Thus the phrase 'on earth peace, good will toward men' (Luke 2.14) is better translated 'on earth peace among men with whom he is well pleased' (RSV) or '. . . to me who enjoy his favour', as the new Jerusalem Bible has it. In the struggle for the closest translation, the finer shades of meaning count most, the dot rather than the 'i' itself.

Though the translations are of the greatest importance for the reading of the Bible, anyone who has a knowledge of the original languages will know how a text or a passage comes much more to life whenever the Bible can speak to us in its own language. It acquires a richer colour, many different nuances begin to stand out, all of which are lost in the translations. This is particularly so because many authors of the Bible have a weakness for play on words. Here are some examples.

In the well-known story of Jacob and Laban in Gen. 30.25-43, in which Jacob acquires, as wages, a great part of the flocks of his uncle Laban through a trick with peeled white sticks, the word white plays a great part. It is used three times in vv. 35 and 37. Now in Hebrew the word for white is laban, *and the reader immediately sensed the mockery of Laban. In order to fit the translation*

entirely to the intention of the story, Laban should be introduced
as Mr White.

In Psalm 39 the contrast between being silent and speaking plays
a part. 'I will guard my ways that I may not sin with my tongue'
(v.1). David feels wronged by God. But he keeps his grievances to
himself 'so long as the wicked are in my presence'. Then it becomes
impossible for him to keep silent any longer, his complaints come
pouring out: . . . . 'As I mused, the fire burned; then I spoke
with my tongue' (v. 3). The reader expects that he will now
hear complaints about 'how can God permit', etc. But instead of
this, we hear a prayer for awareness of our human limitations and
impotence. 'Let me know how fleeting my life is' (v. 4). This meek
prayer might certainly be heard by 'the wicked', of course, but
there is something illogical about the sequence of verses 3 and 4.
The solution can be found in the Hebrew language, which has two
words for 'to speak'. One is 'amar, and this is used when the spoken
words are quoted immediately and verbally. The other is dibber,
which means 'to speak' in general. The latter is used in verse 3.
Now everything is suddenly clear. This pious man has quarrelled
with God. This is allowed! But now he has reached the point where
he realizes that misfortune and illness, suffering and death are
interwoven into the fragile and never blameless life of man (vv.
5, 6 and 11). He may expect and pray, but he has no right to
demand, 'for I am thy passing guest, a sojourner, like all my fathers'
(v. 12).

Another random example is from Acts, written in Greek. In chapter
21.31,32, all translations convey the impression that the Jewish crowd
tries to murder Paul in a riot, but that they do not succeed in this in
the five or ten minutes which is all they have at their disposal before the arrival of the Romans. They had obviously not mastered the
art of lynching properly. Strange! But the word 'beating' of v. 32
does not mean beating with intent to kill; it is the word tuptein.
This word means to beat on the face, mouth or breast (as a sign of
penitence). At the beginning of v. 31 it really only says that they
'try' to put him away ('to kill' is too strong a word here), preferably
in the legal manner, just as they did with Jesus.

When it is realized, partly through the examples we have just seen, how important access to the biblical texts in the original languages is, then it will surely be admitted that it is no luxury for the Church to demand from its preachers and ministers that they have a knowledge of Hebrew and Greek. Surely it must then be admitted that a long period of study, including a university course, is an urgent necessity in spite of all the nasty things which are sometimes – quite rightly – said about theologians. It is indeed very wrong if they use their expert knowledge to push the congregation aside as immature, or to degrade it into being just a listening crowd, instead of serving it and stimulating it to independent Bible study.

Beside the languages, the study of biblical antiquity, of archaeology in the broader sense, is also very important. Knowledge of climate and conditions of life, of moral customs and social institutions, of the civilization of the people of biblical times is essential, if we are to understand all sorts of details, sometimes not even mentioned, which were quite obvious to the reader of the Bible of those days.

The fact that the Bible is so much more accessible to the present generation is due to the enormous labour of the excavations – archaeology in the narrow sense – to which many scholars have devoted their attention in recent decades. The results of this work have come within the reach of the reading public through numerous illustrated publications. This source continues to be productive, making acquaintance with the Bible as fruitful and lively as possible. To supplement the examples which have already been mentioned in the course of this book, we give two others here to show clearly that the Bible must also be read and understood as a book of a particular period and civilization.

In Gen. 31, the story of Jacob's secret departure after his long stay with Laban, every reader is struck by Rachel stealing the teraphim, the household gods, of her father (v.19). The amusing story which then follows cannot conceal from the modern Bible reader that the wife of the patriarch Jacob obviously still clung to primitive, pagan ways. But the whole thing changes when we know that this was not so much a religious matter as a legal one. According to Babylonian law, it now seems, the possession of the household gods brought with it the right of inheritance. They had the same value *as a will has for us. This makes Laban's fury all the more understandable.*

The tax collector Zacchaeus, in the story in Luke 19.1-10, chooses a fig tree from which to have a good view of Jesus; for anyone who knows the country of the Bible from his own observation, it is obvious why it should be a fig tree. This tree is not only low and broad, but it also has the most enormous leaves. We remind the reader of the fig leaves with which Adam and Eve covered themselves. Behind these large leaves Zacchaeus has a marvellous vantage point from which to watch the proceedings without being seen . . . at least that is what he thinks.

Perhaps it is not superfluous to add here that we are not thinking that because of the results of new, scientific research the Bible will be proved more and more 'right' in its stories and historical descriptions. It is indeed true that the premature conclusions of scholars of the period, which presented the Bible as a historically unreliable book, have now to be corrected. We are not, however, concerned whether the Bible is right or wrong historically, but rather with the light which is thrown on the texts by the researches of scientific archaeologists.

In the third place we would like to discuss in more detail (compare I.B.4) the encounter with Jewish spiritual life which is so important to an inside understanding of the Bible.

In the centuries after the Babylonian exile until the first century of our era, Jewish apocalyptic writing especially flourished. In Isaiah 24-27 and in the second part of the book of Zechariah, as well as at the end of Ezekiel, we already find parts which could be included in this, while Daniel 7, the prophecy of the Son of Man who appears before 'one that was ancient of days', fits especially into this category.

But beside all this there are many apocryphal books – that is, books which are not in our Bible – which are very apocalyptic. The word 'apocalyptic' means a strong expectation of the future, expressed in colourful and concrete imagery; interwoven with this are various themes concerning a future solution, after and through judgement and ordeal, both in Israel and also universally for all mankind and creation. From the book of Revelation – *Apocalypsis* in Greek – everyone knows how difficult it is to explain the language and the imagery of the apocalyptic writers, but also how penetrating and concrete their visions and prophecies can be. We shall not attempt to give a watertight characterization of apocalyptic phenomena here. We do, however, want to establish that at the time of Jesus and the apostles, apocalyptic images and expectations are evidently alive, among the Jewish people as well as outside, though this is stronger in some groups and currents than in others. Thus it can hardly fail to be that in the Gospels and Epistles, all sorts of passages, texts and words have their background in Jewish apocalyptic writing. It is often difficult to make out whether these expectations are rejected – as seems to be the case when Jesus more and more consciously rejects certain expectations of the people, as in John 6.15 after the Feeding of the Five Thousand – or that Jesus and the apostles agree with them. It is also possible to assume that the imagery and the form are adopted, but that they are filled with other contents. We are thinking for instance of the parable of the rich man and the poor man Lazarus in Luke 16.19-31, where the latter comes into 'Abraham's bosom' (v. 23). Is this meant to be imagery or reality? Or perhaps both? Or is this one of the contrasts that are impossible to the Jewish mind? In such matters the best thing is to leave the matter open, without maintaining boldly that it must be true because it is in the Bible, nor yet that it cannot be true because we cannot form a picture of it in that way.

Mark 13 is a well-known chapter with an apocalyptic flavour. The often quoted words about 'wars and rumours of wars' are found in v. 7. The verse about the false Christ and false prophets is also well known in some circles (v. 22). The beginning of this chapter is clearly concerned with a future destruction of Jerusalem and the temple, so that it is very concrete and historical. Looking back, we can give the date, AD 70. But can we also give a date, in the past or in the future, for the falling stars of v. 25? Only those who have made a profound study of the Jewish spiritual life of those days may attempt to give a careful answer here, as is for instance done by Hendrikus Berkhof in his book *Christ the Meaning of History*. We are, however, of the impression that in many circles where great stress is laid on expectations of the future, an inner understanding and knowledge of all this is absent. On the other hand, however, it must be recognized that the official theology of the Churches often painstakingly avoids these 'apocalyptic' biblical passages, or

considers the matter finished for us in our day with a reference to
the Jewish background. We shall have to ask honestly and carefully
what the Bible has to say to us in this colourful, concrete and often
exotic language, even in our time, as God's message is truly no
timeless truth, but fulfils itself in the progress of the centuries.

It may be useful to mention here that the many confessional titles
which are given to Jesus by the Scriptures are in some cases coloured
by apocalyptic thinking. This is generally accepted of the expression
'Son of man', as in Mark 14.62. 'And Jesus said, "I am; and you will
see the Son of man sitting at the right hand of Power and coming
with the clouds of heaven".' This should be compared with Dan. 7.13.
One should not, however, forget that this confession has Ps. 8.4 as
background, where man is called 'son of man'. Jesus as the Son of
man would therefore be the man. *The most familiar title of Jesus,*
Messiah (Christ), also has firm roots in the Tanach, but it does not
play as important a part there as is usually assumed. Messianic
longing crystallized particularly in the period between the return
from the exile and the birth of Jesus. This can be deduced from the
apocalyptic writings.

At least as important as these apocalyptic writings from the inheritance of Jewish spiritual life is Rabbinic legal learning. This has been
preserved for us in the famous collection, the Talmud. The codi-
fication of the Talmud is a complicated history into which we cannot
go any further here. From the gospels we know that the lawyers
explained the Torah, the Law of Moses, for the purpose of application
in daily life. The Pharisees were a narrow and nationalistically inclined group of these lawyers, often at loggerheads with the
Sadducees, who would have little to do with detailed explanations,
probably because their attitude to them was rather more lukewarm.
It is unjust to imagine the Pharisees as unqualified hypocrites. There
were hypocrites among them, but in general their great love for the
Law was praiseworthy. They desired nothing but to live entirely
on the basis of what the God of Abraham, Isaac and Jacob had given
to his people Israel. The tragedy, however, is that they did not, or
did not entirely, understand the secret of God's election and love,
as they believed that this could be captured and enclosed in their
own devout theology. That is why they could not understand Jesus

either, who had come to fulfil the Law. Their explanation of the
Torah does, however, express their great love of a living association
with the Scriptures, which they knew through and through. That
is why the explanation – *Midrash* – of the great lawyers Gamaliel and
Hillel, preserved by their pupils and later laid down in writing in
the *Mishnah* by the great Rabbi Judah in about the year 200, is of
exceptional importance to Christendom. We should not forget that
Paul was a Pharisee, a pupil of Gamaliel – Acts 22.3 – and how could
we understand the lively, questioning style of arguing and speaking without this rabbinic background? It is a bitter irony of history
that Christianity, through a premature aversion from rabbinical
legal science, has often fallen into the very mistakes with which it
believed it could reproach Rabbinism. In this respect, too, the
notorious *anti-semitism* of the Church itself has caused much disaster.
It is really only in the last century that the Church and theologians
have deigned to let themselves be taught by Jewish scholars. This
has opened up a whole world, from which a surprising new light
begins to fall on the whole Bible, though more particularly on the
proclamation of Jesus and on the letters of Paul.

*In the well-known passage of Matt. 5, in which the phrase occurs
again and again: 'You have heard that it was said to the men of
old', Jesus undoubtedly had the Torah in mind, as it was explained
by the Rabbis. The German scholar K. Bornhäuser has made it his
life-work to make this rabbinical background, against which Jesus
and the writers of the gospels move, serve to explain the Bible. It
is for the experts to judge whether he has perhaps attached too
much importance to this background, or whether he may be wrong in
some details. It remains true that his work is of pioneering quality.*
   *One final example. 'Then Philip opened his mouth, and beginning
with this scripture he told him the good news of Jesus', we read in
Acts 8.35. This phrase 'to open his mouth' seems superfluous. But
that is the standard expression for the official teaching and explaining of a Rabbi. When we see these words, we know that something
important will be said. The devout Ethiopian will indeed have received some solid catechetical instruction on his journey. We can
be sure that Philip was not content with saying that the lamb in
Isa. 53.7 was Jesus. He will have put in the missing lines and shown
the perspectives, 'beginning from that scripture'. And when they*

finally come to water on that long road, the candidate for confirmation asks: 'What is to prevent my being baptized?' Behind this remark, too, there lies a familiar phrase. The Rabbis knew a great many reasons which prevented a Gentile from becoming a proselyte or an integral part of Israel. The eunuch is sure to have discovered this in Jerusalem. Now he fears that they may be a similar obstacle, but the message is that in and through Jesus – who came to fulfil the Law – the gate has been opened even for this pagan.

During the last thirty years the ideas of *later pious Jews and philosophers* have drawn the attention of Christian theologians and biblical scholars. For centuries, Christian theological thought and Jewish spiritual life had each followed their own course, but now these two streams – each of which forms a considerable delta – are coming closer together and showing much more similarity to each other than had been anticipated, to the great surprise of all the experts. Here we must mention with respect the life-work of Dr K. H. Miskotte, who has suddenly forced Christian theology to consider a field and a problem which fascinates both Church and Christianity more and more. This may prove to be the greatest ecumenical turning point of the century. A living Israel and the Church of Jesus the Messiah have begun another conversation.

All this is personified in the Jewish philosopher Martin Buber. He is one of the many to whom we must be grateful for opening the eyes of Christian theology again to the fact that the Scriptures are concerned with a partnership, an encounter between God and man. This I-Thou relationship is one of his basic concepts. That is why his little book *Ich und Du*, which also appeared in English under the title *I and Thou*, is so well known. In his biblical studies, Buber has laid bare the nerve centres of scriptural thought, which the Christian church cannot neglect without suffering great loss. Buber stands in our midst as the interpreter, the mediator, between Church and synagogue, also because he is, together with Frans Rosenzweig, who died young, the author of a German translation of the Tanach in which the translators have done their utmost to preserve the characteristic idiom of Hebrew. The fact that Buber, in *Two Types of Faith*, definitely rejects Paul's interpretation of the faith in the Messiah Jesus should not obscure the insight that dialogue

with contemporary Jewish spiritual life is of the greatest importance
for the understanding of the Scriptures.

*The question which always rises here, too hastily, to Christian lips,
is whether contemporary Judaism is now perhaps at the stage where
Israel as a whole might possibly recognize Jesus as the Messiah. This
is certainly the central question, very much to the point indeed, but
as we have said, it is put rather too hastily. This is so because the
presupposition is that the Christian Church knows exactly what the
contents of the word Messiah should be. In the course of the centuries the Christian Church has given meaning to this word in
theology and in confession of faith, which is indeed based on the
Gospel, but without keeping in touch with Israel itself, and − it
is fair to say − without asking itself carefully how the Messiah
would reveal himself according to the Tanach, the Scriptures. It is,
however, a striking feature of the Gospels and Epistles that the
real vision of Jesus as the humiliated and exalted one only breaks
through when one learns to understand the Scriptures anew.
Obviously, something was wrong here, even in the time of Jesus.
We remind the reader of the story of the Walk to Emmaus, or of
a text like John 20.9. The disciples did not really know the Scriptures,
and that was why the resurrection was so difficult for them to understand. Then there are the constant references to the fulfilment of
the Scriptures. It therefore seems to us that Mark 11.27-33 is of
unique significance for the conversation with the present prominent
spiritual representatives of the Jewish people. In this passage the
chief priests, the elders and the scribes of Jerusalem come to ask Jesus
on what authority he acts. Obviously they respect Jesus to some
extent and they do not want to condemn prematurely as inaccurate
the enthusiastic belief of the Galilean crowds. Jesus could be a
great prophet, if not the prophet, who clears the temple as Jeremiah
once cleared the temple, in the temple speech of Jer. 7. Jesus then
asks these leading men what they think of John the Baptist. The
leaders, however, do not know how to handle that question, because
John had undeniably been a prophet of great stature. But, as always
in Israel, it is difficult for the leaders to recognize the real prophets:
they are so radical. The same is true of John. Jesus' question therefore embarrasses them greatly. But if the leaders cannot see John
the Baptist, whom Jesus himself acknowledged as the great off-*

shoot and summing-up of all Jewish prophecy (Mark 9.12, 13), in his true proportions, how can Jesus then exchange one significant word with them about his own power? They cannot recognize Jesus as sent by the Father, when obviously they still have the wrong view of the Law and the Prophets, which had as it were been presented anew to them, lifesize, in John the Baptist. Jesus does not put this question about John the Baptist as a smart evasion – why should he not dare to speak about his own authority? – but in order to test their real knowledge of the Scriptures. As long as this is lacking, a conversation about the Messiahship of Jesus is doomed from the start. This question of Jesus still stands between church and synagogue, between Christianity and Jewry. But in the twenty centuries which have passed in the meantime, much has been changed. In the encounter with the leaders of the Jewish people we shall certainly be able to learn much about the basic secret, the real messianic dimensions of the Law and the Prophets. During the centuries which lie behind us, the Jews have learnt that suffering – which was such a scandal in Jesus' day – plays a real part in this and that is our great shame. We Christians will perhaps have to rediscover this, too. But the only way to clear the way for the question whether the evangelists and the apostles were right in witnessing to Jesus as the Christ, is to go back together to the sources of Israel. If we as Christians should refuse to do so, then the question of whether Jesus is recognized as the Son of Israel by the Jews continues to be meaningless.

As a last aid in our attempt to begin an intelligent conversation with the Bible, we must mention the *study of religions*. We refer to what we have already said about this in Chapter I.

It is obvious that a knowledge of the religious life of the nations of the Near East can bear good fruit for our reading of the Bible. If one knows that the Baals were fertility gods, whose worship was intended to ensure fertility and growth, then it is easier to understand that Elijah announced a drought to Ahab, who had permitted the service of Baal in the land since his mixed marriage (I Kings 17.1). When one also knows that in the Baal cult sexuality and absolute kingship are given primary importance (I Kings 21.1-29), then one may have a little more understanding for Elijah's cruel action against the priests of Baal, after the divine judgement on

Mount Carmel (I Kings 18.40), which so offends every contemporary reader. From the sequence, moreover, it is evident that this was in fact what prevented the complete success of Elijah's career (I Kings 19.1, 2). 'I am no better than my fathers', the great prophet complains in v. 4. The study of religions, however, teaches us to refute as unscientific the idea that all religions are the same, so that tolerance must be preached at all costs.

This last remark has already led us to the field of *comparative religions*. This cannot be dispensed with as part of the university studies which future ministers have to complete. Scientific impartiality demands the unprejudiced study of religious phenomena. The aim here is emphatically not to arrive at the conclusion that Christianity is really the highest and most absolute religion, as a result of studying the religions of the Incas, the Eskimos, the Indians and the Chinese – such incredible and varied riches the world affords! What standards could be used in order to reach such a conclusion? The Churches really do not need to fear or control such comparative studies. A situation might arise in which science, unfaithful to its own assumptions, would presuppose openly or secretly that all religious life can ultimately be reduced to one whole, of which Christianity would obviously be one of the facets. In that situation the Church would do well to remind everyone, with the necessary humour and without too much pomp, that this is precisely the thing which cannot be proved scientifically.

A question which has again become most urgent in modern times is what the attitude of the Churches, with the Bible in hand, should be towards the religions of the world. This is the more relevant because of our contact with the younger Churches who live in the midst of primitive paganism or among highly developed old religious cultures.

This, however, is not the place to go into the many questions which always surround this point. Suffice it to say that the Christian Church has every reason to listen with great openness and deference to everything that comes to us from the world of religions. This is all the more true because we can stand secure and free in the world with the Gospel of the Lord who came, not to be served, but to serve.

After the enumeration of the various fields in which we need the aid of scholarship in order to be able to read and explain the Bible responsibly, the reader may well ask dejectedly: 'who is capable of these things?' It might even seem as if the scribes and the Pharisees have again narrowed the entrance to the Kingdom of Heaven (Matt. 23.13). Similarly, it may happen in a conversation about the Bible and faith, when theological know-how is employed to refute pious ideas, that this expert knowledge is irritably pushed aside with the remark that the disciples 'were just ordinary fishermen' who had not studied theology either. But for Paul this is not quite true. Though this remark holds good for the other apostles, it is often overlooked that the prophets and the apostles spoke and knew the languages in which the gospel of the Scriptures comes to us, and that they lived in the spiritual climate of Israel in which all kinds of things were obvious, which we can only discover by patient study.

We must therefore say emphatically that a conversation with the Bible and about its authority can only be significant and true if we do not reject the obvious help which scholarship can render. It is particularly important that the quiet and clear light resulting from an honest scientific attitude should help us in the differences of opinion and in mutual conversations between the Churches and the sects and the groups and movements in the Churches, as well as between Christians and those who do not believe, the doubters and the seekers. We do not say that scientific knowledge will solve all problems, but we do maintain that many superfluous problems can be avoided in this way, so that a real conversation round the Bible becomes a possibility. This brings us to the third practical rule.

3. *Reading and Listening Together*

We always listen to the Bible in the company of others. This does not mean that one should belittle personal use of the Bible. On the contrary! He is a fortunate man who in the noise of modern life still can find quietness in which to commune with the world of books, and in particular with *the* Book. But at that point it will be discovered that one cannot read the Bible alone, because the Bible is the book of the Church. Apostles and prophets, martyrs and patriarchs, reformers but also heretics, forefathers, children and stepchildren of the Church, noisy contemporaries, but also quiet ones, all have opened the Bible before us, or with us, and somehow or other their voices sound in our ears. We would do well to be conscious of this. It will help us to read better and to understand more clearly. Thus we read the Bible in the communion of saints. We will try to see this fact a little more clearly.

(a) *The Bible was partly written by Fellow-readers*

Examination of the manuscripts has shown that some words, texts or passages were not written by the original authors. Every theologian is familiar with this fact, but it may cause problems of belief for a number of readers of the Bible when it comes to their knowledge. In a Bible study group it may cause confusion when a leader with expert knowledge suddenly produces the information that the parable of the sower – in which the listeners are so neatly divided into four groups – is very probably an explanatory addition of the early Church (Matt. 13.18-23). It is also a shock to hear that the end of the Gospel of Mark, 16.9-20, is not 'authentic'. But the manuscripts do not lie, and modern translations indicate it clearly.

An understandable reaction to this is to ask somewhat irritably what we can then be sure of. There is the by no means imaginary danger that people will at once put the Bible aside as unreliable, or reject all this theological learning as human pride, finishing up with 'accepting everything as it is written': the 'fundamentalism' which we have already discussed. Both these roads lead nowhere.

It is better to make a real virtue out of this apparent necessity, and to accept that at these points we hear the unexpected explanations of the first Christian generations. We do not need to cling to the 'authenticity' of these passages in order to 'believe' as much as possible; nor, however, must we skip them because it seems that they do not belong to the Scriptures. On the contrary, in such passages we meet with our first partners in the conversation in which we listen to the Bible. This may be to our gain. Here are three examples.

In Acts 8, in the story of the Ethiopian minister of finance to which we have referred already, this man exclaims in v. 36: 'See, here is water! What is to prevent my being baptized?' At this point a note in the margin adds: 'Other ancient authorities add all or most of v. 37, And Philip said, "If you believe with all your heart, you may".' This verse, of which the manuscripts moreover have many variations, was added later, and in it we hear clearly the voice of the young Church. During the instruction for baptism the candidate had to learn the main points of the Christian faith, and he had to confess these at the time of his baptism. Baptism and confession coincided completely in those days; that is certainly not unbiblical. These two belong together. But what we really have to grasp here is that the intention of God's Word is that for this Ethiopian, who is also a eunuch – and therefore unclean according to the Torah (Deut. 23.1) – the gates of the Kingdom of God are opened without reserve. Philip baptizes him according to the Scriptures without any more ado. The emphasis is not on the baptism, but on the surprising lack of restrictions. This is, of course, very important for questions relating to infant and adult baptism. Those who will take the trouble to look up I John 5 will discover something similar in vv. 7 and 8. The apostle is speaking of belief in Jesus as the Messiah (v. 1), who came 'through water and blood' (v. 6) – perhaps an allusion to Jesus' baptism and death – and says that the Spirit bears witness to this (v. 7). In the AV, however, v. 7 reads: 'For there are three that bear record in heaven, the Father, the Word and the Holy Spirit, and these three are one.' It is difficult to be sure of the meaning of these words, but we can be certain that they were inserted by the early Church, which wanted to add an explanation pointing towards the doctrine of the Trinity in connection with the words 'three in one'. What are we to do with this explanation? One thing is certain: we cannot appeal to this inserted text for support for the dogma of the Trinity, as the Church Fathers did on occasions.

In John 5.3 and 4 we have a different situation. In the story of the healing at Bethzatha there is a reference to a note in the margin at the end of v. 3. Here it is quite obvious that the insertion in the 'other ancient authorities' is nothing more than a piece of popular superstition. In order to explain the healing property of the water of the pool, an angel was introduced, who descended at intervals into the water to give it healing powers. How plainly we see suddenly here the distinction between faith in the living Lord and belief in supernatural miracles. It is abundantly clear that this insertion is like a ship on the beach. Obviously it is not the right approach to the miracles in the Bible.

(b) *With all the Saints*

The Bible is the book of the Church. No wonder that it travels with
the Church on its journey through the centuries, as we have already
seen in the first chapter. The result is, of course, an enthralling
wealth of scriptural explanations, which are very difficult to sum
up : Sermons by Church Fathers and Reformers, marginal notes to
and explanations of parts of the Bible and of whole books of the
Bible; dogmatic writings, in which Bible texts quite obviously also
have their function and which receive their explanation in this way.
The liturgical formula and prayers should also not be forgotten. In
the classic Reformed order of service for baptism, the passage through
the Red Sea is quoted as an image of baptism.

In many hymns, biblical passages and thoughts are passed on in
a suggestive manner. 'Jesus, Saviour, pilot me' and 'Jesus, tender
Shepherd, hear me' pass on Bible messages in the form of songs,
though their romanticism fails to do justice to the power of the
Lord who rules the winds (Mark 4.35-41) and of the biblical
shepherd-figure of Ps. 23 and John 10. We know that many people
are influenced by these hymns. Poets of today are rediscovering the
possibility of expressing the Bible in modern hymns.

The arts played an important part in the explanation of the
Bible, as we already indicated in Chapter I. Most popular as subjects were the creation (Michelangelo in the Sistine Chapel) and the
stories about paradise, as well as the Flood and depictions of the
Last Judgement. The birth and crucifixion were portrayed innumer-
able times. Mention of Rembrandt should be made here, too. His
magnificent pictorial paraphrasing of the Bible illustrates and brings
it to life in a surprising manner, even for our generation. There
is, for instance, the homecoming of the prodigal son, a sermon without words. But . . . we must not forget that very often biblical
art throws more light on the artist and his day than on the Bible
itself, which, for that matter, is also true of the sermons of many
ministers. We say nothing in this context about Passion music,
which is musically so impressive.

*A striking example of the fact that representations of Bible stories
stick particularly in our memories is the number of paintings and
drawings of the offerings of Cain and Abel, in Gen. 4. In imitation
of Rembrandt, as far as we know, the smoke of Cain's offering*

comes down in every picture, as an indication that his offer was not accepted by the Lord. This is still always a trait of stories, meditations or sermons, though the Bible does not say a word about the smoke. Moreover, there are a great many people who only know the Bible from what they remember of Sunday school, a children's Bible or the religion lessons at school. They never get down to reading the Bible themselves. This is a clear instance of reading 'together' – others read, or have read, and we read through their spectacles. How important is the reading of the Bible itself, in the church service, in the catechism class and in the family. This is where the 'togetherness' is at its best, without being over-emphasized.

(c) The Voice of the Fathers

Out of the great variety of the Christian tradition a number of voices reach us, which have acquired a great authority for the whole Church, or for part of it. These men we call 'the Fathers'. We are thinking of such great names as Chrysostom, Augustine, Bernard of Clairvaux, Thomas Aquinas, Thomas à Kempis, Luther, Calvin, Willem à Brakel, Pascal, Schleiermacher, Kierkegaard, Kohlbrugge, Abraham Kuyper, Gunning, Stanley Jones, Roessingh and many others. It can come as a surprise to hear how these fathers of a distant or not so distant past, have listened to the Bible and explained it. Suddenly the Bible may take on a new dimension and open up perspectives which might otherwise have remained hidden. We need a trained ear, for these voices sometimes come to us from far away. It is the task of historical theology to unearth such treasures and to make them available to the present generation. It is of great value when striking explanations of the ancients are given a place in modern Bible commentaries. Ministers can, of course, stand to gain greatly from this in the preparation of their sermons. This is listening together which can be really fruitful.

One obvious remark should not be forgotten here. Not all the Fathers gained authority for everyone. Protestant and Roman Catholics alike will listen to Augustine, but Thomas Aquinas is a different matter. His authority is unassailable in the Church of Rome, but his voice seldom penetrates as far as the Churches of the Reformation. It is the same with the other Fathers we mentioned, as well as with many not mentioned here. They blazed a trail, but it is not followed by everyone. The reason for this may be that their biblical explanation or their message did not reach everyone, through accidental circumstances. But another possibility is that their voice did not strike a chord with some people, or that it met with strong opposition. Then their voices began to serve as flags round which groups of like-minded people gathered. In some cases this led to church formations or even to secessions, or to special currents within one church. Hence the Lutherans, the Calvinists, the Voetians, the Kohlbruggians and the Kuyperians, and of course . . . all the groups within the Netherlands Reformed Church. What can be said about this? The trouble is not that people did not listen to all the fathers at once. How could that be possible? Nor was it wrong to prefer an explanation of Scripture and faith by one particular voice, if that voice seemed sympathetic. What was wrong was, that by continuing along one track, it finally became impossible to listen to other voices, which is usually an ominous sign that the voice of the Bible is no longer really heard either.

Because we are pleading so strongly in favour of this last point, we underline our practical advice that we must listen together. The Bible can only get through to us if we listen to it together – which is not necessarily the same as agreeing with the other person's explanations of the Bible. This is as true as the fact that the Bible is the Book of the Church, as true as that 'communal thinking' is one of its key-secrets (see Chapter III.D: *Our* Father who art in heaven). This 'together' must not, however, remain limited to listening to the Fathers – which in practice often means, to a few very little-known Fathers whose influence is only experienced unconsciously – it must mean reading the Bible today, together with contemporaries. But before we make further important remarks on that subject, we must add one other link.

(d) *The Decisions of the Church*
Down the road through the centuries, the Church has been forced to take *decisions* at every crossroads it has had to pass. These decisions are laid down in dogmas and in the written confessions of faith. They mark the points at which, in the course of human questioning and searching for the real meaning of the Christian faith, the Bible gained ascendancy and the Church confessed. Again and again in this book we have touched on the question of the

relation between God's Word and dogma, between Bible and tradition, which is somewhat larger than dogma.

All we want to suggest in this context is that dogma and confession of faith also in a sense indicate the large biblical outlines in which the explanation of particular parts or texts have to be contained. These are the buoys and boundaries, the main roads and channels which the reader of the Bible does well to keep in mind, even though he will sometimes venture into new and untrodden paths, indeed even though the question may arise whether the buoys should not be changed as the tide has obviously gone out.

There are those who think that they can let the Bible speak to them without any of these aids, so that it will be completely new and unbiased. This is called *biblicism*. Tired of the many doctrinal differences and problems in the official churches, many pious men, especially in the eighteenth and nineteenth centuries, turned again to the Bible without burdening themselves with any doctrine or confessional formulary. This occurred especially in pietist circles. Even though it is clear to us, afterwards, that these devout men were more influenced by the spirit of the time than they were aware of, we must all the same gratefully acknowledge that frequently the Bible was given a new voice in a period when ecclesiastical Christianity no longer saw the biblical wood because of all the dogmatic trees.

It will surprise no one that this biblicism still often occurs today. It is found particularly in movements and groups which are more or less outside the churches, in sects and revival movements, with both good and bad aspects. We give examples of both.

In recent years there have been strong pleas in favour of believing acceptance of the healing powers which emanate from the gospel, particularly in Pentecostal circles. That there are 'Questions in connection with Spiritual Healing' has already been amply shown by the report with this title, accepted by the Synod of the Netherlands Reformed Church in 1959. This report also explained that the liberating message of the Messiah Jesus in any case touches the whole man, and that healing, whether it is considered a 'miracle' or not, is an essential part of the salvation of the God of Israel. Jesus came to redeem man, both in body and in soul. We already knew this from the first question of the Heidelberg Catechism, but in actual fact the redemption of Christ was experienced and confessed as a propitiation of sin and guilt. In most sermons in church the stories of healing were, and still are, usually spiritualized. The very concrete help and healing which can be found from faith in illness and distress are more often just a thing we remember than something which we accept physically. We should therefore, all of us, both in and outside the Church, consider it a gain that spiritual healing has been brought so urgently to the attention of Christendom. Praise the Lord! We can also safely say that these healing powers are definitely not confined to the Scriptures. They have a place in the whole proclamation of the Kingdom, with which the Lord charged his disciples. 'Preach as you go, saying, "The kingdom of heaven is at hand". Heal the sick, raise the dead, cleanse lepers, cast out demons. You received without pay, give without pay' (Matt. 10.7, 8). Peter and Paul heal the sick repeatedly in the course of their journeys, and there are a few references to raising from the dead (Acts 9.36-43; 16.18, and other places). Undoubtedly the biblicism of the groups referred to has had a liberating and enriching effect. All the questions which may be asked concerning the practical working out of this cannot detract from this positive fact.

It is rather different with some other matters which the biblicism of these groups stresses along with spiritual healing. There is adult baptism as the only biblical form, spiritual baptism and speaking in tongues. Here the biblical basis is much narrower, and the texts which are concerned with these matters should be treated with more circumspection than they are usually given in these circles. Moreover, the difficulties connected with the practical application of these things are great, as is clearly worked out in the pastoral letter of the General Synod, De Kerk en de Pinkstergroepen (The Church and the Pentecostal Groups) of 1960. Of the points made in this letter we would particularly like to underline that it is here that it is felt most that these groups have detached themselves from the classical confessions of the churches of the Reformation. If we consider justification by faith alone as the core of the Reformed confession (see Chapter IV. B.1), which characterizes the basic relationship between God and man, then it is quite clear that this basis is lacking in the Pentecostal movements. Suddenly we have Christians who handle the gifts of the Holy Spirit as mark of a true faith, and who are in danger of forgetting that these are gifts of grace. Having left the Reformed channel, they have run aground on the sandbanks of fanaticism and legalism. May we hastily point out to our Pentecostal brethren that we really do not write this in order to reject haughtily and fanatically those biblical elements which they have discovered, but only to give one example of the fact that the explanation of the Bible has to be given without neglecting either dogma or confession. It is dangerous to ignore these recklessly. We suggest that we should really read and explain the Bible together, so that we may bow down together before its authority which wants to convince us spiritually, and not legalistically – on the basis of a few texts. This is impossible with the biblicist method, which neglects dogmatic and confessional decisions.

(e) *The Conversation with our Contemporaries*

By contemporaries we mean those who, each in their own way, bear the imprint of their heritage (confirmation, the Church Fathers and saints), but who now, in this day and age, concern themselves with the questions which surround the Bible. Questions? Of course there are many wonderful and certain answers which radiate from the Scriptures, uniting us and constituting a common property. The Bible really must not be made out to be more difficult than it is. It is, however, a fact that there are many people who cannot really discover the glorious rightness, the positive force, the sure authority of the Scriptures. That is why there are questions from every side, as well as problems and dark patches which have to be faced by those inside and outside the Church, by Christians and agnostics, by simple people and by experts, by ordinary members of the congregation and by theologians. However, the Bible will certainly not relinquish its secrets and convictions if each one of us listens and tries to understand in isolation, nor if we dejectedly or indifferently cease to listen to the Bible. This way of reading and preaching separately, each in our own way, is how the Church of the nineteenth century lost its way. The world of the Churches was hopelessly divided and the Netherlands Reformed Church split into many groups, sometimes separated by deep chasms. People could no longer understand each other, nor did they make the least effort to do so: everyone was convinced that he was right and everyone else was wrong.

The surprising beginning of the renewal movement of the Church during and after the Second World War led to a fresh desire to begin a conversation with each other. The Netherlands Reformed Church in particular had a number of impulses from this during the years after the Second World War, while in the World Council of Churches this conversation acquired such proportions that Rome, too, is now becoming involved.

We feel that this has been a great blessing which God has granted the Church and the Churches in our century. It has inestimable value for the understanding of the Bible, and therefore for the healing of the life of the Church. If we want to conduct this conversation round the open Bible fruitfully, we must not lose sight of the rules of the game.

In the first place, we must not think that the Bible is so difficult or mysterious that everyone must elucidate it or feel it in his own particular way. The conversation would then run into the quicksand of an uncommitted exchange of personal opinions. No, we must start from the fact that the things which the Bible has to say to us stand out clearly and squarely. We must definitely want to find the truth of the Bible together. We would like to express this in the words: *a passion for truth*. This need not lead to a fanaticism which encloses itself in its own fortress in order to shoot arrows at the other party. Even with the passion for truth, the point is to speak to the other party, not to shoot it.

The second rule of the game is therefore that of *openness*. In a conversation about the Bible we must be prepared really to listen to each other. Anyone who can hardly wait for another person to finish in order to put his own point of view is not really in conversation with him. One can only hear the word of God if one is prepared to listen to the other person. Only then will it be possible to reach him with what we ourselves feel we have received from the Bible. Precisely because one is convinced that what has been received is biblical truth, one can listen to others openly and quietly.

Finally, we plead for *humility* in our conversation about the Bible. 'Our knowledge is imperfect and our prophecy is imperfect' (I Cor. 13.9). Who possesses the whole truth? The truth of God is after all not a dead system, but a living truth. We are on our way together. No Christian of any church need be ashamed that there are things about which he is not entirely clear. Conversely, it is not surprising that points of view come forward which were still hidden to earlier generations. As we read the Bible, God's spirit will reveal to our generation things which were seen differently in the past. Humility, not an inferiority complex, is the right attitude.

This conversation with each other takes place in various forms, in the first place in *theology*. Theology is an absorbing and satisfying science, having the Bible as its centre and the world as its field. Its various branches make their contributions scientifically. It is for *dogmatics* to pose the question about truth. This or that comes to us from the Bible, or from church history, or from the field of religions, but how is it really ? Here we would like to plead for more dialogue on theology and dogmatics. The theologians of the various churches and movements must speak to each other seriously in order to clarify all sorts of matters. It is striking how this dialogue is nowadays often sought by Roman Catholic theologians.

To the question what points should particularly be discussed at present, we would answer as follows.

The place of the Bible. Again and again we meet with the question, both in the Church and in Christian circles, of how the Bible should be explained and how one can appeal to the Bible. It is our hope that this book will be a helpful contribution to theological conversation about the place of the Bible.

Christology. This refers to the doctrine concerning the person and the work of Jesus as the Christ. In conversation between Churches it becomes clear repeatedly how various concepts about him after whom the Christian faith is named, cause profound separations. Mistrust in this respect very definitely hinders the process of unification between the Reformed Churches of the Netherlands and the Netherlands Reformed Church. It is certainly necessary for us to re-examine in the light of the Bible those Christological concepts which we have received from the past and which are often handled very thoughtlessly.

Pneumatology is study concerning the Holy Spirit. In the Christian Church there has been much less theological reflection about the Holy Spirit than about Christ. The Pentecostal groups have realized how far the Churches have fallen short here, and they lay great emphasis on the gifts and the powers of the Spirit. According to their view, this is the only way of gaining 'the full gospel'. The

*profound thinker O. Noordmans has shown in a prophetic manner,
in his beautiful meditations, that the gospel can only touch man
through the Spirit, without becoming our property. A. A. van Ruler,
Professor at the University of Utrecht, is devoting his attention
to pneumatology on a high theological level. This theological conversation is therefore not only necessary, but is even now beginning
to take place.*

*Finally, there is study concerning the Church, ecclesiology. What
should be the form of the Christian Church in the world? What
place should be given to the ministry? Is the Church a clearly defined institution, or should its attitude in the world be much more
that of a humble servant? Should it perhaps almost merge with
the world? Clear theological thinking is required here.*

Furthermore, not only theology, but preaching also should have
more of an element of dialogue in it. It is true that in the sermon
the Word of God is proclaimed with authority, but this does not
mean that the hearers of the word should not be invited or stimu-
lated to think, and where possible, to discuss. The preacher must
draw the congregation into a conversation with the text, in order
that God's truth may speak to all of us together. This presupposes
that the church-goer is actively involved with the part of the
Scripture which has been proposed for that day. It is one of the
basic mistakes of many churchgoers that they listen to what the
preacher is saying rather than to what the text says. Because they
do not see the former as an extension of the latter, they sometimes
fail to see the connection, so that the sermon acquires the character
of a religious address, which may or may not be satisfying. Is this
not perhaps one of the causes of the decline in church attendance?
It could be very different, however, if we could become an actively
thinking and speaking congregation, instead of a passively listening
crowd. We, today, are living in the time of transition.

In the third place we would like to point out that Bible study
groups and discussion groups are excellent opportunities. Since the
war years this kind of association with the Bible has become very
popular. We shall not go into the techniques which are necessary
for this kind of work. It has been discovered that the Bible comes
to life in an extraordinary manner when people are really prepared
to study the world of the Bible together. The questions that the

members of the group put to each other prove to be narrow gates which lead to hidden treasure. The theologically trained leader of such a group will have to be careful not to kill such questions with too hasty answers. He himself will be able to learn much from the deadlock into which others may lead him with their questions. On the other hand, the leader must be sufficiently at home in the varied terrain of the Bible, so that he may judge from the questions what difficulty or misunderstanding lies behind them. An insight into the development of Christian thinking, such as we have sketched in Chapter I, should certainly not be absent here. It will be necessary to make use of the key secrets of the Scriptures in order to let the Bible speak for itself. Some of the many people who today are supposed to be estranged from the Church will only be able to regain access to the biblical message through the possibility of expressing themselves freely in an open conversation. A church service is often indigestible to them, but a conversation round the Bible in which their difficulties are taken absolutely seriously may help them over the doorstep. Doorstep: this word indicates a mutual estrangement between the Church and the world, which is certainly unnecessary, and which need not be there if we really try to listen to the Bible. This brings us to the last point of Chapter IV. B.

4. To Stand in the World

The word 'world' has acquired the meaning of 'evil', that which is turned away from God in the Christian Church; the world of man, which has no concern with God or the Redeemer, and which follows its own sinful ways.

> *Safe in the arms of Jesus,*
> *Safe from corroding care*
> *Safe from the world's temptations,*
> *Sin cannot harm me there.*

Remembering this meaning of the word 'world', we might well wonder why we are now being asked 'to stand in the world'. Does the apostle not exhort us 'to keep unstained from the world' (James 1.27)? It would be useful to trace briefly the meaning of the word 'world' in the Bible. We are aware that we are treading on holy ground here, for this is an intricate part of biblical theology.

*In the Tanach the word 'world' only occurs meaning 'the earth'.
'The earth is the Lord's and the fullness thereof, the world and those
who dwell therein' (Ps. 24.1). The Law and the Prophets speak of
'heaven and earth' (Gen. 1.1) when they want to indicate the
universe. The 'ends of the earth' (Micah 5.4; Ps. 2.8) or 'the coast-
lands' (Isa. 49.1) indicate the spaciousness of this earth, and the
'peoples' (heathen) stand beside or over against Israel when there is
talk of the world of man. There is no hint here of a world which
is 'evil'.*

In the centuries before the beginning of our era this situation
changes, in Jewish-apocalyptic writings, that is to say in the
Apocrypha. We find some traces of this in the Epistles and Gospels.
Here two words are used for 'world', namely cosmos and aeon.

The Greek word cosmos really means ornament, or well-ordered
whole, but in the Gospels it has three other meanings, which run
into each other at times, rather like colours.

(a) Everything that is created, 'whether Paul or Apollos or Cephas
or the world, or life or death . . . all are yours' (I Cor. 3.22). 'To
gain the whole world. . . .' (Mark 8.36).

(b) The world of nations, as the stage for God's deeds. 'And truly,
I say to you, wherever the gospel is preached in the whole world,
what she has done will be told in memory of her' (Mark 14.9).

(c) The world which is turned away from God. 'Has God not
made foolish the wisdom of the world?' (I Cor. 1.20, 21). 'Now is
the judgement of this world; now shall the ruler of this world be
cast out' (John 12.31). In the Gospel of John in particular the word
'world' has this dark meaning. We remark here that the evangelist
often thinks in this sense of Jerusalem and the Jewish people, in so far
as they deny Jesus, enclosed as they are within their own piety.
His brothers encouraged him to go to Jerusalem with the words: 'If
you do these things, show yourself to the world' (John 7.4). Many
texts would sound much less general if we could recognize this
meaning in them. 'He was in the world, and yet the world knew
him not. He came to his own home, and his own people received
him not' (John 1.10.11).

The Greek word aeon really means 'century'. It is the Greek
translation of the Hebrew word 'olam, which is most often used in

the Tanach. The root meaning is that which is hidden from the eyes of those living now, the distant past or the distant future. This leads to the meaning 'a period in the history of the world'. In the plural it is used to indicate the majesty and the 'eternal' aspect of God. 'From everlasting to everlasting thou art God' (Ps. 90.2).

The use of the word 'everlasting' for the translation, as in this verse, may conjure up for us thoughts which were far from the writers of the Bible. Usually we think here of time without end, we contrast time with eternity. The Bible thinks, as in the verse of this Psalm, of periods of time strung together, linking Abraham to Moses, and from there to David, and then from David to the exile, for instance. From the exile there stretches another, open perspective, 'in all generations' (Ps. 90.1). How then can this word aeon also be used in the Gospels and Epistles as 'world'? 'The sons of this world' (Luke 16.8). 'Do not be conformed to this world' (Rom. 12.2). Well, in the centuries before the birth of Jesus there developed among the Jews the concept of two world-periods, the old and the new, the age which will be destroyed and the age to come. It is certain that this is under the influence of Persian religion, but it also fits into the proclamation of the Law and the Prophets. The plan which God had wanted to realize with the Torah in Israel has still not succeeded. The Prophets frequently show visions of a coming judgement, but also of coming felicity (Isa. 11.1-5). 'At that time I will change the speech of the peoples to a pure speech, that all of them may call on the name of the Lord and serve him with one accord' (Zeph. 3.9). Then the new world will break through.

Now the apostles are aware that they are standing exactly on the turning point between these two periods. When Jesus begins to preach, the Kingdom of God is at hand (Mark 1.15). Ephesians 1.21 speaks of all power and dominion, not only in this age, but also in the age to come, which is not in the distant future, but has already begun, with Jesus the Messiah.

Thus it becomes clear that on the one hand the (old) world will be condemned, but that on the other hand the faithful are called upon 'to taste the powers of the age to come' (Heb. 6.5).

From all that has been said it will be clear that with the words 'to stand in the world', we want to express the idea that the Church, while listening to the Bible, is involved in this progress of time and in this turn of world history, to which the apostles are living witnesses. The Church cannot take refuge, with the Scriptures, in a religious reserve, far from 'the stir of the world'. That would give it the meaning which John does so often in his Gospel, of a piousness which cuts itself off and encloses itself in its own certainties, without accepting the real Word of God.

On top of this, this examination of the meaning of the word 'world' can help us to gain an insight into the attitude of the Christian, who stands, with the Bible, in the contemporary world, in our civilization. We shall direct our searchlight in three directions.

(a) *Knowledge of Modern Life*

If the Church wants to be able to explain the Scriptures and apply them to man with spiritual authority, then it must possess a real knowledge of the questions and prejudices, of the patterns of thought and life of the man of today. The biblical message is always specific, not directed to man in general, who is generally a sinner, or generally quite a decent sort, but to *this* person. What are *his* sins, *his* virtues, what are the cares or carelessness, the fear or the pleasure with which we have to live today?

Because of frequent pastoral contacts with the members of his congregation a minister is in general less estranged from the world than is sometimes popularly thought. But on the other hand there is a danger that he will view people and the world in general from his own particular angle, because of the special position he occupies. It is somewhat grotesque to hear a minister denounce excesses in sport or amusements, when it is clear from his words that he has never himself experienced the dangers and enchantments of the dance floor or the football field. Many well-intentioned sermons about, or addressed to, the much-discussed 'modern youth' miss their target, because the world of this youth is unknown from the inside.

We are aware that we have said no more than the obvious so far, but we intend to apply it also more specifically to one special subject.

In the report concerning nuclear weapons the General Synod of the Netherlands Reformed Church expresses itself on a matter which is a burning issue of our day. Whatever one's opinion of the position taken in this pamphlet – an unqualified 'no' – and whatever conclusions one thinks can be drawn from this position, one thing about this report seems to us beyond dispute, namely that it has been written with great expertise and knowledge of the matter in hand. The 'no' is certainly not a cheap no, and the writers give evidence that they have carefully examined the military, political and scientific aspects of this problem. This alone would be sufficient to make it worthwhile to pay great attention to what has been written. This is, of course, such a very complicated problem that there are always additions, corrections and further information which might throw a new light on this matter. But the objection that this report was out of touch with reality could only be raised by people who either were themselves insufficiently up to date with the atomic age, or . . . who had not read the report.

(b) Solidarity with Modern Man

It is not sufficient for us to show that we know modern life when we explain or apply the Scriptures. Another element will have to be added to this. The authority of the Scriptures, the urgent appeal of the Gospels – which may also be a judgement – can only be made to come alive, and can only become effective, if the Church or the pastor, or the Bible-reader is prepared, not just to stand over against modern man, but beside him. The Church has no refuge of its own from which it can call out to the world, as Abraham was able to do to the rich man in hell. Then there was a 'great chasm' (Luke 16.26). But in this 'world' the Church is still under way, together with modern man. It is a well-known fact that a Christian can be much more convincing with the Bible when he gets a chance to show that he shares the same fate, or is prepared to share the same fate, as everyone else. This opportunity is sometimes given particularly in unusual conditions such as a prisoners' camp, or under war conditions. In other situations, as for instance the position of the army chaplain, this solidarity should not consist in joining-in-at-all-costs, but in letting it be felt, quite honestly, that one is prepared to share the conditions of the other person's life, to come alongside the other person. It is striking how there may then come an opening for the message of the Bible, which will also be really helpful.

We find this involved solidarity in particular in some parts of the exhortatory sections of Paul's letters. Listen for instance to the impressive opening of Romans 9, where Paul addresses himself, over the heads of the Christians in Rome, to his very own people, the Israelites, who are still not able to see Jesus as the fulfilment of all their privileges. There is also the tone of the beginning of Romans 12: 'I appeal to you, brethren, by the mercies of God . . .' These are not the words of a moralizing preacher, of a man who from a high pulpit explains with authority the words of God, because that is how it is, but a man who stands beside his brothers, and who wants to make the gospel true, right into their very bodies '. . . to present your bodies as a living sacrifice, holy and acceptable to God, which is your spiritual worship' (Rom. 12.1b).

Is this not the real secret of Jesus himself, the Son of God, who shares and takes upon himself the need and the guilt of the people who reject him, even upon the Cross? Is solidarity not one of the deepest dimensions of the Gospel? Of course the Church can only preach this solidarity of reconciliation by showing simultaneously in its life and being that it makes this solidarity a reality by following in the footsteps of its Lord. We remind the reader of the moving exhortations in I Peter 2.18-25.

As a mark of respect we may here mention the name of the theologian Dietrich Bonhoeffer, who was hanged in the early morning of April 9th, 1945, in the concentration camp at Flossenburg. He could have withdrawn himself from the guilt of the German people, which he foresaw long before the war, by remaining safely in America in 1939. He wanted, however, to bear this guilt with and for his people by taking part in Germany in the underground resistance against the criminal regime of Hitler. While the American guns nearby were already heralding the liberation, he had to follow his Lord along the road of martyrdom and death. His beautiful letters, brought together under the title Letters and Papers from Prison, *give us a moving picture of a struggle with the Scriptures, in solidarity with modern man. Something of this spirit should pervade our contemporary Christianity if we are truly to proclaim with authority to the man of today the gospel itself, and not worn-out Christian phrases, however biblical they may be. We believe that this is what the world is waiting for. But this takes us one last step further.*

(c) A *Step Ahead of the Modern World*

Generally speaking, the Church has the name of being rather conservative, of being behind 'the world'. This is very often true in
fact, though we think there are some other aspects which should
be pointed out. What would have become of the Roman Empire
without the new stimulus which came from the gospel? What
would Europe have become without the earthquake of the Reformation? How would things be in Indonesia and the Congo if no
missions had ever gone there? We are just putting these questions
forward. We have no desire to quarrel about historical facts, as we
have already said earlier; but there is one thing, based on the Bible,
which we want to establish firmly: paganism is essentially conservative, the Bible is essentially progressive. Of course these words
should not be interpreted in the accepted civic-political sense. No,
it is the Name which creates history. Abraham leaves the ingrown
paganism of Babylon, and the God of Israel blazes a trail through the
world of the nations which makes it possible for the first time
to speak of a past and a future. 'Remember' is a typical biblical-
Israelite word. That was why the phrase 'and it came to pass', the
event, is a key secret of the Scriptures (Chapter III.B).

> Great are the works of the Lord,
> Studied by all who have pleasure in them . . .
> Holy and terrible is his name!
>
> Ps. 111.2, 9b

Here we refer to what we wrote earlier about the meaning of the
word 'world' in the situation of the Christian congregation, to which
the Gospels and Epistles witness. The situation is that the old world
has become past tense, a new world has dawned. This is the word
'world' in the sense of period of time, past and future. When the
writers of the Gospels refer to this new world they invariably use
the word 'age' (era, a long, incalculable period), because in their day
the word *cosmos* (world) had acquired an unfavourable sense, as we
have already seen in John. But how should we imagine this new
world, according to the Bible? What do the evangelists and the
apostles think of when they witness to 'the coming of the Kingdom'?

*In the nineteenth century, New Testament research was particularly
interested in a reconstruction of 'the life of Jesus'. People tried to*

distinguish the authentic words of Jesus from the inauthentic ones
in order to arrive at a picture of Jesus. In general Jesus was, in this
process, considered as the announcer of the spiritual empire of moral
and religious thoughts. Albert Schweitzer, who was later a doctor
in Lambarene, was also a pioneering theologian because of his
famous book The Quest of the Historical Jesus. This book was at
once the celebration and the funeral speech of this history of
nineteenth-century research. Following up a work written by
Johannes Weiss in 1893, he put forward with emphasis the suggestion that Jesus could never be understood as the preacher of religious
values and truths, because he had lived completely in the Jewish
apocalyptic expectations of his own day. Jesus, Schweitzer held,
saw himself as the 'Son of man' appointed by the Father in Dan.
7.13. He was firmly convinced that the Kingdom of God would still
break through with power in his own lifetime, that everyone would
recognize him as the Messiah, and that 'the end' of history would
appear as a tremendous closing drama. When Jesus sent his disciples
to the towns of Israel, he said: 'I say to you, you will not have gone
through all the towns of Israel, before the Son of man comes'
(Matt. 10.23). When this tremendous event seemed to tarry, Jesus
tried to force his Father, by hastening his own death and permitting
Judas to betray his 'Messiah-secret' to the leaders of the people.
Then Jesus testified before the Jewish council: 'But I tell you, hereafter you will see the Son of man seated at the right hand of Power,
and coming on the clouds of heaven' (Matt. 26.64). That is why the
disciples and the early congregations still lived in the expectation
of the very close appearance of Jesus in glory, the parousia (appearance) and this expectation can be felt right through the New Testament. Schweitzer's own conclusion is a radical one. Jesus made a mistake. The Jewish apocalyptic imagery has lost its significance for
us over the centuries. The manner in which Jesus gave himself
personally and passionately remains for us a guiding light, however,
enough to inspire even the contemporary Christian to deeds of self-
sacrifice and love. Naturally this consistent eschatological vision did
not remain unchallenged (more about the word 'eschatological' in a
moment), and many scholars have racked their brains over this
problem of the 'postponed parousia expectation'. We indicate three
directions in which a solution has been sought.

(a) On the basis of many texts from the Gospels and Epistles it can be shown that Schweitzer and his followers were very biassed. Over against the texts which seem to indicate that the end is near, there are many which leave room for a much larger perspective. 'It is not for you to know times or seasons which the Father has fixed by his own authority' (Acts 1.7). Perhaps there is a certain unevenness in the texts, which can be reduced to an error of perspective. What is in reality further away may from a certain angle seem very near. The expectations for the future, therefore, remain valid alongside what has already been given in Jesus' coming.

(b) The emphasis on the Jewish apocalyptic expectation is one-sided. It does indeed exist, but it belongs largely to the ways and forms of expression of those days. The essential thing is, that with Jesus the Kingdom of God has indeed begun, as is quite clear from all the parables about the Kingdom. When Jesus comes, the end has already become reality. Truly, truly I say to you, he who hears my word and believes him who sent me, has eternal life; he does not come into judgment, but has passed from death to life' (John 5.24).

(c) Though the New Testament writings contain much material which can be ascribed to the realistic expectations of the future, also of the first Christian congregation, Jesus' intention had been to confront man with a decision through his proclamation. Either man must live in his own certainties and with the things provided in our existence, or he must lose himself and risk his life to answer God's call to freedom and love, in order to find the true eternal life. This call, this proclamation, is what should be considered the essential part of the mythological representation of the writers of the Bible. The name of Rudolf Bultmann in particular is connected with this kerygmatic theology.

Professional theologians are asked to forgive us this too condensed and one-sided presentation. It must suffice for our purposes, in order that we may go on to ask how we can apply this in practical Bible reading and in preaching.

It is hoped that by mentioning these problems we have evoked some response in many people. Perhaps they will admit that the Bible and the proclamation often do not touch them because the 'Coming Kingdom' and everything that the Bible has to say about this does not connect with anything in their own lives and thoughts. For

many ordinary Christians it has become a matter of course that every
minister should finish the sermon with a pious remark about the
Kingdom that must come one day (but when?). Church people do
not usually bother too much about this, while in sectarian circles
this 'second coming' is always played as the strong trump-card,
in order to reproach the established Church with slackness and luke-
warmness in the matter of the ardent expectation of Christ's future.

It seems to us that this fog, which has come down over large
sections of the biblical proclamation, is preventing the congregations
from enjoying the wider views, so that they have lost their *élan*, and
are now characterized by middle-class conservatism and staidness.
We have already referred to this in Chapter IV.B4c. How can this
fog be dispersed?

As we consider the various expedients indicated by the theologians,
it seems to us that each of them advanced an important point of
view, Schweitzer as much as any of his correcting or criticizing
successors. But at the same time there remains a feeling that we are
left with too many contradictions to find, as people of the twentieth
century, an insight into this matter which is really convincing and
stimulating, leading us forward.

In this book we cannot pretend to solve the problems upon which
we have just touched in the same style as is for instance attempted
by Jürgen Moltmann in his book *Theology of Hope* (1967). This
book has attracted great attention in a wide circle because of its
vision and scholarship. The writer puts promise and hope in the
centre for biblical theology and for the sermon in church.

We shall content ourselves, however, with a few modest remarks
which might help to lessen the contrasts between the points of view
mentioned earlier.

1. *Hebrew has a peculiarity, that in the verb forms the present
tense does not differ from the future one. In Hebrew, therefore, the
future has always already begun. If there is talk of an expectation
of the future, this is always an expectation of the present. Often it
is of no importance whether the verb is translated in the present
tense, or in the future one. 'The Lord judges his people' also means,
'The Lord will judge his people'. It seems to us that this is not just
a simple question of linguistics, but a matter which is of significance
for the way in which the Jew lives. He does not cut time up into*

separate pieces, but really lives towards the future. If we remember that the writers of the Gospels and Epistles, even if they were Gentile Christians like Luke, thought and felt in Hebrew, then we must not attach too much importance to the difference between present and future in various texts. 'The times of ignorance God overlooked, but now he commands all men everywhere to repent, because he has fixed a day on which he will judge the world in righteousness . . .' (Acts 17.30, 31). At the word 'will' we think involuntarily of a future which obviously has not yet arrived: the problem of Schweitzer. An error of perspective? The Greek text makes it obvious that this judgement is already in progress (mellei) and this word of Paul must be understood as truly Hebraic. From the closing sentences of the chapter it is clear that as a result of Paul's preaching a division (judgement) takes place.

2. The Hebrew expression in the latter days, as in Isaiah 2.2, also quoted by Peter in his address on Pentecost, was translated into Greek by eschaton, which there means final boundary, extreme, end in the absolute sense. Bultmann even writes: 'Eschatology is therefore the doctrine concerning the end of the world, its destruction' (History and Eschatology). But the Hebrew word 'aharit means something that comes as the end of a particular period, after which a new thing is coming. One does an injustice, not only to the apostles, but also to the later Jewish apocalyptic writers, when one thinks exclusively in vertical terms of sudden, unimaginable catastrophes and the fierce descriptions of judgement, heavenly angels and events coming from above – the new Jerusalem coming out of heaven (Rev. 21.2). This vertical dimension is, in the biblical consciousness, always connected with the horizontal one, progress in the course of time. The phrases 'from above' and 'on the clouds of heaven' indicate really much more that it is the God who continues to be the Lord of history, than that history would suddenly cease because of a vertical intervention.

3. The phrase second coming is not biblical, even though it is always used thoughtlessly. Biblical passages always say 'to come' or 'coming', meaning that which has already begun and which is now going to continue; this is what John the Baptist expects from Jesus in Matt. 11.3. We believe that it would help to clarify things if this point were remembered in the explanation of 'future texts'. The 'coming of the Lord' is then not something which is 'delayed',

but something which is already taking place. That is 'the new creation', 'the age to come' (Mark 10.30). In all this it is assumed as self-evident that these coming events, this continuation of the Kingdom from the resurrection of the Lord, will one day have a fulfilment, an end, in the sense of a ripening. This is similar to the fulfilment of the progress of the history of God with his people Israel in the appearance (parousia) of the Messiah Jesus, in spite of all the disappointments and judgements. For this fulfilling 'end' the Greek has the fine word telos which is connected with the word to finish, to complete, as the Lord God completes his work on the sixth day of the creation. It is also obvious that the end has not yet come, and specifically for the Christian there remains much to be hoped for and to be expected, indeed particularly the faithful 'must enter the kingdom of God through many tribulations' (Acts 14.22). We are not advocating the idea of a development of history which is inherent in itself, nor in our opinion does the Bible justify the vision that in Jesus, in his cross and resurrection, the Kingdom is already there, but hidden, so that since that time there is really nothing else to be done but to believe and to wait until suddenly it comes. Even the expression which is so popular today, of 'erecting signs of the coming Kingdom', seems to us to be a little too scanty.

4. When we meet the words 'eternity' and 'eternal' in our translations of the Bible, we should be on our guard. We know that this is a difficult and also a delicate point, especially in view of the Christian's personal expectation for the future. But all the same, we would like to point out that with these words one must in the first place think of the age, the new world (and everything connected with that) which has been given in Israel and for the nations by God in Jesus the Messiah.

5. We did not stop at all these points in order to help in the solving of a theoretical difficulty, which affects the stand of the Christian in this world. 'Therefore, my beloved brethren, be steadfast, immovable, always abounding in the work of the Lord, knowing that in the Lord your labour is not (shall not be) in vain', Paul writes just after those words about 'the last trumpet' which sound so strange in our ears (I Cor. 15.58).

The natural image that we obtain in this way is that of the divine new start, in the Messiah Jesus, which opens up a new future, not just for the people of Israel, but also for the Gentiles. At this turning point stand the first witnesses, and through it the whole Christian congregation lives. Seen from this point the whole world of pagan nations is 'old and transient', and Paul, as ambassador of Christ, may proclaim to the heathen : 'Therefore, if anyone is in Christ, he is a new creation; the old has passed away, behold, the new has come' (II Cor. 5.17). These new elements – and they are not just signs – of the Kingdom of God which is on the march meet with much contradiction and opposition, and the journey is through judgement and persecution. But according to I Peter 1.3-12 this does not temper the joy of the few Christians scattered among the heathen, who since the resurrection of Christ have part in the new world for which the prophets have searched and into which even angels cast envious glances. They reach the goal, the fulfilment, the *telos*, of 'the faith' (not of *their* faith, but of the mighty affair with which the Lord of the nations has been specially concerned ever since Abraham, the father of all believers), the redemption, too, of their lives (v. 9). They experience in their own lives the dominion of the Saviour who was born on Christmas night.

The conclusion must be that through the gospel a progressive attitude may develop. We have the future before us, the future in which the exalted Lord, through his Word and Spirit, is working to make the old world into a new one. There is no room for disappointed expectations, because as a Christian Church we do not go towards a distant and uncertain future, but to a near and certain one, in which every day the joy of Easter and Whitsun sheds its rays over our lives, giving courage and power to perceive new perspectives, while 'the old world' is closed to this future. A Christian is therefore progressive in a radical sense, and as such we are part of our civilization, leading the world in so far as it is still 'old'.

In so far as it is still old, we have just said. Since the gospel made its journey among the nations, the old pagan world has in fact changed profoundly, too, and we are earnestly convinced – see the end of Chapter I – that the present Western world would not have its modern, renewed aspect if it had not been really blessed by the proclamation of the gospel. We must not picture the Kingdom of God as a spiritual, heavenly, or invisible entity, which exists only inside men, or – which would be worse – only as something far off in a supernatural world: it is here and now, on this earth among nations. We think that this is what the Bible says. The famous question of the apostles to the risen Lord in Acts 1.6, whether he would at this time restore the kingdom to Israel, was really not a silly one. They were not thinking too materially and earthily, but on the contrary, they were thinking too little in terms of this earth. They received instructions to proclaim the royal rule of Christ, starting from Jerusalem, to *all* the nations. The current notion that nothing has come of this and that we have now been waiting in vain for the results for twenty centuries, until 'it' will suddenly appear from above, is not realistic.

But it is, of course, also true that the Christian nations may fall back into the old world, and that the 'fulfilment', the end, does indeed appear a long way off. On the contrary: the fearful question may arise whether the modern world, come of age, which has to thank Jesus, the Lord, for such an incredible amount, is not slowly but surely sliding back into a conservative paganism. Though it is technically and scientifically still very progressive – for which we cannot be thankful enough – the future for modern man in our welfare state in particular is beginning to cloud over slowly. Lack of perspective, nihilism, absurdity, these are words which we hear more and more often. The circle of paganism is slowly but surely regaining its suffocating hold on the man whom Christ had liberated. This is where the Christian Church has to be on its guard, and where it has to understand that it may keep the future open through the Bible, in the name of Christ, not as a distant desire, but as a reality on which life can be built. Jesus, the Lord of the Church, goes forward, and the Church may follow and so bless the world.

To read the Bible properly, as it is meant to be read, may therefore also mean very practically that we remain a few steps ahead of the world and of twentieth-century man. It means that the congregation lives the fact that we have a future which has already begun. He who really understands the Bible can only be 'up to date' in that sense.

Because it seems to many people that the contact between the gospel and the modern world, between Church and civilization, threatens more and more to be broken, it is understandable and

praiseworthy that progressive theologians do their utmost to translate the biblical message in such a way that it still has meaning
for the man of today.

Among our German neighbours, who are traditionally a veritable
nation of theologians, some leading figures are doing this, in the
footsteps of Rudolf Bultmann whom we have already mentioned.
All the mythological features of the Bible, including angels, miracles
and supernatural powers, are altered, removed, or considered as mere
background, so that the figure of Jesus alone may come into the
foreground. His faith, his appeal, his call to freedom, to the life out
of grace, these are seen as the proclamation which should be capable
of reaching man in his existence in his real life. The American pupil
of Bultmann, Paul van Buren, goes farthest in this; his book The
Secular Meaning of the Gospel soon became not only famous but
also notorious. These theologians do not hesitate to drop many
of the traditional treasures of faith of the Church. It is therefore
not surprising that many in the German congregations are disturbed,
and that there is much agitation, just as there is in the Anglo-Saxon
countries because of the utterances of Bishop John A. T. Robinson
A great deal has been published there, for and against Bultmann and
his followers.

It seems that unfortunately this theological current is overshoot-
ing its mark. These writings and thoughts bear the mark of the
study too much to be really capable of holding the attention of
people who are estranged from the Church, while the congregations
of the churches are thrown into a disquiet which cannot be called
healthy. On the other hand, we think that it cannot be right
to pull all the weeds of the new 'liberalism' out quickly and radically
in our reaction. We might root up the wheat, which is undoubtedly
there along with the weeds (Matt. 13.29).

If we are to come to a final conclusion in this book, in particular
with regard to the theological currents, then it must be as follows:
too many of these theologians still start from the thought-structures
of the previous century, in which people searched for the core, for
the essence of Christianity, as a truth which must be announced
to man. That is why people are still looking for the basic figure
of Jesus. The secret of 'the event', of God's action in the people of
Israel and in the Messiah, precisely for the nations, is overlooked.
That is why these new thoughts do not come down to earth, into

the real events, but remain floating and tenuous. Therefore they
cannot become really up-to-date, concrete and 'with it'. They are
following modern man (without catching up with him), rather
than going ahead of him. The latter is the aim which we hope to
achieve with this book.

Conclusion

We close this book with an appeal: either oppose it with clear and plain proofs from the Bible as a whole, or otherwise let it stimulate the reader and us into giving the Bible another honest chance to show its living power. In a way we do not have to give the Bible this chance, for it can look after itself. But because the Bible is not a tyrant, it will do nothing without us. Its spiritual authority waits for us. But one day it may be too late, too late for our culture and for the world of nations, too late even for the Church itself. That is why our appeal is urgent.

We address this appeal in the first place to churchgoers and ministers and to those who are in some way or other involved in the life of the Church. Let us cease to ignore and contradict one another, but let us instead, honestly and without any inner reservations, listen to the message which comes to us from the Bible. We are here thinking of the *modes and groups, the currents and movements* inside the Church and outside it, which continue to be separated. We must be ready to give the Scriptures an honest chance, and nobody needs to define his standpoint in advance. We must listen to and with one another. We must listen to the Bible. The nearer we are to the source, the clearer we shall find the water. What unheard-of perspectives might open up if we could find one another again round the Bible which is found in every pulpit. 'So if there is any encouragement in Christ, any incentive of love, any participation in the Spirit . . . complete my joy . . .' (Phil. 2.1, 2).

We also address this appeal to all those who usually pass by the Bible and the proclamation of the Church with a shrug of the shoulder. Is that really right? Could we not try together to hold a thorough spring-cleaning among all the misunderstandings and prejudices, in order that the voice of the Bible may come through

to us as clearly as possible? Are we not doing irreparable damage
to our own civilization and that of Western Europe by neglecting
the source of the Bible in this way? We are also asking this, of
the *humanists* among us, with doubled humility. We believe that
they and we still draw our nourishment practically from the same
roots, but can this go on much longer without our perishing?
We do not want to deny that a man can stand on his own two
feet. We are not harking back to the tutelage of the Church. But
was this independent man not put on his feet by God? Is that not
precisely how he was created and intended by God? If not, then
what are the perspectives which others see for man and for humanity
in the world of today? Would it not be worthwhile in any case
to let the Bible have its say once more in a symposium of all men
of good will?

We are also thinking of the *Roman Catholic Church*, whose
development in recent years we are watching with the greatest
interest. What could prevent us from really reading the Bible together, with or without the ties of tradition?

Finally we appeal, with ashamed humility and modesty, to *the
children of Israel*. What do we possess that we did not receive
through you or from you out of the hands of the God of Abraham,
Isaac and Jacob? If we read the Scriptures in this manner, will you
permit us to sit down beside you again, that we may study the
Scriptures? Could you not then consider once more, seriously,
whether the evangelists and the apostles were really wrong in
recognizing in Jesus of Nazareth the Messiah of Israel? He, the man
of the cross, the suffering servant of the Lord?

Could you try to forgive the sins which we, the Christian
Churches, committed against you, the chosen people of God? We
ask this of you . . . and if you could do this, would it then be altogether impossible to foresee the time when we can together bow
down, with all who are 'in heaven and on earth and under the earth,
and every tongue confess that Jesus Christ is Lord to the glory of God
the Father' (Phil. 2.10, 11)?

For Further Reading

DIETRICH BONHOEFFER, *Letters and Papers from Prison*, SCM Press, London and The Macmillan Co., New York, Rev. ed. 1967.

ALAN RICHARDSON, ed., *A Theological Wordbook of the Bible*, SCM Press, London and The Macmillan Co., New York, 1950.

W. D. DAVIES, *The Setting of the Sermon on the Mount*, CUP, London and New York, 1964.

ROLAND DE VAUX, *Ancient Israel*, Darton, Longman & Todd, London, 1965.

C. A. VAN PEURSEN, *Body, Soul, Spirit*, OUP, London and New York, 1966.

JAMES BARR, *The Semantics of Biblical Language*, OUP, London and New York, 1962.

A. TH. VAN LEEUWEN, *Christianity in World History*, Edinburgh House Press, London, 1964.

L. ALETRINO, *Six World Religions*, SCM Press, London and Morehouse-Barlow Co. Inc., New York, 1968.

TH. C. VRIEZEN, *Outline of Old Testament Theology*, Basil Blackwell, Oxford, 1958.

H. BERKHOF, *Christ the Meaning of History*, SCM Press, London and John Knox Press, Richmond, 1966.

JÜRGEN MOLTMANN, *Theology of Hope*, SCM Press, London and Harper & Row, New York, 1967.

PAUL VAN BUREN, *The Secular Meaning of the Gospel*, SCM Press, London and The Macmillan Co., New York, 1963.

Index of Names

Index of Biblical References